AN ONTOLOGY OF CONSCIOUSNESS

MARTINUS NIJHOFF PHILOSOPHY LIBRARY

VOLUME 18

For a complete list of volumes in this series see final page of the volume.

An Ontology of Consciousness

by

Ralph Ellis

1986 **MARTINUS NIJHOFF PUBLISHERS**
a member of the KLUWER ACADEMIC PUBLISHERS GROUP
DORDRECHT / BOSTON / LANCASTER

Distributors

for the United States and Canada: Kluwer Academic Publishers, 190 Old Derby Street, Hingham, MA 02043, USA
for the UK and Ireland: Kluwer Academic Publishers, MTP Press Limited, Falcon House, Queen Square, Lancaster LA1 1RN, UK
for all other countries: Kluwer Academic Publishers Group, Distribution Center, P.O. Box 322, 3300 AH Dordrecht, The Netherlands

ISBN 90-247-3349-9 (this volume)

ACKNOWLEDGEMENTS

Friends and colleagues who contributed to this study by means of their patient criticisms and kind tolerance are numerous. Carl Berreckman, Lester Embree, Bernard Freydberg, Tom Beuner and Robert Powell read early versions of some sections and Anibal Bueno helped with the crucial second chapter. The psychologist Don Kiesler spent many generous hours candidly discussing with me the methodology of psychological research. My former teachers John Scanlon, John Sallis and Andre Schuwer made the thinking of Husserl and Merleau-Ponty accessible to me when those philosophers were not very popular in America. I thank the editors of the *International Philosophical Quarterly, Man and World,* and *Auslegung* for allowing me to reprint sections of Chapter I and III. I am especially indebted to Lynda Ellis for the diagrams in Chapter V, and more importantly for her encouragement and support. Finally, I must acknowledge gratitude to my parents R.J. Ellis, himself a philosopher, and Frances Ellis, an English professor, for their criticisms, suggestions and encouragement.

CONTENTS

INTRODUCTION

The object of this study is to find a coherent theoretical approach to three problems which appear to interrelate in complex ways: (1) What is the ontological status of consciousness? (2) How can there be 'unconscious,' 'prereflective' or 'self-alienated' consciousness? And (3) Is there a 'self' or 'ego' formed by means of the interrelation of more elementary states of consciousness? The motivation for combining such a diversity of difficult questions is that we often learn more by looking at interrelations of problems than we could by viewing them only in isolation. The three questions posed here have emerged as especially problematic in the context of twentieth century philosophy.

1. The question of the ontological status of consciousness

The question 'What is consciousness?' is one of the most perplexing in philosophy—so perplexing that many have been motivated to proceed as though consciousness did not exist. If William James was speaking rhetorically when he said "Consciousness does not exist,"[1] many behaviorists of the recent past were not.[2] James meant only to imply that consciousness is not an independently existing soul-substance, alongside physical substances. He did not mean that we do not really 'have' consciousness, and he did not provide final resolution for the problem of the causal interrelations between consciousness and the physical realm (e.g., our bodies). Many recent philosophers and psychologists, however, try to proceed as though these problems did not exist. By asking 'What is consciousness?' we posit the question of the ontology or ontological status of consciousness. If consciousness is not a physical thing, or an aggregation of physical material, then what sort of phenomenon is it? And how does its mode of existence differ from and interrelate with that of material things?

One reason for the difficulty of the question of the ontology of consciousness is that this question forms a peculiar kind of circle with the epistemology we use to answer it. While attempts have been made to formulate epistemologies in which consciousness plays no role, the absence of any role for consciousness in such epistemologies generally turns out to be an illusion. Somewhere in the background, consciousness always plays its role—for example, in the experience of the meaning of propositions, or in the intuition that tells us that *this* empiricist criterion for meaning is better than *that* one if it accommodates the kinds of propositions we secretly 'know' are meaningful.[3] Our concept of what kind of thing consciousness *is* therefore influences what kind of epistemology we use. But at the same time, our epistemological assumptions obviously affect the way we conceive of consciousness, just as they affect our conception of anything else we study. Hegel once remarked that a small circle is a vicious circle, whereas a large circle is philosophy. One problem where the study of consciousness is concerned seems to be that the circle between the ontology of consciousness and the epistemological assumptions we make tends too often to be of the vicious kind.

Another fundamental difficulty with the question 'What is consciousness?' is that all conceivable answers to it appear to involve severe difficulties. Chapter Two of this study will discuss in some detail some of the reasons why this is the case. The profundity of the dilemma has frequently been noted, and a great deal of contemporary philosophical work has been done on it, centering mainly around five important types of theories:

(1) Theories of psychophysical identity hold that mental processes and physiological processes in the brain are really identical with each other. The only reason they appear to be different is that it is possible to view them from two different perspectives. From the subjective perspective, they appear as conscious processes such as thoughts and feelings. From the objective perspective, they appear as physiological and ultimately physical processes.

(2) 'Interactionism' maintains (at the risk of oversimplification) that there are two essentially different causal sequences, the one mental, the other physical, and that the two sequences sometimes causally interact with each other. A mental event may be caused by a physical one (e.g., a blow to the head), but it need not be. Similarly, a conscious choice may cause some physical event (e.g., the decision to raise my hand). On this view, consciousness would not be completely explainable in physiological terms.

(3) 'Parallelism,' a view seldom taken seriously anymore, is similar to interactionism except that it denies any causal interaction between the two causal sequences. It sometimes explains the apparent correlations between mental and physical events by positing that the two sequences initially shared a common cause (e.g., that God initiated the two sequences

simultaneously). In an extreme version, it would hold, with Leibniz, that God causes each event individually, thus ensuring their parallel structure.

(4) 'Epiphenomenalism' is the most straightforward of all theories. It simply says that all mental phenomena are caused by physical events, and denies that one mental event can ever cause another. The explanation as to why one mental event may *appear* to lead to another is that the earlier mental event is caused by a physical event which also causes a later physical event, which then causes another mental event.

(5) Alvin Goldman has recently proposed the theory that mental and physiological events are 'nomically' or 'nomologically' equivalent with each other.[4] That is, they behave as though they were identical, and may be treated scientifically as though they were identical, even though they may be different from each other in an ontological sense. He argues that for every mental event, there is a corresponding physiological event and *vice versa,* and that either the mental or the physical causal chain may be considered complete in itself for the purpose of causal explanation. His explanation as to how a physiological event can be completely caused by a previous physiological event, and yet also be partially caused by a mental event, without the mental and physical events' being identical in the ontological sense, is a unique one and will be discussed in Chapter II.

A wealth of distinguished authors have entertained these theories, including Smart, Sellars, Putnam, Nagel, Brandt, Kim, Davidson, Goldman, Malcolm, Noren, Weil, and a host of others.[5] At the same time, there has been little dialogue between these predominantly English-speaking philosophers and the equally important phenomenological authors whose ideas are obviously relevant to the mind-body relation. In particular, a further development of Merleau-Ponty's theory of psychophysical 'forms,' discussed mainly in *The Structure of Behavior,*[6] suggests a sixth possibility beyond the five just mentioned, a possibility hardly touched upon by the above-listed authors: a process-substratum model of the mind-brain relation in which mind and brain are inseparable, in the sense of being necessary and sufficient for each other, yet bear neither a causal relation to each other nor an identity relation, nor a nomic-equivalence relation. One of our purposes here will be to elaborate such a theory.

Someone may have noticed that Cartesian Dualism was omitted from the above list. One reason for this is that dualism, when championed at all in contemporary philosophy, is given a modified interpretation and tends to fall under the heading of interactionism. The truth is that most contemporary authors no longer take very seriously the possibility of a true dualism in the Cartesian sense, and for reasons that are so well-known that it is only necessary to mention them briefly. Dualism, in the pure sense of the word, maintains that mind and matter are different and independent types of substances. Thus it would be possible for consciousness to occur without any physical or physiological correlates or causes. The problem immediately arrises: If consciousness is not a physical thing, then from a physical point of view, its mass is zero. But the amount of motion that an object with a mass of zero can cause in an object with a finite mass should be zero. Otherwise, the object with the finite mass would be observed to disobey the laws of physics, which does not seem to happen. Thus, if dualism were correct, the mind would not be able to cause the body to move, nor *vice versa,* which would be absurd. It is easy to observe that the mental intention to raise my right hand can, at least indirectly, cause the hand to go up. Because of such problems as these, which have been well-known for some time,[7] it seems that we must look beyond dualism for a possible solution to the problem. This leaves the five theories mentioned above, which also have their problems, thus prompting us to turn to a development of Merleau-Ponty's thinking as a possible sixth approach to the issue.

Interactionism, the theory that probably comes closest to the common-sense view, entails serious difficulties when submitted to philosophical scrutiny. In its true or usual sense, we must remember, interactionism maintains not only that mind and matter sometimes interact, but also that they sometimes need not interact—that the mental and physical causal chains are in principle two different chains. They are not the same thing viewed from different perspectives, nor is one completely explainable in terms of the other. A serious problem with the theory is that it does not take into account a basic principle of causation: The sum of all causes of an effect should be in a certain sense both necessary and sufficient to produce the effect, at least 'in the given circumstances.' (While it is true that the notion of causation can be thematized without using the concepts 'necessary' and 'sufficient,' this diversity of causal languages turns out to be of little consequence for our purposes.) The case in which the difficulty becomes most obvious is this: Suppose one state of consciousness brings about a later one, and therefore *ipso facto* also brings about the neurophysiological event corresponding to the later state of consciousness. If the previous state of consciousness is necessary and sufficient to bring about the later one (and therefore also its corresponding neurophysiological event), then no previous physiological event can be either necessary *or* sufficient to produce the later physiological event. We would then be left with a physical event which has no necessary and sufficient physical cause. On the other hand, if a physiological cause could be both necessary and sufficient to produce a subsequent neurophysiological event (and therefore its corresponding conscious event), then any previous state of consciousness, by the very definitions of 'necessary' and 'sufficient,' could be neither necessary *nor* sufficient to produce the later one. This problem can be presented graphically. Let **A** be a state of consciousness which brings about **B**, a later state of consciousness. And let **a** be the physiological event that corresponds with **A**, and let **b** be the physiological event that corresponds with **B**. Then we have **A** bringing about **B** while at the same time **a** brings about **b**.

If there is ever any necessary or sufficient connection between mental events and their corresponding physiological events (as neurophysiology strongly suggests), then we have a dilemma. If **A** is necessary for **B** (as it sometimes seems to be), then **b** cannot be sufficient for **B**. And if **A** is sufficient for **B**, then **b** cannot be necessary for **B**. Thus if **A** is necessary *and* sufficient for **B**, then **b** must have no necessary or sufficient relation to **B**. Similarly, if **a** is necessary and sufficient for **b**, then **B** can have no necessary or sufficient connection to **b**. It appears, at least on initial inspection, that we cannot have our cake and eat it too. To the extent that a conscious event has a physical cause, it cannot have a mental one. And to the extent that it lacks a physical cause, its physiological correlate in the nervous system also lacks a physical cause, which seems to contradict what we observe about physics.

Nor can we escape the dilemma by saying that both a physical *and* a mental cause must combine in order to produce a subsequent mental effect, because then the earlier physical event would not be sufficient by itself to produce the later physical event (i.e., the one corresponding with the later mental event). This, again, would contradict what we know about physics. Though one might initially be prone to assume that there must be some easy way out of this dilemma, it turns out that the more we squirm, the more the knot tightens. The problem can be approached in a number of ways, as outlined in Chapter II, but ultimately, it has no satisfactory solution within the context of an interaction between mind and matter conceived as separable entities, i.e., in the context of interactionism in its usual sense.

Popper and Eccles argued for a kind of 'interactionism' in their classic study on the mind-body problem.[8] However, it would seem that their sense of 'interactionism' is so broad as to include all five of the above theories, since their main argument establishes at best only the *existence* of mental events, not necessarily an interactionist interpretation of them. The argument is essentially to the effect that "World 3 objects"— scientific theories, concepts, etc.—exist because without them it would be impossible to explain the behavior of scientists. And these World 3 objects also have an effect upon "World 1 objects," i.e., physical objects. But, they argue, this effect can only be exerted by means of "World 2 objects," i.e., the thoughts of scientists; therefore, the thoughts of scientists affect the physical world, implying to them an "interactionism." The problem with this argument for our purposes is that, if interactionism is distinguished from other theories of the mind-body relationship, then the argument no more entails interactionism than it does the identity theory, or epiphenomenalism or any of the other theories. It could be, for example, that the *physiological correlates* of the thoughts of scientists cause them to move their bodies in such a way as to build nuclear power plants, etc., which would be just as consistent with epiphenomenalism or identity theory as with interactionism.

For essentially the same reasons that 'interactionism' in the strict sense is problematic, so is parallelism—the theory that there are parallel but non-interacting series of events, one physical, the other mental, which perhaps have some common origin which accounts for their parallel nature, but which only *appear* to be interacting. Not only is parallelism in this sense not capable of accounting for the dilemma resulting from the necessary-and-sufficient relations at the beginnings of the two series (as we shall see in Chapter II), but parallelism also has additional and worse problems. It cannot account for the possibility that a physiologist can cause predictable effects in the stream of consciousness through purely physiological manipulations.

Epiphenomenalism, the theory that conscious events cannot be caused by previous conscious events, but only by underlying physical events, runs into difficulties when we consider the phenomenological observation that we can cause ourselves to have one state of consciousness by having another. For example, the intention to focus my eyes is often part of the cause of my seeing what is there. And, though it is entirely conceivable that a prior 'conscious event' might *appear* to cause another event while itself being only the epiphenomenon of a physical event, epiphenomenalism cannot explain in what sense the prior 'conscious event' is necessary or sufficient for the subsequent one without asserting that the conscious event is somehow 'the same thing as' an underlying physical event. But then it is no longer really an ephiphenomenalism (i.e., the theory that conscious events are *caused by* physical ones) but rather an identity theory (i.e., the theory that conscious events *are* physical ones).

But theories of psychophysical identity also have problems. They are inherently unable to account for the conceptual difference between subjective experiences and their objective manifestations, a conceptual difference that persists even if the consciousness and the corresponding physiology are inseparable from each other, or even if one causes the other. At the risk of oversimplification of this point, which will be discussed at length in Chapter II, we might say that the identity theory resembles the assertion that there is really no difference between the front and back sides of a house because they are 'really' only different perspectives on the same object. But if there were really no difference between the front and back of a house, then there would be no difference between the two different perspectives on the house. On the other hand, it seems equally problematic to assert that the physical and mental realms *are* different, because then we are thrown back to the problems of interactionism, which fails to make sense out of the necessary-and-sufficient relations between events that cross from one realm to the other. Alvin Goldman's 'nomological equivalence' theory, as we shall see, solves this problem for certain kinds of cases, but is incapable of solving it in all cases.

It seems that for any theory of the ontological status of consciousness, a convincing argument can be found somewhere in the contemporary mind-body literature which effactually refutes it. While some epistemologists have lauded 'falsifiability' as a virtue of theories, the situation in which the theory of consciousness finds itself—with all theories seemingly having been falsified—can hardly be what they had in mind.

2. The question of 'unconscious,' 'prereflective' or 'self-alienated' consciousness

Still another stumbling block in the conceptualization of consciousness is the confusion generated by the phenomena of 'unconscious' and 'prereflective' consciousness. The process of psychotherapy and other life experiences seem to reveal that people sometimes have thoughts and feelings of which they are unaware. The person 'suddenly realizes' that he has already been thinking or feeling something, perhaps for a long time, without knowing it. One reason for the difficulty in making theoretical sense out of this phenomenon is the conceptual paradox: How is it possible for a person to be 'unconscious' of his own 'consciousness?' If we conceive of thinking and feeling as conscious events, how can we then conceive their occurrence on an unconscious level? On the other hand, if we do not conceive them as conscious, then how are such phenomena as 'acting for reasons' intelligible?

A physiologist, it is true, might point to physical correlates of an emotion and say that these can be present before we are consciously aware of them; but this would have little to do with our question. Our perplexity does not stem from the question: How is it possible for a person to evidence increased heartbeat or adrenal secretion without being aware that any emotion exists? We ask, rather, how it is possible that he feels an emotion *'about'* some definite object (perhaps even an abstract cultural object), that he behaves *purposefully* in order to contend with the object, and even purposely *communicates* and *exchanges communications* with other people on the subject of the emotion, as we often see described in the clinical psychological literature—all without ever being 'consciously aware' that any of these presumably experiential events are taking place. The subtle and intricate thinking that seems to go into this apparently purposeful behavior would be difficult to explain without reference to cognition—leading to the suspicion that, on some level, consciousness must occur. Yet the person may show every sign of having remained ignorant of this consciousness until the moment it suddenly comes to light— and then he feels certain that he was 'really' conscious of it all along. There seems to be an ontological confusion here which makes those who believe in the existence of unconscious consciousness (or the preconscious, the unconscious, prereflective consciousness, preconceptual consciousness, all entailing essentially the same problem) peculiarly vulnerable to the behaviorists' 'Define your terms!'

The suggestion might at first sound odd that this question of 'self-alienation,' as we shall call it—this epistemological gulf separating consciousness from itself—is one of the pivotal problems not only of action theory, but of contemporary epistemology as well. In a variety of contexts in recent years, the ubiquitous notion of the non-self-transparency of consciousness has begun to thematize itself as crucial for an understanding of the 'prereflective,'[9] the 'transcendental ego,'[10] the phenomenological approach to meaning as an alternative to empiricist criteria for meaning,[11] and the question of the ontological status of consciousness.[12] Perhaps equally important, its clarification is crucial for phenomenological psychology as an approach to the recently renewed interest in studying cognition and consciousness.[13] Of course, the circularity between preconceptions and perceptions was also one of the main problems that prompted the trend in Continental philosophy away from pure phenomenology and toward hermeneutics and structuralism.[14] Also, the solution to the problem has far-reaching implications in the realm of ethical theory.[15] One might thus begin to suspect that self-alienation is an all-pervasive problem in contemporary philosophy; yet, like so many problems which are so close to us that focusing on them poses a problem in itself, self-alienation has received little systematic attention, although it is true that a few idealists, existentialists and theologians have addressed it obliquely and in a somewhat vague, poetic style. These inconclusive attempts to elucidate the problem, while providing some important and suggestive insights, should serve perhaps more importantly as negative examples whose primary lesson is that not only must we penetrate to the depth of the problem, but we should also bring to it the philosophical rigor and clarity of description which it increasingly obviously deserves.

Neither physiology nor behavioral research can come to grips with such questions as 'How is unconscious consciousness possible?' Neither of them studies consciousness directly. If we want to clarify the meaning of the words 'conscious' and 'unconscious,' and the paradox of their interrelations, we must have a discipline which studies consciousness, not as behavioral manifestation, and not as physiology, but simply as consciousness. One discipline which tries to do this is phenomenology.

Phenomenology aims at clear and distinct description of phenomena and their interrelations, 'just as they present themselves' in experience.[16] It purposely refrains from making any statement regarding the physical reality of the *object* of experience, but simply describes what we experience *as* we experience it. It concentrates on subjective reality. But unlike phenomenalism (whose purpose is simply to learn how to predict general patterns in the succession of the phenomena), phenomenology recognizes that no sooner do we attend to our experience of a phenomenon, than we notice that even on the most primitive and immediate level, on the level of the *direct conscious datum,* the phenomenon can only appear to us as already having a *Wesen*[17] (a 'sense,' 'meaning' or 'essence')— as being an instance of one or more generalizable *classes* of experienceable meanings (such as 'taking up space,' 'being colored,' 'having shape', 'being three-dimensional,' 'being a prescriptive rather than a descriptive statement,' etc.). A mass of *presuppositions,* in effect, becomes evident as infiltrating the immediate act of perception itself. In actuality, then, the description of a phenomenon must inevitably make references to the experience of the meanings or essences that the phenomenon evidences—the experienced 'sense' of *what* the phenomenon appears to be. Maurice Merleau-Ponty, whose work we shall discuss in Chapters II and III, points out that the act of perception is inherently an act of interpretation, of 'making sense' out of visual objects.[18] In a similar way, Jacob Needleman, one of the first psychiatrists to apply phenomenological philosophy to psychotherapy, shows that analytical thinking also makes use of preconceptual categories on the basis of which we interpret reality[19] —a notion highly consistent with the thinking of such contemporary cognitivists as Bruner[20] and·Ausubel.[21] In fact, Ernst Cassirer, in his classic book on relativity physics, points out that even the meaning of 'taking up space,' which appears to be an immediate property of objects, and was assumed to be so by Descartes and by Locke, turns out to be subject to a variety of different pre-perceptual interpretations.[22]

These *essences*, of which we see phenomena as being instances, are already partially 'sedimented' in our habitual ways of apprehending phenomena, before the particular phenomenon even presents itself. Although the essence is ultimately based in some way upon direct intuition (intuition either of existing objects, of imagined objects, of objects thought as possible or as impossible, etc.), the essence is largely preconceptual in relation to any given experience. 'Green tree' describes the conjunction of a preconceived color concept with a preconceived botanical concept. Most of us feel reasonably confident that we can clearly intuit the meaning of these concepts, although we recognize the contribution of the human perceptual apparatus in 'coloring,' as it were, such concepts as 'color.' But we intuit such higher-order concepts as 'operant level,' 'anxious behavior,' 'inhibition of conditioned response,' and 'intelligence' with less confidence in their immediacy, their 'eidetic purity,' and consequently their clarity. Certainly, the concepts of politicians and economists, even when precisely mathematicized and based upon tightly controlled empirical evidence, sometimes show themselves in hindsight not to have been as devoid of tacit presuppositions as they might at first have seemed, and therefore not as conceptually clear. But whether a concept is clear or vague, it always partially *precedes* the perception of the individual phenomenon. Gestalt psychology experiments illustrate this point.[23] Each person to some extent comes to an experience with conceptual or preconceptual *categories* which influence what essences he will see a phenomenon as exhibiting. The content of his perception and conception is always colored by this limitation. His description should therefore include not only a description of the thing seen, but also of the system of categories that contributes to his *perspective on* the thing.

Here, however, we encounter a problem: Nothing would seem to be accomplished by a description of this category structure unless the person could somehow step *outside* the category structure in order to describe it. If I describe my category structure from the perspective of the category structure itself, I may well leave out of account precisely those aspects of the category structure which had limited or rendered inaccurate the conceptual categorization of the original phenomenon whose description was attempted. If I am a behaviorist, for example, my description of my own category structure will be contaminated by the limitations and presuppositions of the behaviorist terminology and the legacy of behavioristic theoretical formulations, try though I may to exclude them. If I am a Freudian, it will be contaminated by incipient Freudian concepts. In general, let A be my category structure and B the thing I am trying to see 'as it really is.' If **A** contaminates my perception of **B**, then in order to get rid of this contamination, I must first know what I have to get rid of. But if my category structure, **A**, affects the way I see everything I look at, and if I must look at my category structure in order to find out what it is (so that I can get rid of it), then **A** will contaminate my perception of **A** just as seriously as it contaminates the perception of **B**. Or at the very least, we can say that *there is no guarantee* that A does not contaminate the perception of **A**.

In this sense, it would appear that to attempt a description of my own category structure would be like trying to pull myself up by my own bootstraps or, to borrow Heidegger's expression, like trying to jump over my own shadow. This is essentially the problem we shall refer to as the problem of self-alienation, since it is in effect equivalent with the above-mentioned epistemological gulf which separates me from the 'immediate data' of my own consciousness. We shall soon see that only by under-standing this problem of self-alienation can we ever hope to make sense out of the phenomena which we began by calling 'unconscious,' 'prereflective,' etc. Self-alienation, like Sartre's 'bad faith' and like Heidegger's 'inauthenticity,' will be conceived, not as an inherently neurotic phenomenon, but as a fundamental feature of personal con-sciousness, which nonetheless can be minimized in practice.

The posing of the question in such terms as these presupposes still another fundamental question with which we also must deal: *Is there a 'self' from which one can be alienated or not alienated?* These two questions interrelate in complex ways with the question of the ontological status of consciousness. Since the question of the self seems in some sense to be presupposed by the question of self-alienation, let's proceed to a preliminary outline of the direction of inquiry it necessitates. This in turn may enable us to formulate the question of self-alienation more precisely.

3. The question of the 'self'

Is there a 'self,' an 'I,' or an 'ego' which would provide some sense of continuous subjective identity throughout the changes I undergo from one state of consciousness to another? Or on the other hand, is Hume correct in supposing that the stream of consciousness is a loosely con-nected series of ontologically distinct states of consciousness which have no essential relation to an enduring conscious entity? In the latter case, the word 'I' would simply refer to my present state of consciousness at the time when I use the word—a state which will undoubtedly change in the next instant and could easily be so different from the previous state that it might even contradict it. There would be no enduring 'I' as an existing entity which persists through time. I would always be afraid of heights, as Sartre suggests, because I would continually be afraid that in the next instant I might change my mind and decide to jump.[24] All connections between one conscious state and the next would be merely accidental, resulting from the continuity of physiological processes, the continuity of my spacial location, and my enduring general relation to my world. This would imply that if my relation to the world suddenly changed, then so would the self. There would be no consciousness which transcended the limitations of the immediate perspective. Thus the prob-lem of self-alienation as we have described it could never be overcome.

If there is a self which is capable of transcending the limitations of the immediate perspective of the present state of consciousness, this self would perform a function similar to the one Husserl assigns to the 'transcendental ego,' and therefore might appropriately be called a transcendental ego, though in a somewhat different sense. One good philosophical reason for *rejecting* the idea of a transcendental ego is well summed up by Sartre in *The Transcendence of the Ego*.[25] The ego, Sartre says, is an object *for* consciousness, not a content *in* consciousness. Sartre maintains that if there were a transcendental ego, this ego could only be one of two things: (1) An immediate state of consciousness, experienceable as personally and as subjectively as any other immediate state of consciousness; or (2) something *other than* a state of consciousness—something we cannot immediately experience—which abstractly unifies all the various momentary states that make up the stream of consciousness, welding them together into one unified being. According to Sartre, if 'I' am a state of consciousness (a *pour soi* rather than an *en soi*), then I cannot *unify* all states of consciousness within the stream, since in this case I would be merely *one of* these states—waiting, along with the others, to *be* unified. On the other hand, if the 'I' is something other than a state of consciousness, which unifies all the states of consciousness into one coherent entity, then 'I' would not myself *be* a consciousness, since all the states of consciousness would then be ontologically distinguished from what I am; this, Sartre concludes, would contradict our experience of ourselves as having the status of conscious beings. Thus Sartre does not believe that there is a transcendental ego.

The expression 'transcendental ego' has been used by many philosophers in many senses; even within the realm of phenomenology, there is a lack of consensus as to how the ego is to be conceived, or whether one is even necessary.[26] For our purposes, the basic core of the meaning of 'transcendental ego' will be essential for a concept of a self capable of being alienated from itself. We define it as that which (a) allows a greater *unity and continuity* within the stream of particular experiences of any one person than would be accountable for within a Humean or Sartrean stream of consciousness; and (b) can be *experienced by* consciousness, not merely as an abstraction *posited* by consciousness as existing over against consciousness (which would *automatically* alienate the ego from its own consciousness), but rather as an immanent *content* of consciousness itself, experienceable like any other consciousness. This entails a definition of 'transcendental' that differs from the way Husserl used the term, though it has certain essential elements in common with Husserl's usage. We shall see in Chapter III that the transcendental ego in our limited sense performs certain functions that so strikingly transcend the immediate relation to an intentional object, that this ego must be conceived as a phenomenon whose ontological status consists of complex interrelations and interworkings of lower-order states of consciousness.

Can there be 'self-alienation' within such an ego? We define self-alienation as a condition in which the stream of experience within the ego interrelates in such a way that the subject of experience can think that he is aware of a *direct conscious datum* (in the phenomenological sense) while in fact he is not, or can think that he is not while in fact he is. Thus a phenomenological description of the way in which a phenomenon presents itself would have no guarantee of being accurate unless this problem of self-alienation could in some way be contended with.

For reasons we shall outline in a moment, the answer to this question must be affirmative. The phenomenon to which the word 'I' refers is a 'transcendental ego,' though in a limited sense, and this ego can be alienated from itself. As soon as this answer is chosen, several subsidiary questions arise:

(1) What is the *ontological status* of such an ego? Does it have the same kind of being, for example, that a physical thing has? Is it like a 'property' of things, such as size or color, or does it belong to the class of 'events' and 'occurrences,' or to some other class? What kind of entity is it? Where is it?

(2) Since 'ego' has been defined in terms of experience, the two additional questions arise: (a) What is the ontological status of *experience*, especially in relation to physical things and to the body? and (b) What is the relationship between experience and the *ego or self*?

These questions, pertaining to the meaning of 'consciousness' and 'ego,' will tend to dominate the first half of our study. There are also some subsidiary questions pertaining to self-alienation:

(3) For such a thing as self-alienation to occur would mean that it is possible for there to be contents in my consciousness, in some sense, of which I am unaware. We must try to see how this is possible, and indeed *what it can mean* to say 'consciousness of which I am unaware.'

(4) Self-alienation will be conceived as a force which can influence the *direction* of the flow of experience, and therefore indirectly can influence the *content* of experience. It will therefore be necessary to find

ways of studying the constitutive history of a given 'subject' of experience in such a way as to see how the form manifested by the overall direction of the stream exerts an influence upon consciousness which is relatively independent of the content of the experience in question. It can be asked in this regard: (a) Is there a kind of determinism through which, in conjunction with external events, past events in the stream affect future ones? (b) If there is such a determinism, is it still possible for present consciousness to organize itself in such a way as to counteract the alienating features of this determinism?

4. Toward a coherent theoretical approach

The starting point of this study is a recognition of the possibility that, since even the most naive experiencing of relationships between or among things may often already involve conceptualizations and categories of phenomena, a subject's view of the world may be greatly influenced by the limitations of his category structures. The amount of such influence even on the subject of the *philosophical* experience may not be fully transparent to the philosopher who wishes to make the structures of experience themselves the object of his inquiry. In fact, even an attempt simply to describe the way in which phenomena present themselves has no guaranteed exemption from this influence. It is therefore important for any attempt to faithfully describe experience to try to find out either (1) what the extent of the resulting limitation of this attempt is, or (2) how to compensate for such limitation. Self-alienation, therefore, is an important thematic problem in both 'normal' and 'pathological' experiencing.

We shall show that this problem of 'self-alienation' is a proper topic of philosophical inquiry, and cannot merely be relegated to the methods of empirical psychology. The validity of the methodology with which empirical psychology would approach such a question presupposes some philosophical clarification, whereas the validity of this clarification itself is affected in turn by the problem in question.

The solution offered here is based on a purely phenomenological analysis of some essential features of consciousness, supplemented by some logical analysis. Logical analysis, after all, is not excluded by the phenomenological method, although it is true that Husserl believed that the postulates of pure logic flow from a phenomenological *a priori* 'intuition of essence' and not the other way around. Perhaps if phenomenologically oriented thinkers were more frequently to point out and use this compatibility between phenomenology and logic, a better quality of dialogue could be established among the various contemporary styles of philosophizing.

Our solution to the problem of self-alienation can be outlined as follows:

Some *symbolization* of experience (understood in a broad sense) is ontologically necessary for the continued existence of the experience; therefore, an experience cannot be much more fully experienced than it is fully symbolized—at least not for very long. Experience thus motivates its own adequate symbolization, whenever this is possible given environmental circumstances.

When an experience is adequately symbolized, it *explicates* itself[27] in such a way as to motivate *additional* experiences in the future, or at least instances of some certain class of additional experiences; it also motivates the symbolization of these additional experiences, and of the further experience of the way *these* experiences interrelate. In an interconnecting chain of each adequately-symbolized experiences, the meaning of each is related to the meaning of the others. The category structure constituted by the overall nexus of interrelated meanings is broad enough, and includes fine enough distinctions among its various elements, to comprehend any one element in the chain, although a category structure which succeeded only in comprehending a few elements might not adequately comprehend the others without some distortion of them.

To the extent that such an adequately-symbolized and sequentially-motivated pattern obtains, the stream of consciousness is not likely to be very self-alienated; the category structure is then adequate to the description of any one of the experiences as it presents itself, even though the structure may later change so as to become on the whole *more* comprehensive at the instant when a *new* experience occurs. On the other hand, discontinuity and fragmentation in the motivated direction of the flow of experience—which can result in the comprehension of a phenomenon within an inappropriate category—result from a lack of *opportunity to symbolize* experiences in such a way that the additional experiencing that would be called for by those experiences could be carried through *in* the direction called for.

If the solution to the problem of self-alienation is to involve saying that symbolization is ontologically necessary for the full occurrence of experience, then something must be said about the ontological status that experience itself has, and especially about the relation of this kind of being to the kind of being that the *body* has, since we shall see that symbolization involves the use of the body as well as of other physical things. It will be convenient to approach this topic by examining Merleau-Ponty's discussion of this relation in some of his earlier works.[28] Merleau-Ponty's analysis shows that the body has a *prereflective* consciousness of phenomena, and that symbolization helps consciousness to be aware of these phenomena more explicitly as intentional objects—that is, as objects perceived as having such-and-such complexes of qualities whose character can be focused and further clarified through phenomenological description. By symbolizing the experience (for example, by verbalizing it, by expressing it in music, or by dreaming about it), we learn more adequately to thematize what the (imaginary or real) object of our consciousness is. However, although the intentional object becomes more clear when symbolized, there is a sense in which the intentionality involved is already implicitly present in the body's prereflective relation to objects. According to Merleau-Ponty, we do not first see colors and shapes impinging upon our retinas, and then deduce that there is something 'out there' in the world. Rather, from the very beginning our senses see and intend objects as being 'out there.' Symbolization brings this intentionality to a more *reflective* level, further clarifying *what* appears to be out there, and thus increasing the vividness of the experience.

Since the word 'intentionality' becomes important here, it will be helpful to explore its meaning, especially since it will turn out that there arc different ways of intending different classes of objects, and since the kind of intending relevant to the kind of unification necessary to a transcendental ego is different from the *presentative* or *perceptual* kind of intending (which posits its object as *over against* consciousness) that is usually thought of as primary. We shall find that each 'presentative intention' is preceded by another intention, associated with some past consciousness, which motivates consciousness to *attend* to one aspect of a phenomenon as opposed to another. The class of objects 'intended' by this teleological or *motivational* dimension of consciousness can be quite broad. (For example, 'On the basis of my present experience, I wish to be occupied in the future with *any* topic that is to a given extent relevant to topic X, or is relevant to topic X in such and such a way.') A sub-thesis of the solution to the problem of self-alienation will thus be that the entire stream of consciousness of any subject of experience can be analysed in such a way as to reveal (a) that there is a coherent *general pattern* formed by the motivational dimension of all the experiences; (b) that this unity can be *felt by* the self (because it is essentially of the nature of a subjective state of consciousness) and *is* the self (because it is the only factor *experienceable as a kind of consciousness* which can help to provide unity throughout the stream of experience); (c) that there is therefore a 'transcendental ego' in a sense to be formulated somewhat differently from any of the ways in which it has been defined in the past; and (d) that the *lack* of symbolization which we said leads to self-alienation does so by *minimizing the direct consciousness* of this type of unity within the stream of experiences. In this context, we shall have occasion to discuss the thinking of James and Gurwitsch on the unification of the stream of consciousness.[29]

It will become necessary also to lay a foundation for talking about the ontological status of consciousness by considering the relationship between consciousness and the physiological processes of the nervous system. As mentioned at the outset, we reject all current theories as they stand, and instead will try to develop a new conceptualization based on some of Merleau-Ponty's ideas. The essentially *monistic* account we shall end up giving of the relationship between the kind of being that physical things have and the kind of being that consciousness has can be roughly caricatured as resembling somewhat the relationship between a wave and the medium through which the wave is propagated. While all components of a radio receiver must function in a given way in order to elicit music, there is an obvious ontological distinction between the radio components and the music, though not one which would involve a dualism. The distinction is highlighted by the fact that a different radio receiver could be interchanged with the first, yet still pick up the same music. Perhaps more dramatically, in the case of the wave nature of sub-atomic particles, the distinction between the conservation of orbital symmetry in a given context and the laws which govern the behavior of the relevant individual particles *per se* makes a great deal of difference in our understanding of the transmission of the energy involved, thus underscoring a more fundamental ontological distinction between the process and its substratum. Perhaps we should hasten to add, however, that our reasoning will not depend upon such analogies as these, but is simply summarized here by means of them (in addition to our intuitive grasp of the distinction being aided by them). Another question which is related to this question of the relationship between physical things and consciousness will also become important: What is the relationship between these concrete, conscious experiences and the 'self' or 'ego' that seems to emerge through the unity and continuity of such experience? What is the ontological status of the ego? It is *necessary* to have some concept of an ego, as such a unity of experiences, if the disunity which is called 'alienation' is to be accounted for. It is *possible* to have such a concept on the basis of the 'coherent general pattern' which is formed when we take into account the role of motivation in the direction of attention. Chapters III-V of the present study will construct a fuller picture of the meaning 'self' or 'ego,' in this sense. A rough way to briefly summarize this picture would be to say that the self or ego (the phenomenon to which the word 'I' refers) is of the same ontological *kind* as experience, in that the 'I' is a directly experienceable felt meaning and is like a wave in the above sense. This 'I' differs from experience-in-general, however, in that the medium *through which* it is propagated is *experience itself*, rather than only the physical substrata which support experiencing in general. That is, the ego is a type of consciousness whose ontological status is that of a higher-order process than the processes which constitute the other kinds of conscious experiences. The ego is not just ordinary consciousness being conscious of itself.

Thus three things are to be related here: experience, physical things, and the self. The body is an example of the interaction of experience and physical things. Symbolization is another such interaction. The self relates directly to experiences-in-general in that it helps to tie them together, and it also relates to physical things in the same way that any kind of experience does (it depends upon a physical substratum), since it belongs to the class of experiences. In order to qualify as a self, it must always do these two things at the same time.

The epistemological presuppositions of the study, as discussed here and there throughout, are briefly as follows: It is presupposed that the consciousness I call 'mine' really occurs, although it is not assumed that the true character or content of this consciousness is fully transparent to me. It is further assumed that the true nature of the subjective quality of any conscious state is transparent to that conscious state itself, but not the true nature of any relation to the *object* of consciousness. It is *not* assumed, on the other hand, that the nature of consciousness, either with respect to its subjective quality *or* with respect to its relation to an object, is transparent to 'me,' since 'I' will not be taken as by definition numerically identical with each conscious state in its stream of experiences.

On the contrary, its relation to each conscious state is a complex one, and one that cannot be assumed *a priori*, but must be deduced or inferred in some way. The expression 'conscious state' is admittedly objectionable, for it is difficult to rid this term of the connotation of some sort of static entity existing in a discrete instant of time. Far from assuming that consciousness is composed of static units, in fact, one of our conclusions will be that consciousness is a kind of process.

That consciousness should turn out to be a pattern of change in its material substratum, and the self a pattern of change in consciousness, would support the possibility suggested by David Jones, that whether a person is the same person at two different points in his history is only a matter of degrees.[30] In this case, I would still be very much the same person I was yesterday, whereas I might be only to a slight extent the person I may become a billion years from now—just as a pot of water is very much the same pot of water after a few drops have been replaced, but not at all the same after all the drops have been replaced. In consciousness, however, it is the continuity of the *pattern* which is decisive, not the continuity of the substratum. But we should note at the outset that our main purpose is not to deal with the paradoxes of personal continuity discussed by Jones, Coburn, Chisholm, Nozick and others, such as the 'reduplication' problem, the half-brain transplant, etc.[31] The solution to those puzzles, it would seem, would be independent of (but not wholly unrelated to) the answers to the questions we have posed here.

With the first three chapters having been devoted to preliminary clarification of the meaning and ontological status of the ego in relation to consciousness, the focus of attention shifts somewhat beginning with Chapter IV; we shall now be concerned more directly with those features of the ego that make alienation within it possible, but not inevitable. It will have been seen in Chapter III that there is a motivational or teleological element of consciousness that determines in each case, not what will be thought to be true or false, but merely what will be thought *about*. Ultimately, it turns out that what the ego is motivated to think about is in turn determined by other past events in the stream of consciousness, among them what has previously been thought to be true or false. It will not be necessary to go into the question as to whether everything that happens in the stream of consciousness is ultimately determined by events outside of or prior to the ego and its consciousness, though we have discussed this question elsewhere.[32]

We can then begin to fill in some of the contents of this general blue-print. To begin with, there are at least four elements without which consciousness cannot unfold in a continuous and unified way: attention; memory; some cognitive synthesis (putting two or more conscious events into a surveyable whole so that relations between them can be seen); and some analytic or logical functioning. These four elements can be put together in such ways that consciousness can unfold in two different styles, which we call the 'productive' and 'receptive' styles of attention progression. Roughly speaking, in the 'productive' style, the sequential connection between consecutive events is tight, as in the case of a logical deduction; in the 'receptive' style, it is somewhat looser, as in the case of glancing through the books on a shelf to see what might make interesting reading. We use the productive style when we wish to trace further implications from ideational or emotional material already present in consciousness; we use the receptive style when we wish to introduce new data into our stream of consciousness, 'from the outside,' so to speak.

At any given juncture, many possible future directions for the stream of consciousness present themselves, somewhat in the manner of a crossroads. In few cases is the decision arbitrary as to which direction is taken, as for example whether the productive or receptive way of organizing the four more basic functions in time will be used. Nor is such a decision made by the productive or receptive styles themselves. It is made rather by a further component of cognition which we shall name the 'creative' component. To understand how the creative component of cognition functions so as to determine in part the unity and continuity of the stream of consciousness is to understand a motivational and value-positing dimension of consciousness. We shall see that, because of the ontological structure of consciousness discussed earlier, motivation and value cannot exhaustively be described in terms of drive-reductive tendencies alone, but also must involve something like an actualization motivation. It is this motivation which, when adequately symbolized and explicated, seeks in turn the symbolization and explication of other experiences, rather than merely the reduction of drives. Thus, in a sense, there is an implicit 'ethical' stance or value-orientation on the part of consciousness (although a limited one, and one that does not rule out any additional ethical postulates one might want to posit on other grounds); the explication of this dimension accounts for the influence of the creative component of cognition on the direction of the stream of consciousness.

After these analyses are completed, we can then embark upon a description, in Chapter V, of (1) what the structure of consciousness within a transcendental ego looks like when experience is optimally symbolized; (2) what this structure looks like when symbolized only to a small extent; and (3) the circular relationship between inadequate symbolization and self-alienation, which influences to a greater or lesser extent the preconceptual categorizations which undergird both theoretical and practical thinking. Extending this reasoning further, Chapter V will also explore some of the more important epistemological implications of this theory of consciousness.

CHAPTER I

Some contemporary philosophers, such as Feyerabend,[1] Armstrong,[2] and Rorty,[3] speak as though any distinction between subjective processes and their objective manifestations depended upon the supposed 'incorrigibility' of the subjective processes, i.e., the thesis that I cannot think that I experience a pain and be mistaken. Actually, it is not necessary for this purpose that the subjective knowledge of mental states yield any such incorrigible information, but only that it yield *different* —though perhaps equally corrigible—information about the mental states. We shall attempt to demonstrate in this first chapter that direct phenomenological reflection upon mental states does yield different information from objective observation methods, and that the objectifying methods are incapable in principle of observing consciousness without being supplemented by and correlated with phenomenological data. This is true, we shall argue, in spite of the fact that phenomenological data are by no means incorrigible. In fact, many phenomenologists cheerfully grant that the notion of incorrigible access to one's own subjective consciousness by means of a complete phenomenological reduction went out of style long ago, when the phenomenologists Merleau-Ponty and Sartre (and many say Husserl himself in the *Crisis* and other posthumous papers) pronounced the idea of a complete phenomenological reduction impossible in principle. There are certain items of information about the nature of consciousness which even phenomenological psychology (not to mention objectivistic psychology) cannot ascertain, but for which it must have recourse to philosophy.

Since the mid-1970s, U.S. and British psychologists have begun to reaffirm the thesis, long urged by phenomenologists, that to explain the more complex areas of human behavior (e.g., problem-solving and social behavior), as well as to help people therapeutically, requires in many instances not merely a theoretical organization based on *behavioral* observations alone, but also calls for an empirically-verifiable understanding of *cognition* and *consciousness* as well. Whereas psychology students earlier had been taught that only behavior was subject to scientific observation and measurement and therefore that only behavioral theories were susceptible of empirical validation, many psychology texts now encourage an eclectic approach which would incorporate both behavioral and cognitive theoretical orientations.[4] This new trend obviously reopens some old and fundamental problems in the philosophy of social science revolving around the methodological difficulty in principle of how to observe subjective events objectively.

If we expect to reach any different conclusions regarding the possibility of empirical knowledge of conscious and cognitive events from those reached by Pavlov and Watson in the early days of behaviorism,[5] our attention is naturally drawn to a whole new highly-developed trend which now exists in the form of phenomenological psychology, whose purpose is precisely to develop ways of observing conscious phenomena scientifically.[6] It was phenomenology, in fact, which originally inspired the work of Carl Rogers and Abraham Maslow,[7] and therefore indirectly that of their many disciples and fellow-cognitivists of the 1950s and 60s. This early mass of quasi-phenomenological work, however, is subject to many criticisms, both in methodological principle and in the specific techniques used to gather and assess the data. We shall also demonstrate here that the better and more fully-developed pure phenomenological psychology of the present time is also limited by the same inevitable methodological inadequacies—*unless*, that is, it is willing to base itself on a body of theory which is not empirical in origin at all, but rather is purely philosophical, i.e., the ontological conclusions reached regarding man by the phenomenological philosophers themselves, especially the existential phenomenologists who thematize man-in-existence. Such a rash suggestion, of course, runs counter to the thinking of many phenomenological philosophers and psychologists, who maintain that psychology should only make use of the *method* of investigation outlined by Husserl in his *Lectures on Phenomenological Psychology*; in those lectures, Husserl specifically admonishes psychologists against speculating *a priori* as to the 'essence of man' or the 'nature of consciousness.'[8] Yet phenomenological philosophy has developed and changed in complex ways since that time, and one of the most fundamental changes has been that later phenomenologists such as Merleau-Ponty and Sartre no longer believe that phenomenological philosophy can reflect upon a pure transcendental ego as divorced from a really-existing psychophysical 'I'.[9] One ramification of this reversal is that the basis for the very distinction between phenomenological philosophy and phenomenological psychology, as drawn by Husserl, must again be questioned. Perhaps more important, the phenomenological method of observation in the empirical-research situation simply is not immune to the same inevitable limitations that have plagued empirical researchers all along, resulting in the unreliability of self-reports, personality scales, projective techniques, factor analysis, and all the other traditional attempts to observe conscious phenomena empirically.

In spite of this forbidding complex of difficulties, and really because of it, it will become obvious that if psychology is to genuinely ground a methodological approach to consciousness and cognition, it must have recourse not only to phenomenological *psychological* methodology, but also and more importantly, to the actual conclusions reached by phenomenological philosophers themselves regarding the nature of consciousness—notwithstanding the early admonition of Husserl to the contrary. At the same time, it is obvious that we must proceed very cautiously in this direction because both the methodological issues and the substantial conclusions of various phenomenological philosophers are still hotly disputed and are by no means obviously true. Many phenomenologists, in fact, obviously contradict each other. Moreover, one must search diligently through the phenomenological literature in order to find those ontological assertions which would be directly relevant to psychological theory. The authors who are most apt to offer theoretical statements with direct applicability to the psychological subject are those who assume that there is no distinction between this subject and the transcendental ego, or that because there is no difference between the psychological subject and the ego, there can be no transcendental ego at all. Examples of such authors are Sartre (whose psychological conclusions, however, are highly controversial), Merleau-Ponty, Gurwitsch, and perhaps Heidegger and the hermeneutic philosophers such as Godamer, Ricoeur, Ihde, and Bernstein.[10] Obviously, there are clear differences and contradictions among the psychological implications of these theorists.

In this chapter, we shall focus upon the methodological difficulty of making either direct or indirect observations of conscious events in a way that would be free of unwarranted and obviously biased presuppositions. Specifically, section 1 will select for discussion three general factors that make experimental psychology distort our view of man to some as-yet-unspecifiable extent because these factors show that in psychology, more than in the physical sciences, hypotheses tend to be partly self-confirming in the way discussed by Thomas Kuhn;[11] for these three broad reasons, at least, the inherent inaccuracy of translating subjective into objective data allows—in fact, forces—the investigator to limit the field of possibly disconfirming data in ways methodologically predetermined by the nature of the hypothesis itself: (1) The wider the gap to be bridged between theory and observables by means of extensive auxiliary inferences, the fewer are the concrete instances where such a complex inference can conveniently be made; but when the number of possibly disconfirming instances which can be observed are few, the chances of accepting a false theory (because it fails to be disconfirmed by any objective experience) are great. (2) When a science attempts to connect phenomena which have extremely different ontological status (i.e., consciousness and observable manifestations of it), the number of possible explanations for the same statistical correlations multiplies. Such an attempt also necessitates the assumption, for statistical purposes, that the data covered by the science are homogeneous, which in psychology they may not be, and the consequent prejudice against holistic phenomena; similarly, the lack of any quantitative means for comparing the relative *importance* of variables whose homogeneity cannot be established is an extremely difficult problem. (3) Psychology shows a marked tendency to produce theories which account for different sets of data, while there seems to be no way to determine whether one theory can account for the other's data or vice versa. Combining factors (2) and (3) also shows that objectifying approaches will inevitably lead to reductionistic motivational theories by preference over self-actualization and existential theories. Finally, section 2 will show that phenomenological psychology, as an empirical rather than *a priori* discipline, cannot really escape these three basic difficulties either, although it is less prone, for philosophical reasons, to become reductionistic.

1. Attempts to observe the subjective objectively

Thomas Kuhn, in *The Structure of Scientific Revolutions,* suggests that one problem inherent in scientific reasoning in general is that the researcher, in choosing which tests to perform in order to see whether the facts conform to his hypothesis, may be inadvertently directed toward certain *kinds* of facts by preference over others.[12] His selection of facts is influenced by his theoretical sense of which facts are important and by which facts his experimental apparatus is best equipped to measure. Both these factors tend to be influenced by the hypothesis which is being tested. Similarly, phenomenological theorists such as Jacob Needleman emphasize the pre-perceptual set of the scientist in influencing the way he perceives the objects of his particular science. Disconfirming observations remain possible, but not as likely as they would be if apparently irrelevant facts were not ruled out *a priori* by this system of expectations and selective attention.[13] Observations made in a clinical setting, for example, are seldom relevant to the validation of learning theory, unless a few very limited aspects of that setting can be singled out as focal points accessible to the usual research designs applicable to learning-theory phenomena. Similarly, the behavior of rats would hardly be entertained as a possible source for validation of a process theory such as that of Carl Rogers.

This point is relevant to the empirical study of conscious events in a way more serious than and qualitatively different from its relevance to the physical sciences. Earlier, we mentioned three essential peculiarities of the objective observation of subjective phenomena that tend to exaggerate the Kuhnian problem to more severe proportions than in the natural sciences. Let's examine these peculiarities in a little more detail.

(1) A wide gap to be bridged between theory and observables, by means of extensive auxiliary inferences, indirectly increases the probability that possibly disconfirming data may be ignored—especially when auxiliary hypotheses themselves depend upon theory or previous research. This is true because when the inferences that lead from the postulation of a theoretical variable to its observable manifestations are very complex, as is the case in progressing from psychical variables to objectively observable and measurable manifestations, the number of available instances where such inferences can conveniently and reasonably be made diminishes. For example, the number of known experimental situations that can measure a theoretical connection between extraversion and retroactive inhibition are extremely few and are limited primarily to eyelid conditioning experiments and experiments involving a pursuit-rotary task.[14] But—and this is the key point—the more limited the number of observable facts which can be used as a true test of a hypothesis, the less likely anyone is to be able to observe those facts which, if they *could* be observed, might conceivably disconfirm the theory. The odds are against a direct and conclusive disconfirmation of retroactive inhibition theory, since the elaborate technique of eyelid conditioning was originally perfected by Eysenck and his associates (the proponents of the theory) because its results are in fact congruent with the theory.

(2) When a theory attempts to connect phenomena which have different ontological status (such as the radically dissimilar phenomena of consciousness and behavior), then the statistical correlations between them can be explained in a variety of different ways, depending on one's ontological commitments. These different explanations cannot be tested against each other experimentally because the thesis that a given experimental datum represents an underlying psychological construct would already involve correlating variables at different ontological levels. The purely natural sciences need not preoccupy themselves so much with ontological issues in order to carry out their research, since all the terms to be correlated in any given natural science can be safely assumed to exist at the same ontological level. Moreover, all the phenomena investigated by natural sciences have in common that they present themselves as objects of experience, whereas psychology must correlate some data that present themselves as objects of experience with other data that are directly observable only as subjective events. So in psychology, at least to the extent that it hopes to study consciousness at all, many equally viable theories can explain the same facts, and there is no experimental ground for comparison between many of these theories. This incommensurability between theories leads researchers to ignore data fields associated with rival theories simply because such data could also conceivably be explained by their own theory. The direction of each worker's research interest then narrows so that each is again to some extent predisposed toward the kinds of apparatus and research design likely to favor confirmation rather than disconfirmation. Also, the attempt to correlate data at different ontological levels leads to an imprecision that engenders further selectivity in accepting or rejecting alternative explanations of the same data. When correlations are obtainable only in the range of .30 to .40, with 1.00 representing perfect correlation, researchers are all the more free to interpret the same data as having different theoretical implications. (A .30 correlation, after all, only accounts for nine percent of the variance, a .40 correlation only 16 percent.)

Since the natural sciences connect variables of similar ontological status, compared with those of psychology's attempts to study consciousness, it follows that natural scientists can reasonably assume that their data are somewhat homogeneous. Natural phenomena all exist in space, which can conveniently be divided into homogeneous parts for the purpose of measurement (although, as Poincaré points out, there is no logical necessity for such a division[15]). The assumption that subjective variables are homogeneous, however, is on less solid ground, since there is some evidence that some psychological phenomena may function holistically rather than in *partes extra partes* fashion.[16] Therefore the *isolation* of variables, which is so necessary in statistical reasoning, can easily be done in the natural sciences, whereas in psychology it is always necessary to *assume* that an isolated variable or set of variables is still the same in essential respects when disconnected from the holistic complex in which it participates.

Consequently, ·there is no way of quantitatively comparing the relative *importance* of variables whose homogeneity cannot be established. Self-actualization theorists like Maslow are free to accept the validity of homeostatic drive theory in its entirety while still relegating that theory to a very minor place in the total explanation of the functioning of man as an emotional and intellectual being.[17] And since *where* a given researcher looks for his data is motivated by a sense of the importance of those data, each researcher will be motivated to look for the kinds of data that are more likely to support his own.theory than a mere random sampling of all possible observations would support, if such a random sampling were possible.

(3) That literally hundreds of mutually conflicting psychological theories can respectably coexist is a well-known fact which in itself does not discredit those theories. In any science, more than one theory can successfully account for the same experimental data. A more significant point for our purposes is that in the field of psychology, conflicting theories often account for *different sets* of data, while there seems to be no way to determine whether one theory can account for the other's data or vice versa. The primary reason for this incommensurability of psychological theories appears to involve the difficulty of getting at psychological data in the first place. This inherent difficulty stems from the necessity of translating subjective phenomena (some of the phenomena about which psychology theorizes) into objective phenomena accessible to measurement and manipulation.

The reduction of the subject to an object leads to a reductionism in the realm of motivational theory and investigation where behaviors can only be interpreted as intended to lead to a rewarding end-state—whereas such a *stasis,* once achieved, would deprive consciousness of one of its main essential and distinguishing features (at least according to some philosophers), i.e., that it is a becoming or process rather than a static thing-like entity. The experimental prejudice in favor of reductionism seems to stem from the principle of 'parsimoneity'[18] in the philosophy of science—the modern-day version of Ockham's thesis that 'What can be explained on fewer principles is explained needlessly by more.' The most parsimonious way to explain motivation is to reduce it to as few principles as possible. Also, motivational theories which are not reductionistic are not as amenable to objective observations which might constitute relevant test implications as are theories that reduce motivation to physicalistic or stimulus-response terms. The more physicalistic or behavioristic a theory, the more readily it can be supported through observation in the sense of measurable and operationally-definable experimental parameters.

Use of scientific method in psychology is necessarily objectifying. There is no possibility of making hypotheses and confirming or disconfirming them without translating the subjective into the objective because the scientific method requires operational definition. In order to formulate an operational definition of any construct, we must have reliable methods of observing and measuring the phenomena investigated.

The necessity for prediction and controls in psychological research demands that the experimentor be able to manipulate variables. The psychologist must obtain his view of the phenomena as much through affecting them as by being affected by them. This too is as true in the other sciences as in psychology and should not be construed in itself as a criticism, but it seems to have more of a limiting effect on psychology than on physical sciences. The validation of Eysenck's personality theory, for example, requires the use of an extremely complicated apparatus and research design.[19] A very imaginative experimentor might be able to disconfirm the hypothesis, but only if he has accurately replicated the experimental apparatus and research design originally used to support the hypothesis, since, as mentioned in point (1) above, the number of relevant test implications at an objectively observable and quantifiable level are so few. The proponent of the hypothesis plays on his home field, whose terrain works to his advantage. The more difficulties stand in the way of inferring from the theory to possibly disconfirming test implications *which could be objectively observed,* the less susceptible the theory is to disconfirmation even if it is false.

So the facts investigated by any psychological researcher are necessarily extremely selected, much more so than in sciences that take naturally-occurring objective phenomena as their subject matter. And the facts are as much actively created as they are passively observed. This, again, does not automatically present any methodological difficulty. That the split atom is a creation of the scientist does not keep it from yielding useful information. The discovery that a manipulation can even successfully be performed may in itself constitute an important statement about the way things are. But the problem does arise that the intensely selective and creative aspects of psychological observation are bound to vastly exaggerate the propensity of psychologists to see only, or at least primarily, what they are looking for and to ignore what they are not looking for. Perhaps this problem is not correctable, as it is to some extent in the other sciences, but rather is essential to the process of making the subject matter present itself in a guise which at best has an entirely foreign ontological status, i.e., the process of making the subject of experience appear as an object of experience.

The problem appears still less correctable when we explore some further implications of point (2) above. If a variable is to be accessible to statistical manipulation, it must first be isolated. (Otherwise it would be impossible to determine that one specific variable really does statistically correlate with another.) But to study a variable in isolation is precisely to ignore the point that it is in holistic equilibrium with other variables. In effect, this means that use of the experimental or hypothetico-deductive method to study the subject of experience enforces a prejudice against holistic phenomena and leads to the interpretation of them as though they were not holistic. For example, paper and pencil personality scales usually have as their goal the statistical grouping of responses into 'clusters' with high correlations between items within each cluster and low correlations between clusters. The ideal result would be to devise a test whose clusters would be perfectly orthogonal to each other, so that the experimentor could conclude that the clusters are relatively independent of each other and therefore constitute personality 'factors' or 'traits.' But by isolating the variables (i.e., test items), the designer of the test must take out of their natural context the behaviors and feelings about which he inquires. The test thus removes the variable from its role in some ongoing, holistic picture of the motivated functioning of the personality structure which the subject himself would see in terms of the context and purpose of each specific behavior. A procedure which must isolate variables in order to define them cannot ask the holistic question as to whether the personality structures being measured may not constitute a larger equilibrium in which teleological interactions between and among factors may be more important for the functioning of the

organism than the absolute quantity attributable to any particular factor. The meaning of a phenomenon *to the subject* may be definable only
in terms of its relationships with other variables.

Someone might argue that the very fact that such tests produce correlations between variables at all speaks for itself. This argument, however,
forgets that psychological research as a whole yields correlations at best
in the neighborhood of .30 to .40, accounting for nine to sixteen percent of the variance—hardly an impressive indication that some systematic
sources of error are not at work even in the rationale behind the very
design of the research. One of these sources of error might very conceivably be an unavoidable prejudice against holistic phenomena.

An interrelated methodological problem is determining *what* a given
test or procedure 'really' 'measures.' (Absolutely pure behaviorisms,
which would not need to concern themselves with this problem because
of their strict operationism, are not relevant to this discussion because
they are not relevant to the study of the human *psyche,* which is the
psychological correlate of the subject of experience.) If we want to
measure a predominantly subjective condition, it may be possible in principle to construct tests and behavior observations to indicate what the
underlying feelings and states of mind are, but the connection or correlation between the subjective state and the test or behavior observation must be grounded in one of two ways: either through a 'face validity' procedure such as that of Spence[20] (which is really an informally
phenomenological analysis of the *meaning* of the test items), or through
factor analysis as employed by Catell[21] and many others who use the
purely statistical manipulations of factor analysis in order to construct
operationally self-defining variables which need not appeal to any
common-sense or phenomenological interpretation of the meaning of
the variables being manipulated and correlated. The 'face validity' procedure is open to the charge that the test may not really measure what
it claims to measure—that the connection between the observable
responses to the test items and the variable these responses are supposed
to measure is not scientifically demonstrable or assessable. Use of factor analysis as an operationally self-defining technique, on the other hand,
requires ostensive definition (for example, defining intelligence as 'that
which' an intelligence test measures) and makes difficult any assessment
of the extent to which the test orders the subject's responses in terms
of categories preconceived by the experimentor, as in the case of the factor
on Catell's 16PF that measures "Bohemianism," defining it either *a priori*

or through theoretical interpretation as "hysterical unconcern; favors the abstract over the concrete."[22] In fact, only if the designer of a factor-analytic test has some thoroughgoing theoretical preoccupation can he hope to obtain orthogonality between clusters of items. (These theoretical preoccupations in practice usually derive from a factor's reliable tendency to correlate significantly with clinical diagnoses, with other measurable behavior parameters or, sometimes, with learning curves; in order to be significant, however, a correlation need not be extremely high.) The task of designing a test that will yield truly orthogonal or even nearly or-thogonal dimensions is an extremely ambitious one which has only been achieved by two or three factor-analytic workers, and then only after years of trial and error and repeated revision of the test items themselves. Strictly speaking, this process of repeated behind-the-scenes revision violates one of the fundamental tenets of hypothetico-deductive reasoning itself, that a theory should *predict* previously unknown facts rather than merely accommodate itself to facts already known. There are also some logical problems peculiar to the factor-analytic method, as employed in this way, which are irresolvable except through analysis of the meaning of the test items themselves. For example, if we could find two ques-tions which consistently failed to correlate, such as 'Do you consider yourself Republican?' and 'Do you dress before shaving?', we could con-ceivably rephrase the question in fifty different ways to produce a test which would give the appearance of yielding orthogonal dimensions of personality. An implicit and imprecise presupposition of the factor-analytic method is that the test items must each ask a really different question from each other item, rather than merely repeating essentially the same question—whereas no known procedure can determine whether in fact they do so on any given test. In constructing personality scales, some kind of face-validity analysis of the meanings of the items, whether implicit or explicit, seems unavoidable. Here again, the lack of homogeneity in subjective phenomena precludes precise measurement.

The difficulty of determining what a given test or procedure really measures combines with the other methodological problems discussed above to lead to situations in which different researchers actually *see* different and contradictory data while looking at the same phenomena. A case in point is the famous Spence-Eysenck controversy. This as-yet-unresolved controversy illustrates, not merely the well-known fact that psychological theories disagree in their interpretations of the same facts, but that their methodology leads them to observe the *facts themselves* in mutually contradictory ways. Researchers working with the Maudsley, Guilford and Eysenck personality scales have found that "C" (an alleged "conditionability" factor) correlates significantly in a negative direction with E (extraversion) but not with N (neuroticism, or anxiety). The procedure used to reveal these correlations is eyelid-conditioning.[23] At the same time, researchers working with the predictions from Spence learning theory and using Janet Taylor Spence's Manifest Anxiety Scale (MAS), have used the same eyelid-conditioning procedure to yield data that contradict the Eysenck data—correlations between conditionability and MAS (anxiety or neuroticism) but not between conditionability and E, even though Janet and Kenneth Spence and their associates used Eysenck's own personality scale to measure for E.[24] Eysenck and his associates have also used the MAS test, finding no significant correlations with conditionability. Eysenck's data are indeed predicted by his theory, whereas the Spence data—data that directly contradict Eysenck's —are predicted by Spence learning theory. For years this paradoxical controversy has stood as a suspicious-looking stumbling block in the way of much realistic progress toward the attainment of the 'true facts' in an area of investigation which originally seemed so promising because the wide-range implications of both the Spence and Eysenck theories are so diverse and all-pervasive.

In sum, then, Kuhn's point about the partially self-confirming nature of hypotheses in the hypothetico-deductive method is vastly more applicable to psychology than to the natural sciences. The problems discussed above all derive from the fact that psychology must study subjective phenomena or phenomena that interrelate with subjective ones, whereas in order to make these phenomena amenable to hypothetico-deductive reasoning, scientists must first translate them into objectively observable data. The possible contributions of phenomenological psychology to this problem will be discussed next.

2. Phenomenological psychology encounters similar problems

Since phenomenologists have criticized empirical psychology for treating the subject as an object, one might expect to find in phenomenological psychology an alternative to the experimental method. Rather than an alternative method, however, phenomenology seems to offer a complementary method, to be used alongside the experimental method in order to get at facts which are inaccessible to the experimental approach. Amedeo Giorgi, one of the most articulate and systematic spokesmen for phenomenological methodology in psychology, emphasizes that phenomenology does not rule out the use of experiment. Rather, it uses experiment where appropriate, and uses the method of phenomenological description where experiment is not appropriate.[25] As far as validation of findings and theories is concerned, phenomenological psychologists seem to do three things that experimental psychologists do not do: *Experiential* observation on the part of the researcher, experiential observation on the part of the subject, and 'eidetic' or 'meaning' analysis on the part of the researcher and/or the subject. The third factor, eidetic analysis, always accompanies one or the other of the first two.

Experiential observation on the part of the researcher adds to mere empirical observation an additional technique—phenomenological reduction—which is intended to overcome the prejudice against holistic phenomena. Before subjecting the phenomenon to be studied to mere empirical observation, the phenomenologist attempts to determine *what* is being observed. By bracketing out theoretical presuppositions of all kinds (phenomenological reduction), including the unwarranted assumption that the meaning of a phenomenon is the same as the method of measuring it, the phenomenologist attempts to see the phenomenon as it immediately presents itself in the total context in which it naturally seems to occur. In the total context, its full and authentic *meaning* can be explicated (eidetic analysis)—something which may very well not happen if the phenomenon is isolated before the research begins. ''By analyzing meaning the significance and relevance of an experience for the whole person becomes intelligible. Furthermore, a knowledge of the essence of the phenomena of consciousness is indispensable for an understanding of them,'' says Giorgi.[26] ''The approach of phenomenology is characterized by the attitude of openness for whatever is significant for the proper understanding of a phenomenon. The subject is required to concentrate on the experience of the phenomenon exactly as it is given to him, and not to pre-judge it nor to see it through any specific perspective simply because of previous knowledge about the phenomenon.''[27] The phenomenological method of observation is essentially similar to that of the experimentalist (empirical intuition through the senses) except that it is cleansed, through the reduction, of the sedimented presuppositions that ordinarily contaminate perception, and it is complemented with a clarification of the meaning of the phenomenon presented.

Experiential observation on the part of the subject of the research works essentially in the same way as experiential observation on the part of the researcher, except that the subject also has access to a more immediate perspective on his own conscious events. The researcher can only see signs that the subject may be thinking or feeling a certain way, whereas the subject can actually think his own thoughts and feel his own feelings. If he can be induced to adhere to the phenomenological techniques of reduction and eidetic analysis in reflecting on these subjective events, he can then provide a way of getting at them that is not available to mere objective observation on the part of the researcher. As Schultz says, "Perhaps, then, the best way of investigating the nature of man is to ask him."[28]

Eidetic meaning analysis may also be used in isolation from any particular experiential observation. The psychologist may choose first to do phenomenology in its purely philosophical sense in order to investigate essential and necessary aspects of the phenomenon of consciousness *per se*; he may ask, "What does it mean to be a conscious being in general? Are there ontological dimensions in the absence of which it would make no logical sense to call a being 'conscious'?" R.D. Laing relies heavily on this method, first exploring the meaning of pure possibilities for consciousness and then attempting to apply what he has learned through such analysis to his particular cases.[29] Sartre uses it in that half of his *Psychology of the Imagination* which deals with "The Certain" (before turning to "The Probable").[30] And Needleman and Binswanger use it in the work by those authors previously cited. Husserl, however, cautions psychologists against its use; we shall see why in a moment. We shall also see that experiential observation on the part of both the researcher and the subject of the research are subject to the same validational problems encountered by empirical psychology. Ultimately, Needleman's point about the dependence of observation upon the category structure of the researcher, and Kuhn's point about the partial self-confirming of hypotheses, remain all-pervasive even in the context of phenomenological psychology.

On an abstract level, the differences in principle between naturalistic and phenomenological psychology seem clear cut. But in practice they tend to break down, for in practice it seems unavoidable that the psychologist must, and in fact does, rely on objective experience and interpretation of this experience. It is well known, for example, that

Merleau-Ponty in his psychological work began with observed facts and encouraged his students to take a controlled, experimental approach to the verification of their hypotheses (this is evident, for example, in his essay "The Child's Relations with Others").[31] Satre, too, in his psychological writings, cites the results of experiments as integral parts of his reasoning (for example, in his *Psychology of the Imagination,* cited above, and in his *Esquisse d'une Theorie des Emotions*).[32] Phenomenologically oriented clinicians tend to rely in their practice on the valid specifiability of what the real as well as intentional object of their experience is, as opposed to attending to the experience itself as phenomenologically reduced. (Moreover, we shall demonstrate later that in the context of Husserlian phenomenology not only the *real*, but even the *intentional* object of an experience cannot be precisely specified without presupposing a great amount of self-knowledge and unity in the functioning of the transcendental ego.[33])

Even if one takes an empathic rather than an inferential approach to the subject's (i.e., other person's) experiencing, as Carl Rogers attempts to do, the overwhelming tendency of psychologists, including Rogers, is to test the appropriateness of procedures and the validity of conclusions against positivistically and objectivistically oriented methods of verification. Rogers, for example, in his use of the "experiencing scale" which he and Gendlin constructed, validates the results by correlating the seven stages of therapy with other measures that have grown out of the experimental and factor-analytic traditions, such as Q Sorts, inter-rater correlations and scores on various personality scales such as the MMPI and the 16PF; and the overall structure of Rogers' and associates' reasoning in such instances is hypothetico-deductive. Thus it might appear that the perceptions and conceptions that come out of empathic observation in therapy situations have to be supported with inferences, even if inference is not used in the empathic process itself. In attempting to support the results of phenomenological investigations by using these hypothetico-deductive techniques, certain alien assumptions are carried over into phenomenology itself, such as the theory of the self-concept implied in the use of Q Sorts, or the inexplicit theoretical presuppositions originally used in defining the categories to be quantified or already having been quantified in factor analytically oriented scales and their accompanying statistical techniques. This approach in effect puts the entire phenomenological side of the thinking and practice of psychologists like Rogers in the position of one among many hypotheses to be confirmed or disconfirmed by the traditional objectifying modes of experiencing criticized by Kuhn and Needleman; such an approach therefore carries all the mistakes pointed out above into the validation procedures of phenomenology itself, in full force. For example, if the validity of phenomenologically derived results is going to be tested against Catell's 16PF, this presupposes the validity of Catell's category structure, whereas that category structure is phenomenologically naive. Catell has never pretended to be a phenomenologist or to reflect on the categories in terms of which he proposes to measure people from the standpoint of their subjective context, importance or validity. He has never proposed to integrate these *partes extra partes* 'traits' into an overall picture of the motivated functioning of a holistic personality structure in terms of the purpose and context of each type of 'behavior.'

Suppose we ignore for a moment the traditional validational tools of research and ask what kind of validation might come purely from experiential methods, such as relying on the therapeutic setting itself as a means of finding out what is going on with the other person. Then we would seem to be stuck with one of several presuppositions: (1) Either I presuppose that the person is simply telling me the truth about himself, which implies that he knows the truth and that he is telling himself the truth—in short, that he is wholly and simply transparent to himself, which is doubtful in view of the propensity of human beings to misconstrue, misrepresent or just plain not recognize their own feelings and thoughts. Or (2) I presuppose that I can tell whether what he says is true and that he is wholly and simply transparent to me, that I know what he is experiencing better than he himself knows, which is anti-phenomenological. Or (3) I presuppose that the client-centered or some other therapeutic technique is going to help him to become more and more transparent to himself, which is a serious way of assuming the very thing I need to establish, an assumption made by many proposed therapeutic techniques in need of validation, many of which may be capable through hook or crook of convincing the person that he now more fully understands himself, while in fact he only covers over an already intricate web of defenses with additional ones. (One might cite the Divine Light Mission as an extreme example of this alternative.) Since none of these presuppositions can reasonably be made, it would appear that phenomenology must rely on empirical validation of facts as much as experimental psychology does.

With regard to the possibility of purely eidetic meaning-analysis as

divorced from the epistemic validation of any empirical observations—
i.e., phenomenological examination of ontological structures of consciousness *per se*, which does not rely upon any empirical generalizations —the problem becomes one of application to particulars. How and
when do we know that a given particular case is in fact an instance of
an eidetic meaning or essence which has been arrived at independently
of particular factual claims? Merleau-Ponty is skeptical on this issue:

> [Husserl] was, therefore, well aware of the danger of self-
> deception in proceeding by 'eidetic intuition.'. . . Though
> a knowledge of facts is never sufficient for grasping an
> essence and though the construction of 'idealizing fictions'
> is always necessary, I can never be sure that my vision
> of an essence is anything more than a prejudice rooted
> in language—if it does not enable me to hold together
> all the facts which are known and which may be brought
> into relation with it. Failing this, it may not be an essence
> at all, but only a prejudice.[34]

But some of the "facts that are known" may already be distorted due
to previous prejudices rooted in language or in the misapprehension of
essences. Thus cases are quite possible in which this mutual support of
facts and eidetic intuitions may become like the blind leading the blind.
For example, consider Laing's description of the following eidos:

> Jill is married to Jack. She does not want to be married
> to Jack. She is frightened to leave Jack. So she stays with
> Jack and *imagines* she is not married to him. Eventually
> she does not feel married to Jack. So she has to imagine
> she is. "I have to remind myself that he is my husband."
> A common maneuvre. Elusion is a way of getting round
> conflict without direct confrontation, or its resolution.
> It eludes conflict by playing off one modality of ex-
> perience against another. She imagines she is not mar-
> ried and then imagines she is. Elusive spirals go on and
> on.[35]

But, given any Jill who finds herself pretending to be married and pretending not to be, this analysis may or may not apply. How is she to know

whether Laing's account applies to her particular case? There are many other eidetic descriptions that might apply to the same factual situation, as far as the facts are known. For example, she may indeed want to be married to Jack although communication problems have led to the present state of affairs. The same problem applies in Berne's 'transactional analysis,' for no way is given to determine in any given case which of the 'games' Berne describes is the one in fact being played.[36] This is essentially the objection Georg Lukacs raises against Max Scheler's use of eidos. Once the eidetic description of the Devil is complete, he says, then the brackets must be removed, whereupon one should hope to be confronted with the Devil himself.[37] But no eidetic description of the essence of the Devil can ever tell us whether a given phenomenon is in fact a Devil. There simply is no way around the necessity in psychology of ascertaining what the facts actually are. Ultimately, the facts must be obtained either through a researcher's empirical experience or through the subject's internal (but equally fallible) experience.

It seems that eidetic analysis alone provides no access to consciousness as an object of empirical study, since the application of any eidetic description to any real case would require further empirical information. And, given that we cannot simply step outside our preconceptual category structures in order to rid empirical experiences of the kind of implicit presuppositions and structural problems we have been discussing, little certainty is likely to result by combining eidetic analysis with empirical observation (although we grant that this combination is better than the empirical experience by itself). So where does this leave us? Is there no way to get reliable information about the nature of consciousness?

Somehow, we must find some solid information in which to anchor ourselves—some set of universal truths which we can assume applicable to *any given* consciousness. Then we could use these truths as presuppositions to ground empirical inquiry. The problem is not to proceed on the basis of *no* presuppositions (for this would be impossible), but to proceed on the basis of correct presuppositions. The way to get at these presuppositions and their validation is through the methods of inquiry available to philosophy, not through those available to psychology.

Let's return for a moment to Laing's example. The real reason for Jill's inability to determine whether Laing's eidetic description applies to her particular case is that she is *not fully conscious of her own consciousness.* If this paradoxical issue of 'unconscious consciousness' could be cleared up, and if the subject of any actual research could develop a method of focusing on his own consciousness in a way that would be verifiably purified of 'prereflective' and 'unconscious' effects on the thematization of his reflective apperception, then we would have reliable results and then the purely abstract, philosophical conclusions reached through eidetic analysis could be applied. But here we would finally and definitely have crossed the nebulous line separating phenomenological psychology from philosophy, for two basic kinds of philosophical problems would now have to be solved: First, how to arrive at a phenomenologically 'purified' and universally-applicable eidetic description of some aspect of consciousness, in the face of the possible presence of unconscious and prereflective motives at work in the preconceptual category structure or perspectival limitation of the subject of experience (his 'existential *a priori*'), which is now widely considered to follow from the impossibility of a pure transcendental ego in reflection; secondly, how to deal with the problem of 'unconscious consciousness.' The answer to the first of these two questions also depends partly on an answer to the second, for the perspectival limitations of the philosopher himself come into play when he attempts to describe a pure eidos, as will be discussed more fully later. Unless the problem of 'unconscious consciousness' is dealt with, involving as it does the question of the meaning of 'prereflective consciousness,' then the philosopher will remain unable to reflectively 'read off' his eidetic intuitions in a way that remains unlimited by distorting biases and free of prereflective prejudices. Needless to say, the subject of phenomenological psychology experiments (or the experimentor/therapist acting in his behalf) would be equally subject to this limitation.

With regard to the debate over the 'incorrigibility' of subjective information, it should be clear by now that no such incorrigibility is to be found. But it should also be evident that whatever is going on in consciousness cannot be ascertained by means of purely objective methods divorced from the use of previously-acquired subjective information and assumptions about how subjective and objective events correlate with each other. Thus there is subjective information which is different in kind from what can be acquired objectively. Even if one wanted to assume that someday it will be possible to diagnose a headache purely by means of objective instrumentation, there is still a difference between *identifying the presence* of a headache and *feeling* the headache. Only by means of some previous subjective consciousness would we know what the experience is that we are identifying by means of our objectifying instruments.

In sum, our conclusion must be that no one has yet worked out a very reliable way to empirically observe conscious events independently of the biases discussed above. The most promising direction in this regard appears to be phenomenological psychology, which still cannot avoid the biases, however, unless it is furnished with two things by phenomenological and/or other kinds of philosophy: A pure, *a priori* theory of the nature and ontological structures of consciousness *per se*, which proceeds from eidetic intuition and logical analysis of the meaning of being conscious; and a viable way to understand and overcome the problem of reflection upon 'prereflective' and therefore essentially 'unconscious' consciousness. How can this reflection bypass the subject's notoriously limited, category-structured and thus distorted perspective on his own consciousness? That question must be given a well-grounded epistemological (therefore philosophical) answer before phenomenological psychology's attempt to penetrate into an individual subject's consciousness can become scientifically reliable. The danger is that the phenomenological analysis of the nature of consciousness, particularly with regard to its category structures and to the prereflective and unconscious, will become one of those perennial philosophical questions to which many reasonable solutions are possible but none are strictly provable. Then the study of consciousness, in both psychology and philosophy, might become an endlessly unfolding dialectical process, which nonetheless could sometimes demonstrate that some solutions make more sense than others. But if there is any truth in the 'coherence' theory of epistemology, this problem would exist for all the other sciences as well. And if not—such an approach would still be preferable to a situation in which psychology seeks no information from philosophy about the nature of consciousness.

The common sense supposition which regards psychology as a purely empirical science, containing no room for any philosophical speculation except as regards the philosophy of scientific methodology, has only become prevalent in the last hundred years and is fundamentally the result of a positivistic approach to philosophy itself. But if it is true that strict behaviorism is an inadequate approach to some learning phenomena, and therefore that some way must again be sought to study consciousness and cognition, then it appears that some information regarding consciousness must seriously be sought from philosophy.

The next chapter will attempt to lay a groundwork for determining what the ontological status of consciousness is—i.e., what kind of entity or function it is. Once this ontological question has been resolved adequately, it will turn out that the solution implies some interesting consequences which bear crucially upon our other questions about consciousness, notably the enigma of the ontological status of the self, and the interrelated problems of 'prereflective' consciousness and self-alienation. These implications will then be pursued in subsequent chapters.

CHAPTER II

THE RELATION BETWEEN CONSCIOUSNESS AND PHYSIOLOGY

U.T. Place's statement that consciousness is a "pattern of brain activity"[1] is obviously intended as a theory of psychophysical identity. Yet strictly speaking, and taken for what it literally says, Place's statement does not necessarily imply a true identity theory—at least not if we assume that the identity thesis says more than merely that there is a *correlation* between mental events and brain processes. For the question remains: Is the 'pattern' of the brain activity caused by the specific physical processes in the brain, or on the other hand, does the 'pattern' itself perhaps impose itself upon whatever matter it finds existing in the brain, just as a sound wave imposes itself upon whatever medium it passes through? It would be odd indeed to speak of a theory of 'sound-wood identity' simply because it is found that the sound is a 'pattern of wood activity' when it passes through a wooden medium. Of course, sound cannot occur without a medium; furthermore, it needs an appropriate type of medium—not just any kind of matter is a good conductor of sound. But these facts would not be inconsistent with a denial that sound and wood are identical, any more than a dualist like Aquinas should be considered an identity theorist on the basis that he says mental events cannot be predicated of just any old kind of material substratum. While there is a sense in which the vibration of the wood and the sound are in fact identical as the sound passes through the wood, this type of identity is a weaker one than the identity theorists mean to assert. It remains true that the removal of the wood and substitution of some other medium—for example, air—would fail to alter significantly the pattern of activity which 'is' sound. The pattern could therefore exist without this or that particular material medium, though it is true that it needs *some* material medium. It may also be, then, that this type of identity statement, as applied to the relation between mind and brain, is correspondingly weak. It does not necessarily deny that the consciousness causes the brain activity, for example, which would be a form of epiphenomenalism which reverses the terms from the usual epiphenomenalism that would treat the physical events as the causal agents.

On the surface, it may seem that it should be easy in principle to check this reverse form of epiphenomenalism against the facts. We can simply observe physical events in the brain and determine whether they do or do not follow the same causal laws as the same chemical elements in the same physical circumstances would follow in some context separate from the human brain. But here again, in the analogous case of sound passing through wood, we know that it is the sound wave originating elsewhere that causes the wood to vibrate, not the wood that causes the sound wave to be produced. In the case of consciousness, we can manipulate chemical events in the brain, thereby causally affecting consciousness; or we can cause changes in chemical events by manipulating our consciousness. Such manipulations thus still leave us in the dark as to whether the relationship is one of identity or of causation.

Such an experiment would leave us, in fact, with almost all the theoretical alternatives mentioned in our introduction. Only parallelism would be ruled out. Even if we grant that consciousness is a 'pattern of brain activity,' it would still be perfectly possible to entertain the theories of interactionism, epiphenomenalism, nomological equivalence, or a process-substratum model which regards consciousness as a process which takes physiological events as its substratum, yet is not equivalent with this substratum. We shall see in section 2 of this chapter that there are strong reasons for rejecting interactionism, parallelism, epiphenomenalism and the 'nomological equivalence' approach. Interactionism cannot account for the necessary-and-sufficient conditions in the causal interrelations of mental and physiological events. Epiphenomenalism regards physiological processes as the cause of conscious events; analysis of the notion of directionality in the causal relation in section 3, however, will show that directionality as a general rule cannot be established in the relationship between consciousness and physiology. Parallelism, when worked out in detail, is too far-fetched a hypothesis to account for the correlations between consciousness and physiology (though it is conceivable that there might be isolated instances of parallel occurrences which would not causally interact except in relation to a common cause). Nomological equivalence, though one of the better theories, will turn out not to be able to account for all the kinds of phenomena that need to be included in the explanation. Since psychophysical identity and the process-substratum approach emerge as the two dominant theories, let's begin by analysing some of the important contradictions between these theories.

1. Identity theory *versus* the process-substratum approach

The identity theory has received a considerable amount of attention recently, but has not been able to reach any ultimate resolution of its internal difficulties—especially its inability to add anything which even in principle could possibly be *verified* to the non-controversial 'principle of simultaneous isomorphism' (or regular correlation between mental and physiological events), as Jaegwon Kim and Richard Brandt have pointed out with admirable clarity.[2] The process-substratum model, on the other hand, has hardly been discussed at all, though it seems to have been strongly implied by Merleau-Ponty.[3] Merleau-Ponty's ideas seem to have been left out of the contemporary discussion of the mind-body relation primarily because the participants of the discussion have been Anglo-American philosophers who are not familiar with or interested in the work of phenomenologists like Merleau-Ponty. Strangely, while phenomenology has traditionally been extremely concerned with the elaboration of the subjective side of conscious events, those involved in the mind-body controversy never mention phenomenology at all, except by way of allusion to a certain 'phenomenological fallacy' which consists of thinking that if I see a green thing, then there must be something green in my brain. One sometimes wonders whether it is tacitly assumed that phenomenology as a whole is guilty of this 'phenomenological fallacy,' though such an assumption would be patently absurd.

A certain argument which has been advanced by Wilfrid Sellars serves as a good lead-in to the question of the ontological relation between consciousness and brain events.[4] Sellars points out that the phenomenological data of consciousness, or what he calls "raw-feel predicates," can never have the same logical use as predicates in any brain theory. Against this point, someone could charge that Sellars' argument is somewhat like saying that Clark Kent and Superman can never be the same person since the term 'Clark Kent' can never mean the same thing as the term 'Superman.' To this, however, Sellars could well reply that the relationship between Clark Kent and Superman is not analogous to that between raw-feel predicates and brain-state predicates. A better analogy would be the relationship between water and procrastination, for here we have two terms which cannot possibly occupy the same 'logical space.' It makes sense to say that I drink water, but not that I drink procrastination; thus it is logically impossible that water could be identical with procrastination. Thomas Nagel has made a similar point as well.[5]

This response, however, also is not completely decisive. For there is a relationship between the type of thing procrastination is and the type of thing water is; it is the same as the relationship between the kind of thing flight is and the kind of thing wings are. It would make sense to say that we eat chicken wings, but not that we eat the chicken's flight. Yet flight can be characterized as a 'pattern of wing activity'—just as Place calls consciousness a 'pattern of brain activity.' Thus the fact that the brain and consciousness do not occupy the same logical space does not preclude consciousness from being a pattern of brain activity.

In the case of wings and flight, however, it is more appropriate to say that the pattern of wing activity *causes* flight than to say that the pattern of wing activity *is* flight. This is true, that is, if the pattern of wing activity we are thinking of consists of 'flapping up and down.' On the other hand, if we are thinking of a *broader* notion of 'wing activity'—such as 'moving across the sky while flapping up and down'—then we have a 'pattern of wing activity' which is identical to flight. The problem then becomes avoiding any confusion between the two notions of 'wing activity' we are speaking of: 'flapping up and down' on the one hand, and 'moving across the sky while flapping up and down' on the other.

Notice also that in our broader notion of 'wing activity,' there is a superfluous element. 'Flight' is equivalent with 'moving across the sky while flapping up and down' but it is equally equivalent with 'moving across the sky.' Our only motive in adding 'while flapping up and down' would be to suggest, implicitly, that the flapping up and down is important because it is what *causes* the moving across the sky. But if the flapping up and down causes the moving across the sky, and if moving across the sky is equivalent with the flight, then the flapping up and down causes the flight; therefore, the flapping up and down cannot be the same thing as the flight, for to say that **A** causes **B** is to imply that **A** and **B** are two different things. By substituting 'brain' for 'wings' and 'consciousness' for 'flight,' it is easy to see that whether the consciousness-brain relation is one of identity, one of causation, or some other relation may well depend upon which notion of 'brain activity' one has in mind.

It seems likely, then, that when identity theorists say that consciousness *is* a pattern of brain activity, they are really running together two different patterns of brain activity. There is one pattern of brain activity—let's call it pattern **X**—which they want to say *causes* consciousness, and another pattern of brain activity, pattern **Y**, which they want to say *is* consciousness. And the real point of contention between the identity theorists and their opponents is not so much, as it appears to be, whether or not consciousness *is* pattern **Y**, but rather whether or not pattern Y is caused by pattern **X**. Most anti-identity theorists would probably willingly grant that consciousness might conceivably be identical with pattern **Y**, *if* in doing so they could still deny that pattern **Y** is caused by pattern **X** (i.e., a disguised form of epiphenomenalism). On the contrary, they would like to hold open the possibility that pattern **Y** causes pattern **X** in some way similar to the way a sound wave causes particles of wood to move as it passes through the wood; this would contrast sharply against the assumption that pattern **X** causes pattern **Y** in the way that the motion of a bird's wings causes its flight. To say that consciousness 'is' pattern **Y** would even be consistent with a dualism, since patterns **X** and **Y** might even be entirely different and independent types of patterns. It would be no more consistent or inconsistent with any of the six possible theories of the mind-body relation. But what especially irritates the anti-identity theorists is that the identity theorists seem to be trying to sneak in through the back door the claim that pattern **X** causes pattern **Y** by means of a subtle equivocation. I.e., they speak as though pattern **X** and pattern **Y** were the same pattern, or as though they were both parts of a larger coherent pattern, so that the meaning of 'brain activity' would include a certain atomistic-reductionist notion of the causal interrelation of all 'brain activities.'

The essential problem of reducing pattern **Y** to an epiphenomenon of pattern **X** is that there seem to be certain patterns *of* patterns which use feedback mechanisms of some sort in order to maintain a formal equilibrium between or among the lower-order patterns of which such patterns-of-patterns are comprised. For this reason, the sum of the causes of each of the lower-order patterns may not be sufficient to account for the pattern-of-patterns which is maintained between or among the lower order patterns. Nor can all of these patterns *of* patterns (let's call them second-order patterns) at a given level of activity be characterized as just more complicated first-order patterns on the same level.

Let's illustrate this last point with a non-brain-related example. If two saxophonists play "Bird Lives" at imperfect tempos on different occasions, the tune can be described in each case as the vibration of the reed in a certain pattern (a first order pattern). But the simple addition of these two patterns as such would not suffice to produce the second-order pattern, '"Bird Lives" played on two saxophones together'—i.e., in synchronization with each other. The synchronization is an additional element which must be introduced over against the isolated renditions, which in turn must be modified to produce the synchronization. More important still, the sum of the *causes* of the two first-order patterns, considered separately, may not be sufficient to cause the second-order pattern. That is, a certain amount of musical training will enable the saxophonists to produce melodies describable as "Bird Lives" separately, whereas this same amount of training will not be sufficient to enable the two of them to play "Bird Lives" *together*, in coordination with each other. The truth of this fact presupposes that the *synchronization* of the two renditions of "Bird Lives" is a pattern which is not reducible to the mere sum of the two renditions.

In a similar way, the mere sum of certain activities of the cortex and of the hypothalamous is not sufficient to produce the synchronization or coordination of these patterns which accounts for the difference between sleep and waking consciousness. There is now considerable physiological evidence that wakefulness results, not so much from an increase in the absolute quantity of neural activity, as from a certain type of synchronization or coordination between the activity of the cortex and that of the hypothalamous.[6] Both cortex and hypothalamous may continue functioning during sleep very similarly to the way they do during wakefulness (and in fact they do); what is different is that their activities, though present, are not coordinated. It is true, of course, that something must be done in order to *produce* the necessary synchronization; it does not occur magically. For example, the reticular activating system is intimately involved. By blocking out stimuli, it prevents the synchronization of cortex and hypothalamous—most likely by slowing the rate of cortical activity, or changing its pattern in some more complex way. Conversely, the reticular activating system, by letting through stimuli which it 'considers important' (in some metaphorical sense), restores the pattern of coordination between cortex and hypothalamous, thus bringing about wakefulness. Also, it seems that 'messages' are somehow exchanged between hypothalamous and cortex which maintain the desired coordination for wakefulness. Other patterns of this coordination will produce dreams, still others complete absence of consciousness.

The important point for our purposes is that waking consciousness is a higher-order pattern which may or may not become established, on any given occasion, between or among relatively lower-order patterns such as those which exist in the hypothalamous itself or in the cortex itself. To say, for example, that waking consciousness exists *in* the cortex or *in* the hypothalamous would be absurd—still more absurd to say that it exists *in* the reticular activating system. Nor does it exist simply by means of the sum of the three; it is a certain pattern of *interaction* among the three which produces consciousness. This is an important point not only because it suggests that consciousness is a pattern of the higher-order type, but also because Norman Malcolm is shown to be at least partly correct in that, if consciousness can be localized at all, its localizability is at least different in meaning from the localizability of physical things and lower-order patterns.[7] To say that consciousness, or any given state of consciousness, is located in any specific spot in the cortex, the hypothalamous or the reticular activating system, would be like saying that a wave exists in one particular drop of water whose upward and downward oscillation is necessary to the wave, or again, like saying that the wave exists *in each* of the water drops. We can say in a sense that the wave is located in the total space which includes all the drops in all the points covered by their oscillation. In the same sense, we can say that waking consciousness is located in the *whole* brain or, better still, in the *whole body* (the activity of remote parts of the nervous system is necessary to maintain wakefulness, else there would be nothing for the reticular activating system to 'let through' to the cortex). But this is a different kind of localizability from the localizability of a simple physical object. One essential difference seems to be that simple physical objects show difficulty in being superimposed over each other, whereas patterns of the higher-order type do not. Two water molecules cannot occupy the same place, whereas it is possible to set up a concentric wave pattern, by dropping a stone into a body of water, and simultaneously to set up a rectilinear pattern from one end of the body of water to the other. Any number of radio waves can occupy the same space; it is only necessary to adjust our receiver to the right frequency to pick up one of them. A still more important difference between the 'localizability' of simple physical objects and that of higher-order processes may well be that a physical object can be said to be located in a particular place in a given instant of time; a higher order process, because its pattern involves higher-order temporal rhythms and synchronizations as well as spacial configurations, cannot be located in a given space at a given instant of time. Its configuration does not exist at any given instant, but requires the interrelation of configurations which exist at different instants of time. To freeze such a temporal form in a single instant is to focus only upon its spacial form, leaving out of account precisely those interrelations between its configuration at one time and at another which characterize it as a temporal pattern.

This notion of higher-order patterns or processes is similar to Merleau-Ponty's application of the Gestalt concept of 'forms.' According to Merleau-Ponty, a 'form' exists in the functioning of an organism if the whole has the power, when confronted with a change in one of its parts, to rearrange its parts in such a way as to preserve the same functions on the part of the whole.[8] A case in point is the development of a 'pseudo-fovea' in instances of loss of the peripheral vision of only one side of the retina. The standard physiological explanation of heightened color perception in the fovea and heightened motion perception at the periphery is in terms of the relative distribution of cones and rods in these areas. But when the left half of the retina becomes blind, the center of the visual field shifts to the center of the still-healthy half of the retina. This new center then becomes the point of heightened color perception (though not naturally endowed with an abundance of cones), whereas the locus of the *original* fovea—now become the periphery of the half-blind eye—loses much of its color perception but becomes more sensitive to motion (in spite of a poor natural endowment with rods). Merleau-Ponty concludes that anatomical structures are *used by* the organism to achieve its purposes in the most convenient possible way, rather than additively *causing* the organism to behave according to a sum of discrete reactions.[9]

Another example cited by Merleau-Ponty is that, when some of the legs of a centipede are shortened by partial amputation, the centipede changes the order and rhythm of its leg movements while walking on a smooth surface; yet, when presented with a sufficiently rough surface, it reverts to the use of all its legs, and to the former order and rhythm of movements. The notion of reflex arcs cannot account for the body's ability to alternate these patterns in this way; according to classical reflex theory, such a change should require a lengthy process of conditioning. The body's ability to change patterns at will shows a link to a higher-order pattern or process which coordinates the lower order ones, yet is built up from them.[10]

Because Merleau-Ponty's main purpose in bringing up these examples is to refute classical reflex theory, there is a tendency to overlook the fact that he is also doing something perhaps more important with them: He is calling attention to a whole new (or at least generally ignored) *type* of entity. There are beings whose ontological status consists of being patterns of patterns, whose causation is not perfectly reducible to the sum of the causations of the patterns which make them up, and which are defined by rhythms in *time* in much the same way that most patterns are defined predominantly by configurations in *space*. It is true that we often draw graphs of waves with an understanding that one of the dimensions represented in the graph is time; but once we move into patterns *of* such patterns, our intuitive grasp of them tends to be lost, so that we tacitly assume that such patterns of patterns could in principle be described as just more complicated patterns at the lower level. Because of the emphasis upon rhythm and synchronization in the ontological make-up of these types of beings, they might appropriately be referred to as temporal forms, or as higher-order patterns or processes.

Of course, it would be a rather rash leap from this point to conclude that higher-order forms have *no* causal explanation at the lower-order level. The point is only that, if pattern **X** is composed of lower-order patterns **A**, **B** and **C**, arranged in a certain order and rhythm, some *further* causal explanation may often be required in order to explain **X** than simply citing causal factors which would suffice to explain **A**, **B** and **C**; it may still be necessary in some types of cases to explain why **A**, **B** and **C** occur in the particular pattern that they do, without which **X** would not exist. In this sense, it is quite misleading to speak of **X** as 'identical with' **A**, **B** and **C**, as though this would lead to an understanding of the nature of **X**.

Having now examined the difference between the identity theory and the process-substratum hypothesis, we still need to consider which of the six possible relationships between consciousness (the higher-order form) and brain physiology (the lower-order forms) is the *correct* one. This question will turn out to be unresolvable by empirical means alone, but requires the help of philosophical analysis. From what has been said so far, it should be obvious that we are going to end up leaning toward a certain kind of process-substratum model. Before explaining the reasoning behind this preference, though, we should consider three influential types of anti-identity argument and see why they fail to resolve the issue, so that we can avoid getting ensnared in similar problems in our own treatment.

Approaching the problem from the standpoint of action theory, Alvin Goldman argues against the Anscombe-Davidson type of identity by denying that Davidson is correct when he says, "I flip the switch, turn on the light, and illuminate the room. Unbeknowst to me I also alert a prowler to the fact that I am home. Here I do not do four things, but only one, of which four descriptions have been given.'' Goldman responds as follows:

> Suppose there is a light bulb missing from a certain socket and that George fetches a bulb and screws it into the socket. A moment later John comes along, flips the switch and thereby turns on the light. Now consider John's act of turning on the light. If we tried to list all the causes or relevant causal factors of John's turning on the light, we would certainly include George's screwing the bulb into the socket. . . . On the other hand, George's action is not at all a cause, or causal factor, of John's act of flipping the switch.[12]

Goldman's argument ceases to be very forceful, however, when we realize that he is using the word 'cause' to refer to antecedent conditions which are *necessary* but not *sufficient* to produce an event. He distinguishes between John's flipping the switch and John's turning on the light by pointing out that George's earlier having replaced the light bulb is a causal condition of John's turning on the light, but not of John's flipping the switch. But the Davidsonian identity theorist would not *literally* claim that John's flipping the switch *simpliciter,* under any conditions whatever, is identical with John's turning on the light; the identity theorist would assert, rather, that John's flipping the switch *under certain circumstances* (i.e., when there is a good bulb in the socket, etc.) is identical with his turning on the light. As J. L. Mackie points out, nothing is ever sufficient to cause anything else except *under certain conditions* or *in certain circumstances.*[13] George's replacing the bulb is a causally-necessary (but not sufficient) condition for John's turning on the light; it is also a causally necessary condition for John's flipping the switch under those specific conditions which are necessary in order for flipping the switch to be identical with turning on the light.

In the same way, Goldman argues that moving a pawn to king's-knight-seven is different from checkmating my opponent in chess because it would be possible to move the pawn to this same space (under other circumstances) without checkmating the opponent. But here again, the Davidsonian identity theorist only claims (or should only claim) that moving the pawn to this space *under certain circumstances* is the same thing as checkmating the opponent—not moving the pawn to this space under any conditions whatever. Now it may be more convenient, for the purposes of Goldman's theory of action, to analyse actions in terms of 'act-tokens' and so forth, as he proceeds to elaborate, and there seems to be nothing wrong with taking such an approach. But it is not *necessary* to do so because of any supposed inconsistency in the Davidsonian theory—at least not because of any inconsistency that Goldman has pointed out. (There are, however, still other problems with Davidson's identity theory, which we shall mention in section 2.)

Of course, it is true that Davidson does not do a very good job of defending himself against Goldman's argument. His response is that he holds flipping the switch and turning on the light to be identical with each other only *under a certain description*. Goldman rightly counters by pointing out the difficulties of attributing such importance to mere verbal conditions, such as how an event is to be described.[14] But the better solution, of holding that causal connections hold only *under certain circumstances* is not subject to this type of criticism. And as Mackie so clearly points out, a cause must be both necessary and sufficient for its effect *under the given circumstances.* The notion of causality, of course, is crucial and we shall return to it.

Some theorists, such as Thomas Nagel, have attempted to make the person or human being, rather than the body, the subject of mental predicates.[15] One problem that has been pointed out with this approach has been that it is too vague because it is equally consistent with a physicalistic or a dualistic account of the mind-body relation.[16] It also has left unanswered, so far, the question: What is a person? One of the most important conclusions of the present study will be that, from an ontological (as opposed to merely linguistic) perspective, not only are conscious events not predicates of the person, but almost the exact opposite is true. The person has his being only by means of the continuity established through complex interrelations of experiences or mental events. Beginning with Chapter III, we shall see why this must be the case. But perhaps a more important objection to the Nagel type of approach, as far as its relevance to the mind-body problem is concerned, is that it tries to make the logical and linguistic subject-predicate relation serve the purposes of an entity-property relation. While it may be true that, gramatically speaking, a 'person' 'has' experiences, it does not follow that persons are entities of which experiences are properties; it could just as well be that experiences are entities of which persons are the properties, or that the body is an entity of which both experiences and persons are properties.

At the other extreme from Nagel, Strawson makes persons predicates and the body their subject.[17] While a number of logical problems have been pointed out in this approach, notably by Bernard Williams,[18] a sufficient impediment to its bringing much clarity to the mind-body problem is the same as with those theories which make the person a subject and experiences properties. That is, it tries to make a linguistic relation into an ontological one, to make a grammatical subject-verb relation into an entity-property relation. Since it makes just as much sense to say that persons are properties of complexes of experiences as *vice versa,* it becomes clear that bringing the person into the problem of relating the mental and the physical cannot help to answer the question, but on the contrary raises still more questions.

Bearing these points in mind, let's turn now to see if we can find reasons for preferring one of the six possible mind-body theories over the others. For this purpose, an analysis of the different ways in which mental and physiological events can be 'necessary and sufficient' for each other will prove decisive in enabling us to make a decision.

2. The inseparability of mental and neurological events

It is often supposed that the only way to maintain that mechanistic and voluntaristic explanations of consciousness and action are compatible with each other is by means of a Davidsonian kind of identity theory which would hold that mental events and the corresponding neurophysiological events are 'really' the same thing as each other, but viewed from different 'perspectives.'[19] Such a theory has been criticized by Malcolm[20] and by Noren[21] among others, and is also subject to criticisms similar to the ones Kim and Brandt raise against identity theories in general. We should note, however, that no such identity theory is needed in order to preserve the kind of compatibilism just mentioned. Rather, compatibilism only needs to establish the *inseparability* of any given mental event and its neurological substratum. This inseparability thesis is not vulnerable to the various criticisms of the identity thesis, and ultimately ends up confirming that the process-substratum model is the most viable approach to the mind-body problem.

The essential problem for compatibilism relevant to this distinction can be stated as follows: If mental event **A** is accompanied by neurophysiological event **a**, and if subsequent mental event **B** is accompanied by neurophysiological event **b**, and **a** 'causes' **b** with iron-clad necessity, then the question arises as to what sense it can make to say that **A** acts as a reason for, or in some sense brings about **B**. The problem is aggravated still further when we begin to use the terms 'necessary' and 'sufficient' to define what we mean by 'cause.' For if neurophysiological event **a** is sufficient to produce neurophysiological event **b**, then mental event **A** would not appear necessary to produce it; whereas if, on the other hand, **A** is sufficient to produce **B**, then **a** would not appear necessary to produce it. Similarly, if **a** is necessary to produce **b**, then **A** would not appear sufficient to produce it; whereas, if, on the other hand, **A** is necessary to produce **B**, then **a** would not appear sufficient to produce it. Worst of all, if **a** is both necessary and sufficient to produce **b**, then **A** would appear neither necessary nor sufficient to produce it, and *vice versa*. Thus either **A** and **B** or **a** and **b** would be reduced to the status of mere epiphenomena, so that **A** is produced by **a** or *vice versa* (but not both) and **B** is produced by **b** or *vice versa* (but not both). Therefore, either **A** would not produce **B** or else **a** would not produce **b**.

In spite of these difficulties, something about our intention when we say 'cause' seems to make us want to hold that if **a** causes **b**, then **a** is at least *sufficient* to produce **b**; we also tend to mean that **a** is *necessary* to produce **b**, at least in the sense that we could say, 'If only **a** had not happened, or had happened differently, then **b** could have been avoided.' In the case of conscious choices especially, we want to mean that 'If the agent had chosen differently, then he would have acted differently.' We are therefore tempted to conclude that either (1) neurophysiological event **a** causes neurophysiological event **b**, which in turn generates the conscious state **B**—and in this case conscious event **A** is a mere epiphenomenon caused by **a**—; or else (2) conscious event **A** leads to conscious event **B** by means of reasoning or some other connection between the *ideas* present to consciousness in its successive conscious acts, in which case consciousness seems to have some almost supernatural (or as Gilbert Ryle says, "ghostly"[22]) power to prevent the supposed 'laws of causation' from operating in their usual way in the case of neurophysiological processes. The first alternative seems to leave no room for freedom, not to mention that it contradicts the common observation that we do seem to have the power to act on the basis of rational or at least conscious decisions (which does not easily square with (1) above even if we are prepared to give up the 'freedom' supposedly attaching to the conscious decision). The second alternative, on the other hand, seems to contradict the general tenor of everything that has been learned about neurophysiology, i.e., that the brain viewed in its physiological dimension functions according to regular causal principles, just as do all chemical and physical phenomena.

One resolution for the problem involves saying that mental event **A** and neurophysiological event **a** are really the same event viewed from different perspectives. This view has been criticized with some justification (as we shall see), notably by Norman Malcolm. We suggest, however, that a compatibilist resolution for the problem can be preserved without positing the identity of **A** and **a**. It is only necessary to posit that **A** and **a** are inseparable—that is, that they are necessary and sufficient for each other in some sense other than one's causing the other. For example, they could both be caused by a third thing; this possibility, however, is best exemplified by parallelism and turns out to be untenable. Another alternative is that one of the phenomena in question could be subject while the other is its predicate, as Feuerbach has it.[23] Or, conceived in more contemporary terms, we could posit that one is a wave while the other is its substratum or the medium through which the wave is propagated. There are thus alternative ways in which **A** and **a** could be inseparable without being identical and without causing or being caused by each other. But it is only necessary that they be inseparable—not that they be identical—in order for the compatibility of mechanistic and purpose-oriented explanations to make sense. For, if conscious event **A** and neurophysiological event **a** are inseparable without being identical, while the same is true for **B** and **b**, then **A** may be necessary and sufficient for **B**, *and* **a** may be necessary and sufficient for **b**, *and* **b** may be necessary and sufficient for **B**, all at the same time and without entailing any contradiction. We shall show that for **A** and **a** to be inseparable (and therefore necessary and sufficient for each other), without being either identical or the cause of each other, is perfectly natural and unparadoxical, and that in this sense, two events can *each* be both necessary *and* sufficient for some third event, but only if the first two events are necessary and sufficient for each other. In the process, we shall find that the terms 'necessary' and 'sufficent' in the context of causal theory tend to be ambiguous and misleading in this respect. With this clarification, the problem for compatibilism mentioned above—which forms the essential core of Malcolm's and Noren's criticisms of compatibilism—becomes solvable.

Sections 3, 4 and 5 of this chapter will attempt to establish three basic clarifications: (3) The confusion about the compatibilism problem results partly from the 'necessary-and-sufficient' conceptualization of the meaning of the word 'cause'. (4) In cases where events **A** and **B** are inseparable, the principle does not apply which would say that if **A** is necessary for **C** (some third event) then **B** cannot at the same time be sufficient for **C**. (5) The clarification of the meaning of 'cause' in (3) and the limitation imposed on the principle that **A** cannot be necessary for **C** if **B** is sufficient for **C** in (4) combine to elucidate the fourfold interrelation of mental event **A**, neurophysiological event **a**, mental event **B** and neurophysiological event **b**, where **A** may be necessary and sufficient for **b**, yet neither a causal relation nor an identity relation exists between **A** and **a**. We shall also show in this context that Malcolm's critique of the 'identity' theory is well-taken in spite of Vivian Weil's recent response to it.[24] For essentially similar reasons, Goldman's 'nomic equivalence' thesis is almost as unacceptable as the identity thesis in solving the problem. Finally, we shall attempt to describe the sense in which **A** and **a** can be inseparable without being either identical or causally related. It will turn out that the process-substratum model of the mind-body is no metaphor, but literally describes the only reasonable compatibilist resolution for the problem.

3. Necessity and sufficiency in the causal relation

That neurological events can be controlled by voluntary intentions in some cases is a phenomenological datum. For example, if I survey my book shelf, select a book and open it, this choice in some sense causes or brings about the neurological event corresponding to the paying attention to the words on the page, which I do accomplish. But if the choice to read these words is sufficient to bring about the corresponding neurological events, then any antecedent neurological events would appear not to be necessary to bring them about and certainly would appear not to be a sufficient explanation of them without some reference to the choice involved.

One possible compatibilist way of preserving the physical cause-and-

effect sequence would be a form of interactionism which ends up proving to be untenable. A compatibilistic interactionism would posit that
some previous neurological event caused me to make the choice as I did,
and that conditioned responses to the words on the page caused the
neurological events corresponding to the thoughts expressed by the words.
In this sense, the decision to pull down the book might still *cause* the
pulling down of the book and therefore indirectly might cause the
thoughts resulting from reading the book. Thus a conscious event would
cause a physical event which in turn would cause another conscious event,
etc. In this way, the conscious events might all cause other conscious
events (by acting indirectly through the medium of the physical), and
all the physical events might similarly cause other physical events (but
in the case of *some* conscious events, they could do so only by acting
indirectly through the medium of a conscious choice).

An obvious problem with this response, however, is again that if the
conscious choice is necessary to bring about the event, then the
neurological correlate may be present as an epiphenomenon but would
not be sufficient by itself—in fact, would not even occur unless the conscious choice were made in the first place; or, alternatively, the conscious
choice may be present as an epiphenomenon, but would be neither
necessary nor sufficient as an explanation by itself, and in fact would
be only the surface appearance of a more basic dimension of the
phenomena (namely, the chain of physical causes and effects) which
would be sufficient by itself. It is important to note that this is not merely
a case of causal 'over-determination,' where either of two antecedents
would be sufficient by itself to cause the event, yet both occur together;
rather, it is a case of mutual exclusivity, where if one antecedent is
necessary, the other cannot be sufficient, and if one is sufficient, the
other cannot be necessary.

Still another problem with interactionism is less decisive, but should
be mentioned. Interactionism, in any form, would entail that many
physical events have no direct physical cause (but rather are caused by
mental events); this would be inconsistent with what we have learned
so far about the physical and chemical behavior of the matter in the brain,
which as far as we know operates by causal laws similar to those of any
other matter.

It should also be obvious that parallelism becomes untenable for similar
reasons. Parallelism is really just an extreme form of interactionism. It
holds that, at least at one moment in the stream of consciousness (usually

the first moment), a mental event shared a common cause with a physical event and that, for this reason, the chain of mental events and the chain of physical events run parallel with each other. Besides being subject to the same criticisms just given of interactionism, this also contradicts the well known fact that we can introduce a predictable variation in the stream of consciousness by manipulating physiological factors.

Compatibilism, then, must maintain that in some sense the choice to pull down the book and read it does cause—i.e., is necessary and sufficient for—my reaching for the book and my eyes' focusing on the words on the page; while at the same time the neurological events corresponding to the choice are necessary and sufficient, on a purely physical level, to make me pull down the book and read it, which causes the words on the page to cause neurological events that correspond to the thoughts expressed by the words on the page. But if any choice on my part is *required* (i.e., necessary) as an intermediary or in any other sense, then the antecedent neurological event seems insufficient, of itself, to bring about the consequent ones. A rupture therefore seems to be created in the supposedly universal laws of nature—unless, of course, the antecedent neurological event and the choice are presumed identical. Malcolm, however, points out good reasons for regarding this identity thesis as untenable, as we shall see in section 5.

In the case of conscious sequences, then, there is no escaping that we normally want the meaning of 'Smith decided to act and did so' to include that if he had not so decided, he would not have so acted, and that his decision to so act would (in the given circumstances) enable him to do so (i.e., would be sufficient to produce the action in the given circumstances). There is a temptation, nonetheless, to remove the counterfactual conditional or to remove the sufficiency of the cause (saying that both the conscious and the neurophysiological antecedents are necessary to produce the consequent, thus doing away with the need to claim that either is sufficient by itself). But in addition to an apparent conflict between this interpretation and what we normally intend by causation in cases of conscious sequences, a consistent analysis of causation *per se* (whether in mental or purely physical instances) would show that the removal of either the necessity or the sufficiency requirement would be both incorrect and incapable of solving the problem, just as it is incapable of solving any causal assymetry problems in general.[25] There are two primary difficulties with the solution of doing away with either the necessary or the sufficient stipulation. In the first place, the temptation to drop the requirement that a cause is necessary for its effect arises from the realization that there may be more than one possible cause for some event. *In a sense,* it is often false to say, 'If **A** had not occurred, **B** would not have occurrred,' because something else might have stepped in and caused **B** if **A** had failed to cause it. But *in another sense*—the sense really intended in the definition of 'cause'—it is always true that in any specific context, given all other circumstances exactly as they in fact are, except for the deletion of **A**, then **B** must fail to follow or else **A** does not qualify as the cause of **B**. The fact that in other possible contexts **C**, **D** or **E** might also be capable of causing events like **B** is irrelevant. So in this sense, **A** must be necessary for **B** if it causes **B**.

A second reàson why **A** must be necessary for **B** is that if we say that an event is necessary but not sufficient for the occurrence of another event, we mean that it is one of the causal factors which brings about the event, but not the only one; thus we mean that all of the causal factors taken together are both necessary *and* sufficient to cause the event.

Obviously, then, since we cannot *subtract from* the necessary-and-sufficient definition, we must *add* something to it. J. L. Mackie has explored some of the possible stipulations that might be added in order to convey the sense of directionality in the causal connection. While we need not agree with every point of Mackie's analysis, he clearly shows problems with most possible stipulations that have been proposed to meet this problem (such as, for example, stipulating that the cause must precede the effect in time); his conclusion is that a present event may be "fixed" in a sense that can never apply to the corresponding future event for which it is necessary and sufficient.[26] Mackie does not, however, seem adequately to address the objection that if the present event is fixed and is necessary and sufficient for a future event, then the future event by the same token becomes just as 'fixed' as the present one. Nor does he elucidate how this concept defines the direction of causation when the cause is simultaneous with the effect. But a slight modification of Mackie's view will serve our purposes here: Let's add to the necessary-and-sufficient stipulation that if **A** causes **B**, then any experimental manipulation of **A** which leads to a corresponding change in **B** does so of necessity, whereas a manipulation of **B** in the same circumstances will not necessitate any corresponding change in **A**. If **a** is the necessary and sufficient cause of **B** in the circumstances, then to change the circumstances so as to alter **B** does not necessarily alter **A**; whereas to change the circumstances so as to appropriately alter **A** will necessarily alter **B** (unless we simultaneously introduce still another change in the circumstances so as to purposely *avoid* altering **B**). For example, if turning a switch (A) in the appropriate circumstances causes a light to come on (B), then not only is **A** necessary and sufficient for **B** (and *vice versa*), but also the deletion of **A** from the situation necessarily prevents **B**, but not *vice versa*. The need for invoking this 'manipulability' stipulation is especially obvious in the case of a simultaneous cause and effect.

A complete analysis of this concept of manipulability would be beyond our scope here and is not necessary to the points that follow. It was only necessary to establish that both the 'necessity' and the 'sufficiency' stipulations are necessary to the concept of cause, and that with the addition of some stipulation to make the causal relation assymetrical (such as the notion of manipulability), the necessary-and-sufficient characterization makes enough sense that we can still analyse the fourfold interrelation of consecutive mental events with their corresponding consecutive neurological events in terms of which of these events are necessary and sufficient for which others.

In the following section, we shall see that the 'exclusivity' principle of necessary-and-sufficient relations in general—the principle that if **A** is necessary and sufficient for **B**, then **C** cannot also be necessary and sufficient for **B**—is not universally applicable. This point is extremely important in the context of the compatibility problem, for it shows that no contradiction is involved in saying that mental event **A** is necessary for mental event **B** while at the same time neurophysiological event **a** is necessary and sufficient for neurophysiological event **b**, which in turn is necessary and sufficient for mental event **B**.

4. Problems with the exclusivity principle

If we presuppose that the necessary-and-sufficient relation is 'exclusive', i.e., that if **A** is sufficient for the occurrence of **B** then **C** cannot be necessary for **B**, and *vice versa*, then not only Taylor's fatalism (see note 25) but even more glaring difficulties result. One of these difficulties is pointed out by Alvin Goldman,[27] and can be illustrated with the following example. Suppose three dominos are lined up such that the first falls, causing the second to fall, causing the third to fall. Let's call these three events **A**, **B** and **C**. Then, according to the axiom that if **A** is necessary and sufficient for **B** then **C** can be neither sufficient nor necessary for **B**, we find the following perplexing state of affairs:

(1) If **A** is necessary and sufficient for **B**, and if **B** is necessary and sufficient for **C**,

(2) then **A** is necessary and sufficient for **C**.

(3) But if **A** is sufficient for **C**, then **B** is not necessary for **C**.

(4) And if **B** is sufficient for **C**, then **A** is not necessary for **C**.

(5) Furthermore, if **A** is necessary for **C**, then **B** is not sufficient for **C**.

(6) And if **B** is necessary for **C**, then **A** is not sufficient for **C**.

Note that the conclusion of the conditional in each of (3), (4), (5), and (6) contradicts (1) in some respect, even though each of them follows directly from (1). Goldman tries to solve the difficulty by proposing that the causal relations involved are "nomologically equivalent" with each other and therefore the 'exclusivity' principle of the necessary-and-sufficient relation does not apply. It is true that we must deny in such cases that if **A** is necessary and sufficient for **B**, then no other event can also be necessary and sufficient for the same event. But not all instances of non-exclusivity can be gotten out of so easily, as a different and more serious dilemma will show. Suppose the dominos are lined up in such a way that if the first falls (event **A**), it causes the second and third to fall (events **B** and **C**) by striking them both simultaneously:

(1) If **A** is necessary and sufficient for **B**, and if **A** is necessary and sufficient for **C**,

(2) then **B** is impossible without **A**, which entails **C**, and **C** is impossible without **A**, which entails **B**; therefore **B** is necessary and sufficient for **C** and *vice versa*.

(3) But if **C** is necessary for **B**, then **A** is not sufficient for **B**.

(4) And if **B** is necessary for **C**, then **A** is not sufficient for **C**.

(5) Furthermore, if **C** is sufficient for **B**, then **A** is not necessary for **B**.

(6) And if **B** is sufficient for **C**, then **A** is not necessary for **C**.

Here again, the conclusion in each of (3), (4), (5), and (6) contradicts (1), even though each of them follows directly from (1). And here too, the culprit must be the exclusivity principle of the necessary-and-sufficient relation which we presupposed at the outset. We must therefore deny that if **A** is sufficient for **B** then no other event can be necessary for **B**, and we must also deny that if **A** is necessary for **B** then no other event can be sufficient for **B**. But in this case, Goldman's 'nomological equivalence' explanation does not work. We cannot regard the relationship between **A** and **B** as equivalent in any sense with the relationship between **A** and **C**, although in the given circumstances the two relationships are inseparable.

Giving up the exclusivity principle seems odd, though, because to give up the claim that the sufficiency of **A** precludes the necessity of any other event for the same purpose seems to strip the words 'necessity' and 'sufficiency' of all meaning.

But we do not in fact have to give up this claim in all cases. We may grant that if **A** is necessary and sufficient for **B**, then **C** can be neither sufficient nor necessary for **B**, *unless A and C are inseparable.* Thus, in the case of the three dominos, the exclusivity principle is not applicable because the causal connection between the first and second dominos is inseparable from the causal connection between the first and third dominos (even though these two relationships are neither identical nor nomologically equivalent). In general, we can define **X** and **Y** as 'inseparable' whenever neither a causal nor an identity relation necessarily exists between them, yet the two are necessary and sufficient for each other by virtue of some other relationship, such as both being simultaneously necessary and sufficient for some third event.

By the definition of 'cause' in section 3, we can determine that **X** and **Y** lack any causal relationship unless the directionality of this relationship can be established as outlined above (or could in principle be so established). In the case of consciousness and its physiological correlates, however, this directionality cannot be established because to manipulate a conscious event is *ipso facto* to manipulate its physiological correlates and *vice versa*. The relationship between them is therefore either one of identity or one of inseparability *per se*. The following section will give reasons for rejecting the identity thesis and will attempt to develop the inseparability thesis. Ultimately, this inseparability will have to be conceived in terms of the process-substratum model of the mind-body relation.

5. Inseparability without identity or causal directionality

Malcolm objects to the solution which says that conscious events and their physiological correlates are identical with each other because he says a conscious event and its physiological correlates are not always located in the same place, and because a neurological event does not have all the same properties as a state of consciousness (otherwise, we would not have distinguished them in the first place.[28]

Most remarkable among the differences between mental event **A** and corresponding neurophysiological event **a** is that any objective observer can experience and measure **a**, whereas only the person who directly and subjectively feels **A**, and who is identified with the series **A, B, C**, etc., can experience **A** as such. Conversely, the most complete subjective knowledge of **A** does not guarantee any knowledge whatever of **a**. Moreover, the subjective description of **A** (from a phenomenological point of view) would not make the appropriate kind of sense, i.e., would not *be* an adequate description (as Michael Simon points out[29]) unless described in terms of references to other items in the series **A, B, C**, etc.; whereas a description of **a, b,** or **c** *can* frequently be adequate without references to other items in the series **a, b, c**, etc.—especially to items in the series which have not yet occurred at the time of the one which is to be described. Consciousness sometimes only makes sense holistically, whereas its physiological substratum can usually make sense in *partes extra partes* fashion. (While it may be true, as Goldstein suggests, that the brain sometimes shows a holistic unity,[30] this holism is not nearly so often observed in brain physiology as in the subjective stream of consciousness itself.)

Given these fundamental differences between subjective consciousness and its objective correlates, we cannot with good reason regard the two as identical. Davidson would of course respond that the reason for the differences is that **A** and **a** are the same event, *but viewed from different perspectives.* The main problem with this response is that the 'perspectives' which are supposed to be different would not in fact *be* different if **A** and **a** were not different in the first place. Davidson's position here is like saying that the front and back sides of a house are 'really' the same thing, only viewed from different perspectives; if the front and back were not different, then the different perspectival views would not present different images in the first place. Also, if Davidson were correct on this point, then Sartre would also be correct in his absurd assertion that Peter can have just as intimate an intuition of Paul's emotions as Paul can.[31] But the qualitative difference in principle between Paul's experiencing of his own emotions and Peter's apprehension of them is a phenomenological datum, as we have seen. Chapter III will pursue this point still further.

The position advocated here is not that events **A** and **a** cannot satisfactorily be *explained* on the basis of the physical cause and effect chain alone; we agree that they may possibly be so explainable (and probably are). The point is rather that, just as **B** and **b** can both be explained by **a** (since **a** is necessary and sufficient for both **B** and **b**), so **B** and **b** in principle could also be explained by **A** (since **A** also is necessary and sufficient for both **B** and **b**). At the same time, either explanation taken by itself tends to be misleading because it either denies the existence of one or the other of the '**B/b**' pair, or else it interprets one as the cause of the other. But neither can be the cause of the other, since to manipulate either one would be *ipso facto* to manipulate the other, thus no causal directionality can be established. The only viable solution is therefore to regard the two as distinguishable but necessarily inseparable events.

Vivian Weil takes issue with Malcolm's objections by arguing that when Malcolm says that if mechanism were true a man would move up a ladder whether he wanted to or not, he confuses the event to be explained—the 'action' of climbing a ladder (purposely climbing it)—and the unconscious or sleepwalking climbing of a ladder which is not an 'action' at all. Weil says, "We regard mental components as essential to actions. Holding that reasons are components of actions makes it possible to avoid the bog of the reasons-causes debate."[32] Thus Weil thinks she has saved compatibilism from Malcolm's argument, whereas in fact she has only begged the question. Malcolm's point is precisely that the *action* of climbing a ladder cannot be explained mechanistically; if the compatibilist wishes to deny Malcolm's contention, he must show, not merely that if no purposes are present then the event is not an action, but that even if the event *is* an action, there is no contradiction in accounting for it mechanistically and purposefully.

If two events are inseparable, non-identical, and non-directional with respect to causation, the only remaining explanation would seem to be that the one is a complex *process* while the other constitutes a *substratum* for the process. Obviously, since carbon, oxygen, hydrogen and nitrogen atoms would behave according to similar predictable laws whether associated with a human organism or not, their activity must be the substratum for the more complex process which is consciousness, and not the other way around. On this hypothesis, then, consciousness would become a process, or a higher-order wave-pattern in some sense which must be clarified, which could not possibly exist without some substratum through which to move; conversely, the particles which make up the substratum could not possibly move in the pattern they do without the wave's existing with the particular character and properties it has.

When we say that consciousness is a wave pattern which takes neurophysiology as its substratum, we must be careful not to push too far the analogy between consciousness and other forms of waves. In the case of a transverse wave, for example, the wave seems to have some properties which the motions of its individual particles do not have. For instance, the wave may move a great distance in a horizontal direction from the source, while none of the particles move more than a tiny distance, and most of this motion is in a vertical direction. But there is still a sense in which the motion of the wave can be reduced to an ontological equivalence with the totality of the individual motions of its particles. In the case of consciousness as compared with its physiological correlates, however, we have seen that consciousness is not perfectly equivalent with the physiological substrata, even though the conscious events and the physiological events are necessary and sufficient for each other in some other way than mere identity.

Nor, in the case of consciousness, would we be forced to conclude that it is the motion of the individual particles, each acted upon by other individual particles, which 'causes' the wave to have the pattern it has. It may be possible that consciousness has the capacity to find and use other substrata to perform its functions if some particles which had been used suddenly become dysfunctional or unavailable. For example, to a certain extent, the brain in Kurt Goldstein's experiments was able to replace cells that had been destroyed and to incorporate other cells into the needed functional continuity.[33]

While we cannot conclude that the motion of individual particles acting upon each other, in the case of consciousness, 'causes' the wave to have the pattern it has, neither can we conclude that the wave 'appropriates' particles and 'causes' them to serve as its substratum. Rather, we can conclude only that if the particles did not behave as they do, neither would the wave, and if the wave did not behave as it does, neither would the particles. Bearing in mind the stipulation which lends directionality to the causal relation—that removing the cause will remove the effect, whereas removing the effect need not remove the cause—we see that consciousness cannot be caused by the motion of its substratum, nor *vice versa*.

We would then be left with a view not entirely unlike that of William James when he says that consciousness is not an entity but a function,[34] although precisely what James means by an 'entity' would remain to be clarified. The main difference between the present view and that of James would be that, given James' rigorous empiricism (as dramatized by his immediately preceding statement that consciousness "does not exist"), it is clear that he means to reduce consciousness to the status of an epiphenomenon which is more or less 'caused by' its underlying physiological correlates. In light of the foregoing analysis, however, we must agree with him at least in saying that consciousness has the ontological status of a process rather than a stasis—more resembling a wave than its substratum. A pattern or process is as different from its substratum as the activity of walking down the street is different from the street itself and the feet which walk on the street. The latter have the status of 'that which' is in motion, whereas the former has the status of the motion itself.

Consciousness would therefore seem to exist with the ontological status of a complex process constituted by interrelations among simple 'things in themselves' (if there be such). It should not be at all surprising, then, if the point at which consciousness makes contact with the world turns out to be in this same realm of complex processes, where the 'things' we perceive are not really 'things' at all but rather relationships among 'things' (a visual object, obviously, is a complex relationship resulting from the activity of subatomic and simpler kinds of beings); if we could ever arrive at simple 'things' (again, *if* there be such), we would first have to carry out complex analyses of the processes with which our perceptual processes are capable of making contact.

The words 'thing' and 'motion' may not be the best ones available to describe this relationship. Less misleading might be the terms 'content' and 'relation among contents.' An example of why these terms involve fewer ontological presuppositions can be seen clearly in the case of music. Here the relativity of what we mean by 'form' or 'relationship' on the one hand, and 'content' on the other is easy to see. If we regard the form of a musical composition as its overall structure, such as sonata or fugue, then the individual parts—the themes and the development sections—become the contents for this form. But if we regard a melody as a form, the chord progressions and phrases that make up the melody become contents. If we regard a chord progression as a form, the chords become contents. But if we regard a single note as a content, then a single chord can be a form. Any element, it would appear, can be either a content or a form, depending upon the ontological level or degree of formal complexity we choose to bring into focus. Even the 'simple' tone in itself can be analysed, if we wish, into still lower-order contents—the vibrations of molecules, which in turn can be analysed into atoms, etc.

The advantage of the word 'content' is precisely that it has meaning only in relation to 'relation' or 'form.' Any relation can also be one of several contents which together form a higher-order relation. Thus the term 'content' implies no metaphysical concept of a simplest-possible-substance. Yet the logical relationship between contents and relations can be maintained. For example, the fact that a 'wave' is a process (therefore a relation) to be distinguished from its 'medium' (or content) does not imply that the medium itself may not also be a process in its own right. The wave theory of light, therefore, does not imply the existence of a material ether, nor does the fact that water forms waves imply that the atoms of which the water is composed are not themselves processes. The ontological status of the medium of a wave might itself consist of a set of 'relations' among other contents, while at the same time serving as content for the relation which is the wave.

It follows that the relationship between 'subject' and 'predicate' implies neither (a) a metaphysical relationship between 'thing-in-itself' or 'substance' on the one hand, and 'property' or 'relation' on the other; nor does it imply (b) that relations could necessarily ever even in principle be analysed into simplest-possible, self-subsistent entities or things-in-themselves. Formal logic, therefore, is not in the least dependent upon any metaphysical concept of its terms. It remains as valid if it stands for 'relationships' among 'contents' (which in turn may be relationships themselves) as it would be if it stood for 'substances' and their 'properties.' It remains possible to designate lower-order and higher-order predicates, processes or relationships even if no lowest-possible-order relationship or simple substratum of the relationships exists. If **A** and **B** are both relationships, but **A** is a relationship between **B** and some other contents, then **B** is a content for the relationship **A** and therefore is a lower-order relationship than **A**.

It is entirely conceivable that **A** may be a lower-order relationship than

B in one respect, while **B** is a lower-order relationship than **A** in another respect. For example, 'walking down the street' is a relationship between someone's body and the street, whereas his body is a relationship between some other contents (loosely termed 'material,' e.g., cells, atoms and subatomic particles) and the bodily processes which include, for example, walking-down-the-street. To say that 'my body walks down the street' does not imply that my body is ultimately either a lower-order or a higher-order predicate than walking-down-the-street; it implies both that it is and that it is not, in different respects.

In sum, then, not very many metaphysical assumptions are needed at all in order to preserve the compatibility of mechanistic explanations of mental events on the one hand, and on the other hand the possibility that conscious choices have power to bring about actions. It is only necessary to find a viable way to conceive the way in which a mental event and its physiological correlates can be necessary and sufficient for each other in some other way than by one's acting as the cause of the other—and to show that if **A** is necessary and sufficient for **B**, it does not follow that **C** cannot also be necessary and sufficient for **B**, as long as **A** and **B** happen to be inseparable (otherwise, inadmissible consequences would follow even in a straightforward case of falling dominos). If we accept Malcolm's argument that mind and physiology cannot be identical with each other, the possibility that they can still be inseparable remains if we hold that consciousness has the ontological status of a pattern or process. In fact, we must grant consciousness such an ontological status on pain of either being unable to solve the paradox of the fourfold necessary-and-sufficient relations among conscious states **A** and **B** and neurophysiological states **a** and **b**, or else being forced to deny that consciousness exists at all. But clearly, nothing could be further from the data of experience than to deny that this experience itself exists. The only cogent alternative, then, would seem to be that consciousness has a process nature and takes physiological events as its substratum.

CHAPTER III

Bernard Williams, in the context of his discussion of the possibility of multiple personalities, says

> I shall . . . speak of our having individuated a personality when, roughly, we have answered enough questions [pertaining to whether the different pieces are 'part of the same thread' of personality] for us to have picked out a certain personality from the pattern of manifestations. I shall not here examine the complexities involved in a proper formulation of these concepts.[1]

The main purpose of our present study is precisely to examine these complexities, so as to arrive at a formulation of this concept of 'pattern' or 'thread.' We shall conclude not only that the 'pattern' is a *criterion* that the person is still the same person as he was before (a criterion which Williams, by the way, ends up rejecting); we shall also conclude that the pattern, in certain of its aspects (and we must specify which aspects these are) *is* the person.

Williams rejects all criteria for selfhood which would rely upon the continuity of conscious processes, insisting that only the body can provide such continuity. But, as our previous chapter showed, the opposition between bodily processes on the one hand, and conscious processes on the other, is artificial. That is, there are certain bodily processes which are inseparable from corresponding conscious processes. The real opposition, if there is one at all, would be between those bodily processes which are necessary to conscious processes on the one hand, and on the other hand those bodily processes which are not necessary to conscious processes. It is not as though we could say that anyone who argues for a criterion of personal identity in terms of the continuity of conscious processes were committed to the thesis that consciousness would be possible without any body whatever.

Consider, for example, Williams' argument that memory cannot be used as an adequate criterion of continuity of personal identity—i.e., we cannot use a person's memory of events that happened in Guy Fawkes' life, and lack of memory of anything else, as a criterion for saying that the person is Guy Fawkes. Williams' basis for this conclusion is that it is logically possible for two people to have exactly similar memories without being the same person.[2] Of course, this argument is inconsistent with Williams' own definition of 'memory': "To say '**A** remembers **X**', without irony or inverted commas, is to imply that **X** really happened; in this respect 'remember' is parallel to 'know'."[3] By this criterion, it would be impossible for two people to have exactly similar memories without those memories' being identical. If we require that a memory be the memory of something that really happened in order to qualify as a memory (as Williams does), then it would be impossible for me and you both to remember having sat in the first aisle seat in Professor So-and-so's 9:00 philosophy class in the Fall semester of 1970, without our having been the same person at that time.

But perhaps this is a quibbling objection. What Williams really means for us to suppose is that two different people both *claim* to remember having sat in the same seat at the same time, that both feel justified in their claims, though only one really is, and that with regard to every event in their histories, both claim to remember exactly the same thing, feeling equally justified in their claims. This possibility, however, is denied by the thesis of the inseparability of mental and physiological events. If you really did sit in such-and-such a seat, whereas I didn't, then there is a real historical difference between your body and mine, which should lead to some corresponding difference, however slight, between your consciousness and mine. Multiply these differences by millions of physical differences between your history and mine, and the result is two entirely different consciousnesses. In the case of at least *many* 'memories,' then, your consciousness of the 'memory' will be different from mine. (We might grant an exception in the case of the far-fetched logical possibility that your *body* and mine are also exactly the same in every respect, including not only their structure, but their function as well, while having reached these identical states by means of different causal chains. In that case, the 'reduplication' question would arise—i.e., if two people were exactly the same both physically and psychically, would they be the same person? That question, however, would be equally relevant to a theory of the self based on bodily continuity as to one based on continuity of conscious processes, and is of no concern to us here.) There is also another reason why two different people could not share absolutely identical memories: It would be possible on phenomenological grounds to distinguish between an imagined memory and a real one, in some way similar to the way Sartre distinguishes between a perception and an imagination by pointing out that in a perception of the Parthenon we can count the columns, whereas in an imagination of it we cannot.[4] The consciousness of an imagined memory is not precisely the same as the consciousness of a real one.

Williams mentions another important objection against his view. It might be argued, he says, that memory is so much what makes someone a certain person that when provided with certain memories, he cannot doubt who he is. "Or, the objection might be put by saying that a man might conceivably have occasion to look into a mirror and say 'this is not my body', but could never have occasion to say 'these are not my memories'. Or, again, a man who has lost his memory cannot say who he is."[5] This last phrasing of the objection obviously does not mean exactly the same thing as the others, yet Williams responds only to it, thus making it serve as a straw man. He refutes it by saying that a person who has lost his memory not only cannot say who *he* is, but "cannot say who anyone else is, either, nor whether any object is the same as one previously presented."[6] But what would be true of a man who has no memory *whatever* is irrelevant, just as what would be true of a man with no body whatever is irrelevant; the question is not whether someone with *no* memory can be identified as Guy Fawkes, but whether a person with Guy Fawkes' memory can be identified as Guy Fawkes.

Williams is correct in pointing out that it would be impossible for one person's body to have another person's personality, because one body may not be capable of executing the conscious processes involved in another person's personality. But only some aspects of the body are relevant here. Obviously, losing an arm does not stop me from being the same person. Moreover, as Merleau-Ponty points out, within certain limits, the body is capable of physically and chemically reorganizing itself in order to preserve a continuity of function. It is possible, then, that if we were to take the body of an embecile and give it the 'mind' of an intelligent person (as in the film *Charly*), this would not involve replacing any of the material components of the body, but simply rearranging them so that they would interrelate differently in terms of their temporal configurations.

It is also interesting to note in this regard that rats which have been subjected to a lifetime of complex learning experiments turn out, upon dissection, to have 4% more acetylcholinesterase in their cortexes (a chemical known to be involved in memory) than a control group of rats who did not participate in the learning experiments during their lifetimes. There also proves to be an increase in the number of glial cells, which are also believed to be involved in learning, and an increase in the weight of the cortex as a whole.[7] The implication is that rats who are genetically less intelligent can actually change their physical and chemical composition over time so that they become more intelligent. It is thus logically possible that the mind can act in such a way as to change the bodily substrata so that they better suit its activities and purposes. This ability is not unlimited, of course; the rats in Kretch's studies worked very hard for a lifetime for only a 4% increase in acetylcholinesterase. The point is simply that we cannot speak of structure as though it were independent of and separable from function any more than we can regard function as independent of and separable from structure. Furthermore, the issue is not whether structure or function has *causal* primacy, but rather whether it is the continuity of structure or of function that is referred to by the concept 'I' or 'self.'

To return to the example of memory, then, our thesis is not that having certain memories is what makes a person who he is (or makes him still be the same person he was before). The thesis, rather, is that memory is inseparable from something which makes the person who he is— namely, a very complex *temporal form,* a way of patterning responses and states of consciousness which is not only unique to a given individual, but which in fact *is* the given individual. Even in cases of amnesia, the short-term memory from one moment to the next is inseparable from this temporal form. A person *is* a patterning of conscious events in time, or in Merleau-Ponty's sense, a 'form.' This patterning cannot be simply reduced to its elements, because the configuration of the elements as well as the elements themselves is necessary in order to make the person who he is. We shall find that this pattern is an experienceable conscious process, that it is tangible enough to be a definite entity, and that it functions as a limited Husserlian transcendental ego, providing the unity and continuity within the stream of experiences that renders possible an incomplete phenomenological reduction and allows us to escape encapsulation within the immediate perspective of a momentary conscious state. It will also be necessary to give a specific account, in terms of the phenomenology of conscious experiences, of exactly what kind of consciousness the self consists of.

In the next section, we shall attempt to show why a concept of the self is necessary, and that this self functions in such a way as to accomplish (to a limited extent) the function Husserl assigned to the 'transcendental ego.' This concept of the self must satisfy the requirements that (a) its ontological status is clarified; (b) self-alienation and prereflective consciousness can be explained on the basis of it; (c) it is revealed as a real consciousness rather than merely an abstract concept; and (d) its unifying function in the role of 'transcendental ego' can be understood in concrete terms.

A. DIRECTIONALITY AND FRAGMENTATION
IN THE TRANSCENDENTAL EGO

In *The Transcendence of the Ego,* Sartre denies that there can be a transcendental ego in the Husserlian sense or in any sense resembling the Husserlian one.[8] The ego, he says, is an object *for*, not a content *in* consciousness. Consequently, Sartre does not regard the ego as having the status of a pure, disengaged consciousness which would remain intact after all implicit but questionable presuppositions had been bracketed out by means of the phenomenological reduction. Rather, in Sartre's view, the character and identity of the ego become uncertain and nebulous as a result of the reduction. This denial of the subjectively conscious transcendental ego then becomes one of the basic tenets of the worldview he develops in *Being and Nothingness*.[9] We shall suggest, however, that such a denial puts the whole phenomenological movement in jeopardy by needlessly removing an essential element from its methodological foundation. The transcendental ego, at least in some limited sense, is necessary if consciousness is to be free enough from self-alienation that even an imperfect phenomenological reduction—in the sense of disengaging our presuppositions about a phenomenon from our immediate consciousness of it—can be performed with any confidence or clarity.

According to Husserl, (1) the transcendental ego consists ontologically of our immediate consciousness in its subjective purity;[10] because this immediate consciousness remains unaffected by the phenomenological reduction, it is transcendental.[11] At the same time, (2) "One consciousness is bound up with another so as to constitute *one* consciousness, of which the correlate is *one* noema."[12] Husserl credits the "unity of the immanent time-consciousness" with this accomplishment of "[binding] consciousness with consciousness."[13] Because of this essential unity, pure consciousness has the structure of an *ego*, and not a mere succession of transcendental 'consciousnesses.' It is both *transcendental* and an *ego*—a transcendental ego.

Sartre considers it impossible that the same immanent consciousness as reduced can be both transcendental and an ego. He begins with Eugen Fink's thesis that the reflecting and the reflected-upon 'I' can never be identical.[14] The reflected-upon 'I' is not immanently given in the act of reflection, but only the *object* of this reflection (the reflected 'I,' the 'me') is given; and this *object*, the 'me,' can never serve as subject-pole for a phenomenological reduction, for the obvious reason that, as reflected upon, it is an object. It stands outside the brackets of the reduction, just as does any scientific or historical claim. Essentially, then, says Sartre, if the transcendental ego cannot be immediately given to me in any of the particular moments of my consciousness, then it is nothing but a hypothetical construct which is both unknowable and unnecessary; but, on the other hand, if the ego *could* be given in some actual moment of consciousness, then it would no longer be the transcending *unifier* of all these moments of consciousness, but would be merely the *content* of *one* of them. Thus it would be no transcendental ego at all.

We shall maintain on the contrary that the transcendental ego can be simultaneously *both* a principle of unification *and* an immanently experienced concrete consciousness; that to reflect on this consciousness is merely to attend to the respect in which it is directly and immediately conscious of itself as an unfolding (. . . 'from' background noetic meaning contexts, 'toward' ones yet to come. . .) which is part of the essence of phenomenological time. Any conscious experience, no matter how instantaneous or unitary, must in principle be experienced as more resembling a line segment than a point, in the sense that it shows this *directional* dimension. This directionality of the immediate experience, which is experienced as such when we focus upon the subjective meaning of the experience (the *noesis*), gives the subject of the experience a more direct affinity with the immediately preceding and the immediately following experiences than it could ever have with a mere *object* of experience.[15] Sartre can ignore this point only by failing to take adequate account of the impossibility in principle of there ever being experienced an exact present moment in the stream of consciousness. To experience an exact 'now' in the temporal dimension would be analogous to experiencing a figure without a ground in the spacial dimension. Even the closest we could conceivably come to experiencing a 'now' would reveal itself as already having part of its meaning inseparably bound up either with the immediately preceding moment, or the immediately following. And because of this inherently time-consuming character of even the simplest experience (which Sartre of course does not deny[16]), it becomes possible for consciousness to reflect upon an essential aspect of itself, without thereby reducing itself or this aspect of itself to an object external to its own reflection.

That our thinking here could be derived directly from Husserl would not seem completely far-fetched if we were to follow commentators like Ludwig Landgrebe[17] and Gerd Brand.[18] But whether we do or not, it is clear that in order to contend with the Sartrean problem we must further clarify that property of the transcendental ego which allows it to become coincident with our concrete consciousness at the instant when a reduction is performed, and this property, we assert, is the felt experience of directionality in the immediate consciousness.

With regard to the danger of psychologism, we must also show that this subjectively-sensed meaning which immanently discloses the direction of consciousness in its unfolding is the residuum of a *phenomenological* and not merely a *psychological* reduction—which it is, precisely because the reduction *produces a coincidence* between human and transcendental consciousness in the particular instant when the reduction is accomplished. Furthermore, 'I,' the human being who performs the reduction, prereflectively already was essentially my transcendental ego.

The argument then hinges on the question: Must we equate 'reflection' by definition with making oneself into an object, or is it possible for 'me,' as my ongoing process of relatively unified experience, to 'reflect' upon the immanent consciousness (which has and can subjectively experience itself as having this directional aspect) in some other way than by making it into an intentional object? If so, then to focus upon a 'moment' in the flow as inherently meaningful only in terms of other moments is to disclose, in however limited fashion, the Husserlian transcendental ego.

The importance of this problem has become increasingly obvious since the publication of *The Transcendence of the Ego* in 1937. If the possibility of reflecting on the prereflective negates the possibility of a transcendental ego, then the philosopher performing the reduction can never be sure whether he has escaped the prejudices and limitations of this immediate perspective, as Merleau-Ponty points out.[19] What seems to be an intuition of essence may be merely a "prejudice rooted in language,"[20] or possibly rooted in the prevalent theoretical concepts and research paradigms and values of our historical situation.[21] Nor could we ever be sure an imaginative variation had indeed varied culturally-relative attitudes of which we still may be unaware. In short, the whole phenomenological enterprise would be jeopardized, for there could be no method of overcoming the fragmentation of consciousness.

Thus we must ask two interrelated questions, and answer them on Husserlian grounds, or at least on grounds that support the essentially Husserlian view: (1) Is there a transcendental ego, as distinguished from particular states *of* this ego's consciousness? (2) If so, how does the ego escape from the prejudices of the particular perspectives that limit all of its particular moments (thus rendering possible a phenomenological reduction)? (Conversely, how can we know whether the 'essences' we intuit in the reduction are indeed true essences and not prejudiced and distorting category structures arising from the limited nature of each perspectival state of consciousness within the flow of consciousness?)

1. The motivated direction of attention as a unifying function

In the *Crisis* and in some of the later manuscripts, Husserl did in fact express an uneasiness about the relationship between his concept of the pure, disengaged transcendental subjectivity on the one hand, and on the other hand the corresponding concrete and human experiencing which necessarily sees and thinks from a situated point of view.

> Who are 'we,' as subjects performing the meaning- and
> validity-accomplishment of universal constitution? . . .
> Can 'we' mean 'we human beings,' human beings in the
> natural-objective sense, i.e., as real entities in the world?
> But are these real entities not themselves 'phenomena'
> and as such themselves object-poles and subject matter
> for inquiry back into the correlative intentionalities of
> which they are the poles, through whose functions they
> have and have attained their ontic meaning?[22]

If transcendental subjectivity ultimately disengages itself from the real, psychophysical entity that 'I' am in my everyday being, then from an ontological perspective the question arises: Where can the consciousness we call 'transcendental' reside? Does not consciousness-as-experienced become a mere phenomenon alongside others? And if so, then where is the 'subjectivity' of transcendental subjectivity? Must it not derive from my own shadowy consciousness and thus remain pulled this way and that by my own prejudices, value-laden thematizations[23] and limited category structures?[24] Can the subject of the philosophical experience bracket himself?

To confront this problem, we must proceed from Husserl's earlier discussions of attention, especially in the Fifth Logical Investigation, and then analyse the process whereby the consciousness of the present moment succeeds in transcending the limitations of the immediate perspective, thus becoming the purely transcendental subjectivity which sees this limited perspective as a phenomenon in its own right. We shall demonstrate that (1) for a particular state of consciousness to decide to divorce itself from its own limited perspective, in order to relate this perspective to other actual perspectives and to a whole horizon of other possible perspectives, is to *become* one's own transcendental ego. (2) To become one's own transcendental ego is to attend to a kind of consciousness which is already taking place within one, but on a prereflective level, which has the function of unifying one actual perspective with another, and finally with possible perspectives. This becomes most evident when the reduction is performed. Implicit interconnections which tie one intentional thread to another become visible when the reduction loosens those threads from their ordinarily constricted meanings. When consciousness attends to this preconscious network of interrelations of felt meanings, it becomes transcendentally unified by seeing the respect in which on a 'preconscious' level it already is such a unity. (Here Sartre's discussion of the impossibility of 'unconscious consciousness' will come into play.)

It is true that Husserl concludes in the above-quoted passage that the transcendental ego, *on the whole*, is different from the human, psychophysical ego. But he does not elaborate enough at this juncture in his writing as to what the ontological status of such an ego would have to be in light of the problem as later posed by Sartre, and as to whether the two egos can ever coincide in consciousness. However, if we compare what he says here with elsewhere, we can see at least one possible answer to the ontological question. Four pages after the above passage, Husserl says,

> . . .Each human being 'bears within himself a transcendental "I"' . . . insofar as he is the self-objectification, as exhibited through phenomenological self-reflection, of the corresponding transcendental 'I.'[25]

The human person is therefore not to be considered ontologically prior to the transcendental ego. He merely *is* the *self-objectification* of this ego. 'Self-objectification' does not seem to refer to the process in which I, as the person I happen to be, objectify the person I happen to be; but rather, I as a person somehow get constituted in the process wherein this transcendental ego objectifies *its* self, and I end up *being* this objectification. At each instant, my transcendental ego seems to have already existed in some rudimentary form before I became the exact person with the perspective from which I now see—but to have existed pre-reflectively. By combining with the particular accidents of my life, it seems always previously to have produced a changing, idiosyncratic field of consciousness with the capacity to focus attention from any number of limited points of view, but floundering often aimlessly from one set of prejudices to another. My everyday consciousness, stuck in its own point of view, then becomes like a beam of light that shines forth but cannot illumine its own source.

That the transcendental ego somehow precedes or underlies the concrete human being is also suggested by Husserl's view that there is a different transcendental ego for every person.[26] I have my transcendental ego and you have yours. This would be consistent with the supposition that the transcendental ego, which is achieved or would in principle be achieved in the performance of a complete phenomenological reduction, is not some ideal state of consciousness which would be the same for everyone and which would do away with the individuality of the human being, but on the contrary is to be found already there in the existing consciousness of a human being, as the directed tendency of that person's consciousness toward its own amplification through explication, symbolization and the unpacking of meaning.

Why does Husserl choose to introduce this theme of self-objectification at this point, rather than merely citing imaginative variation and suspension of the naturalistic viewpoint as means toward the reduction? It appears that, like Sartre, he regards these procedures alone as inadequate to the solution of the dilemma. The function of the reduction is to describe phenomena as they present themselves. But phenomena already present themselves as having meanings or essences, so a description of a phenomenon cannot avoid making references to the phenomenon's essence or essences. Although imaginative variation can help us to decide what is or is not properly called an essence, imaginative variation has its practical limitations, which in terms of the problem we are considering are crucial. Natural philosophers of old could not *imagine* a physical event without a material substratum, whereas modern physicists go so far as to question the *meaning* of the word 'material.' One thinker may see a unity of meaning exhibited where another denies it, as in the case of Kurt Goldstein's 'impairment of abstract attitude,' which many psychologists cannot intuit as an essential organismic phenomenon, but instead see as a manifestation of several more limited phenomena working together. In general, we may indeed try to vary the imagined objects along the lines of 'existing in this or that cultural milieu,' or 'in light of different theoretical presuppositions,' but never know for sure whether we have forgotten to vary just those aspects of phenomena which our cultural and theoretical attitudes do not easily dissociate, thus contaminating our seeing of the genuine essence or essences involved. Thus each person to some extent comes to an experience with conceptual or preconceptual categories which influence what essences he will see a phenomenon as exhibiting. Ideally, then, as mentioned earlier, his description should therefore include not only a description of the thing seen, but also of the system of categories that contributes to his perspective on the thing.

But, as we have seen, this will not work. For to describe a category structure from the perspective of the category structure itself would be like trying to stand on my own shoulders. Such an attempt would be just one instance of the strange conflict between human and transcendental consciousness. If my present consciousness is to be seen as merely an element of a larger totality, who sees it as such? And in seeing it as such, would not that consciousness necessarily have to reduce my consciousness to an intentional object?

Husserl, as we shall see, was aware of this question long before Sartre and Merleau-Ponty asked it, yet he did not think that it necessitated any major revision of the basic fabric of his thought. He certainly did not abandon the transcendental ego, and with good reasons which the body of his work discloses. Without some transcendental function, the stream of consciousness would be like listening to an endless series of speeches, all equally elegant, all contradicting each other, and feeling swayed by each in its turn, with no appeal to any higher authority. Such a consciousness would more resemble the consciousness Straus attributes to an animal and to a person dreaming[27] than it would the consciousness of a wakeful, thinking person capable of remembering past consciousnesses almost at will, and of creating a more comprehensive viewpoint which enables him to relate them to each other. Consciousness with no transcendentality would not be consciousness as it in fact presents itself.

So conscious was Husserl of the problem of relating human to transcendental experience, that he at first rejected the transcendental ego as an idealistic hypothesis.[28] At that early stage in his development, Husserl did not rule out the possibility that self-consciousness might be non-intentional in some cases, but neither did he explore the possibility. But after making the transcendental function one of his main themes, he began also to allow that the *hylé* or 'stuff' of consciousness can be non-positionally conscious of itself without thereby necessarily making itself into an intentional object for some further consciousness.[29] Transcendental subjectivity is a unity which we achieve by becoming aware of the unity which we achieve by becoming aware of the unity already functioning (in the way described in the lectures on time consciousness) on a preconscious level.[30]

At this point, Sartre's analysis of the absurdity of positing an 'unconscious consciousness' becomes crucial. How can the transcendental subjectivity be something *already* on-going in consciousness, which the concrete consciousness of this moment needs only to attend to in order to achieve its own transcendentality? Would this not involve positing the previous existence of the transcendental element (before we reflect on it) as a kind of unconscious consciousness? To answer this question, we must recall Husserl's treatment of attention as a conscious act.

2. The motivation to focus: 'looking for' and 'looking at'

In the second chapter of the Fifth Logical Investigation, Husserl says that the process of attention is always intentional.[31] That is, it always 'intends' or posits some object *over against itself*. His remarks on this subject become especially important for any attempt to treat the transcendental ego as something that is always prereflectively conscious until I suddenly choose to attend to it. Obviously, there can be such phenomena as prereflective consciousness in the sense, for example, that I can know that I know a name, yet not be able to remember it at that moment; or, again, I can make logical inferences without realizing that I am doing so (many logical fallacies probably occur for this reason). If such instances do occur, this means that in some sense there is a content in consciousness to which at present I am not attending. But since any consciousness upon which attention is not focused is in this sense a *prereflective* consciousness, and since Husserl says that attention is always an intentional act, it would seem to follow that any consciousness to which attention is directed is a *reflected* consciousness, and therefore that if there is any consciousness which is not an intentional act, it can be non-intentional only in the mode of a prereflective consciousness. Any consciousness which is reflected upon would automatically become an object of consciousness rather than an immanent noetic content within the subjective dimension of the stream of consciousness.

Thus, if we were to assume—as Husserl apparently does—that attention must always be intentional in the usual sense, then it would follow that any consciousness which is not intentional (i.e., which does not posit an object as over against itself) is as such doomed to a permanently unreflected-upon status. If attention is intentional, then to become attentively aware of a consciousness which is already there is to make this consciousness into the intentional object of this attentive awareness, which means that, insofar as I am *attentively* aware of a non-intentional consciousness (such as the non-positional self-consciousness of the transcendental ego), the latter is no longer a content in consciousness, but becomes a mere object of consciousness. As Husserl himself articulates in his lectures on time consciousness, "What is caused to appear in the moment-actual [*Momentan-Aktuellen*] of the flux of consciousness is the past phase of the flux of consciousness in the series of retentional moments of this flux."[32]

The absurd consequences of interpreting this statement as meaning that phenomenological reflection always reduces the reflected consciousness to an intentional object can be seen in Sartre's theory of emotion, which seems to follow from the assumption of strictly universal intentionality.

> But fear is not originally consciousness of being afraid,
> no more than the perception of this book is consciousness
> of perceiving the book. . . . Emotional consciousness is,
> first of all, consciousness *of* the world. . . . The emotion
> is a certain manner of apprehending the world.[33]

The main purpose of part B of this chapter will be to contend with the confusing status of prereflective consciousness. For now, suffice it to say that, precisely in order to avoid the absurdity of the Sartrean kind of position, which would deny in principle the possibility of genuine reflection, and would deny that the feeling of fear, for example, is an immanent subjective consciousness to which we can attend without automatic distortion of it, Husserl insists upon allowing that consciousness can be directly and non-intentionally conscious of itself in the sense of its pure flux-character as revealed simply in the experience of directionality and already-ongoingness. If we assume a doctrine of radical transcendence such as the one Sartre expresses in his analysis of emotions, then it would be difficult to understand why it is that I take up *this* particular motivational stance toward the world as opposed to so many other motivational positions I *could* have taken up, and which ultimately would have resulted in different emotions. The teleological or emotional (and therefore temporal) directedness constituting my basic motivations and influencing in this way my interpretation of reality (through perspectival limitation, 'bad faith,' etc.), cannot be so reduced to consciousness *of* some object. If the motivation is not originary, but is rather a second-order property of a perception, then there would be no way to account for the fact that what we see is always already motivated by our designation of the important parameters to look *for* as we bring phenomena into focus. This seems to be one of the important Kantian influences on the development of the phenomenological interpretation of the existential category structure.

If it is true that our pre-perceptual category structure functions by means of selective attention (and selective inattention) so as to motivate us to see certain things and ignore others, then the motivational stance out of which I implicitly *decide* to attend to *this* while ignoring *that* (a motivational stance therefore partly constitutive of my perspectival limitations and category structures) must be logically prior to the decision in question. This perspectival limitation has an important role in choosing which objects to make thematic. The motivational stance which influences the perspectival limitation in this way may well be intentional in a sense, but in another sense it cannot be. It is conscious on the level of 'looking-for' rather than 'looking-at.' In the same way, it is possible for the human person to 'become' his own already-functioning transcendental unity, without thereby making the subjectivity previously at work in that unification into an object. We must clarify what we mean by this 'looking-for' kind of intentionality.

Consider the example of a man who is told to check through a stack of tickets for all the ones numbered '7': He may not really *see* the other numbers besides 7, but may only see in each case whether the number he glances at is or is not a seven. To a certain extent, we see only the aspects of phenomena we are interested in, and we come to an experience equipped with categories that reflect our interests. Categorial intentionality (as we shall call this broader type of intentionality) functions to facilitate experiencing, precisely *by* limiting it. If we had to approach the world without categorial intentions, we could never make enough 'inferences' from 'sense data' to organize our experience meaningfully. The distinction is not merely between being presentatively aware of a generality of meaning, and being presentatively aware of a more specific fulfillment of that meaning. Rather, the meaning-intention is a looking-*for* the fulfillment of a certain experienced meaning, whereas the presentative-intention which fulfills this meaning-intention is a looking-*at* the object that fulfills the meaning. The word 'intend' in the two cases describes two entirely different functional relations to the object.

For Husserl, of course, the meaning-intention is itself a presentative intention having the pure species as its object. But, in principle, this presentative meaning-intention itself presupposes some other, prior categorial intention or looking-for which would lead me to look at and to grasp the essence of the species in question. And when I look *at* this looking-*for*, I find that some other looking-for must have led me to be interested in making this apprehension as opposed to others I could have made instead. Every *presentative* intention (whether of an individual or of a species) is a figure which presupposes as its ground a *categorial* (more general and 'looking-for') intention. This movement from categorial to presentative intentionality is one instance wherein the moment-transcending quality of experiencing makes itself self-evident in reflection, without becoming an intentional object in its own right.

The intentionality (if any) accompanying such a way of experiencing must be a very broadened kind, and certainly not the narrower mode of looking-at. And at the same time, it must be the hyletic phase to which Husserl points when he says,

> *Not every real phase* of the concrete unity of an intentional experience has itself the basic character of intentionality, the property of being a 'consciousness of something.' This is the case, for instance, with all sensory data, which play so great a part in the perceptive intuition of things. . . . The content which presents the whiteness of the paper as it appears to us . . . is the *bearer* of an

intentionality, but not itself a consciousness of something. The same holds of other data of experience, of the so-called sensory feelings, for instance.[34]

There must be a variety of instances in the experiencing process wherein I am able to be conscious of the on-going experiencing process *subjectively*, and not merely by reflecting on it in an *objectifying* sense, which would make it the object for some other state of my consciousness to inspect as if from a distance; otherwise, it would never be possible to feel anything at all, but merely to be presentatively aware *that* I was feeling or had been feeling some way, which would be absurd if I did not in fact feel that way.

The question remains, can we apply these concepts to Sartre's argument against the transcendental *ego*? 'Ego,' for both Sartre and Husserl, implies the transcending unity across time of the many moment-actuals comprising the stream of consciousness. Sartre says that the transcendental 'I' would have to be either the direct consciousness of this particular moment, or a transcending unity which 'has' all of these particular feelings. If I am the former, then the transcendence across time cannot be explained; if the latter, then 'I' would not myself *be* a consciousness, since all the states of consciousness would be ontologically distinguished from what 'I' am.

However, it would seem that there is the possibility, in fact the necessity, that I am *both*. In the directional experience of the 'looking-for,' for example, I am this motivation to see, which at the same time is already *felt* on the one hand (thus it is a concrete consciousness), yet on the other hand also unifies all the *other* consciousnesses of the intentional complex by motivating the order and pattern in which my circumspective gaze looks around in its looking-for and therefore also in its looking-at. One unitary source, from which this gaze ultimately takes its direction, at the same time that it is consciousness of a transcendent object, can also be directly conscious of itself (as having the character of a directional, on-going process). In the naturalistic viewpoint, when I live primarily in the looking-*at* which results from the process, this self-consciousness is non-thetic and prereflective. (It is also possible to look *at* myself in this objectifying way, but then no coincidence is guaranteed between the human and the transcendental 'self.') But if this always-presupposed 'looking-for' categorial intentionality should choose to involve itself in a phenomenological reduction, to just this extent I become aware of the hooks and arrows connecting my seemingly objective world-view with the prior interest-motivated pattern in the systematic *direction* of attention, that is, with my category structure or perspectival limitation. The perspectival limitation, which is now part of the directly felt subjectivity of the time during which this experience takes place, becomes conscious of itself. Then in the instant when this limited category structure attends to itself intentionally, it automatically *changes*: At least some of the prejudice which formerly limited it (and which it formerly *was*, in part, *being* its own limitation through selective attention) is now in the process of dropping away. And precisely in this experiencing *of* the change *in* our perspective, we experience consciousness itself as having a direction, *from* something *to* something (and these somethings themselves are not at this moment experienced as isolated moments of consciousness, but as further-away segments of the same flow). We then see that its meaning cannot be described in terms of an immediate 'now' which in reality is only an abstraction. The experience, rather, exhibits the unity of a flow from one perspective to another, and this flow—which is both *unifying* and *directly experienceable*—is the transcendental ego.

We do not therefore conclude, too simplistically, that 'I,' in the instant that I become conscious of myself as my transcendental ego, am exhaustively and exclusively defined as the total teleological directedness of my category structure (nor, certainly, would Husserl say this). We need to develop more refined concepts with which to deal with the problem of the definition of the 'I.' But experienceable directionality in general allows a commensurability between human and transcendental subjectivity, which is at least one example of what goes on in the 'self-objectification of the transcendental ego.' Thus we can at least conclude, at this point, that a transcendental ego is possible. The possibility of this commensurability between human and transcendental consciousness in turn ensures the possibility of a phenomenological reduction, though perhaps not one which could ever be complete or absolute.

Some would deny that selective attention in the form of a motivating category structure has anything to do with the unity of ego function, insisting, on the contrary, that the objective unity and continuity on the side of the world is sufficient to account for the unity of the self. Some, for example, might interpret Gurwitsch as holding this contrary view. The objective unity on the side of the world, however, is not immanent to consciousness and therefore would not be able to withstand Sartre's argument.

The relevant passage from Gurwitsch comes in his discussion of James.[35] James speaks of two factors both of which provide differentiation and integration within the stream of experiences: selective attention, and the 'saliency' of certain aspects of the realities represented in the experiences themselves. Gurwitsch denies that selective attention can have these functions. "Since, as we have seen, sensible totals are, according to James, the primary data and their decomposition into parts is subsequent, the problem of the first segregation of a component or group of components arises unavoidably."[36] Gurwitsch goes on to say, "Let us suppose the first segregation of a datum or group of data has been performed by selective activity operating at random. To become stabilized, this segregation must be repeated. . . . [But] the very process of [the subject's] singling out [the sensible total into its parts] again must also be accounted for."[37] Therefore, selective attention cannot account for the separation of sensible totals into their constituent parts. For the purposes of the present study, this also would imply that selective attention cannot account for the differentiation and integration which makes possible the unity and direction in the stream of experiences.

Notice that Gurwitsch says "selective activity operating at random" is not capable of providing such differentiating function. This would seem to imply that, if selective attention did *not* operate "at random," then it *would* be capable of performing such a function. Gurwitsch assumes that selective attention operates at random because he agrees with James that "We are endowed with the faculty of cutting, delimiting, and singling out parts from the concrete continuous stream of experience. The cuts thus performed are artificial in the sense that they are in no way motivated by the structure of the stream of experience, but are introduced from without into the latter which in its original form exhibits no separations and demarcations."[38] Thus Gurwitsch concludes that selective attention is not an adequate vehicle to allow organization to be an "autochthonous feature of the stream of experience"; the only other alternative, then, is that the saliency of certain preferable ways of organizing experience arises from the experiences themselves rather than from within the organism. But this leaves out the possibility that James may be wrong here—that selective attention *may be* motivated in a systematic way from within the organism: In fact, the notion that selective attention *is* motivated would seem to be a phenomenological datum, since we have all experienced such phenomena as motivated forgetting and the ignoring of data we would prefer not to see. Section B of this chapter will show how such a motivational structure *can* be a unifying feature within the stream of consciousness, and this unifying feature will ultimately turn out to *be* the self. Our position, then, is that *both* selective attention *and* the saliency of certain inherently-better ways of organizing data are capable of providing the differentiating, integrating and unifying functions that finally cause the stream of consciousness to assume a certain unique direction in its unfolding. Selective attention, moreover, is motivated by a great many more factors than the saliency of patterns of the data themselves, and it is this motivated pattern that grounds a concept of the ego capable of standing up under Sartre's anti-transcendental-ego argument. Of course, it is also true, as Gurwitsch implies, that without a desire to attend to 'salient' features at all, there would be nothing 'transcendental' about this ego in the sense of being able to ground even an incomplete phenomenological reduction.

In order to understand more exactly *what* the nature of the self is, we must explore the phenomena of selective attention, symbolization and prereflective motivation in more detail. This will be the purpose of the remainder of the chapter.

In *The Phenomenology of Perception*, Maurice Merleau-Ponty describes consciousness in a way that is very congruent with the notion that the ontological status of consciousness is that of a process whose substrate is the body. An important element of this description is that consciousness originates in the body in the form of prereflective consciousness.[39] One of Merleau-Ponty's major problems, however, is pinning down the meaning of 'prereflective' in relation to 'consciousness.' If we suppose that we cannot become fully aware of a prereflective consciousness until we reflect on it (for example, the way the shoe on my right foot feels at this moment), then 'prereflective consciousness' seems as paradoxical as 'unconscious consciousness' is in Sartre's critique of Freud.[40] Moreover, if attention is always intentional (as Husserl suggests[41]), then to attend to a prereflective consciousness would seem to make that consciousness into an intentional object rather than merely making it 'reflective'; to reflect upon prereflective consciousness thus appears impossible. Merleau-Ponty's treatment of the problem, as we shall see, does not overcome the Sartrean objection that 'prereflective' consciousness is meaningless unless clearly distinguished from 'unconscious' consciousness. On the other hand, Sartre's alternative—that reflective and prereflective consciousness differ only in that the former makes the latter into an intentional object—ultimately destroys the temporal unity of consciousness which Husserl rightly insisted upon.[42]

Our solution to this paradox involves a re-evaluation of the meaning of 'intentionality.' We propose that there are two very different kinds of intentionality: a 'presentative' or 'looking *at*' intentionality and a 'categorial' or 'looking *for*' intentionality. Consciousness which is intentional in the latter sense is not necessarily intentional in the former sense but strives to become so. 'Looking for' intentionality determines the focus of our attention in the 'looking at' sense. Since 'looking for' intentionality does not (we propose) necessarily have a specific intentional object, then the focus of attention is determined by a form of consciousness capable of becoming self-conscious without reducing itself to an object. The way we accomplish this focusing is by using the process symbolization. For a state of consciousness to move from a 'prereflec-tive' to a 'reflective' state means that the ongoing project of moving in a motivated direction in the stream of consciousness prompts us to use symbols to help us experience a particular phenomenon more fully (one that figures into a general class of experiences we have been 'looking for'). By 'symbolization' here we mean not merely putting a conscious meaning into words, but rather any activity through which the meaning becomes more sharply focused through physical embodiment in some medium (whether this medium be language, music, dance, or some other suitable embodiment). Consciousness strives to become adequately sym-bolized because through symbolization it becomes more fully conscious.

Section 1 of this part will develop the problem of prereflective con-sciousness in the context of Merleau-Ponty's use of the term. Section 2 will show how this problem is intensified in the light of Husserl's treat-ment of intentionality. Section 3 presents a proposed solution, derived from an account of the process of symbolization not far from resem-bling that of Richard Wagner, whose writings on poetry and drama can be generalized to shed considerable light on the problem. The work of Eugene Gendlin will also prove immeasurably helpful in this regard.

1. The problem of prereflective intentionality

Merleau-Ponty's first major work, *The Structure of Behavior* begins with a *reductio ad absurdum* of the philosophical position implied by modern materialism (or the 'naturalistic attitude' in Husserl's usage). He begins by analysing the idea of 'reflexes,' the radically empiricist and materialist doctrine of *partes extra partes* physiological functioning wherein the 'stimulus' efficaciously determines the 'response' in conjunc-tion with previous conditioning. Merleau-Ponty shows that the very sen-sing of the stimulus *as* a discriminative stimulus presupposes that a 'response' has already taken place in the sense of a previous orientation to the environment which is actively perspectival. (Pavlov's 'orientating reflex' and the behaviorists' 'operant level' might be interpreted as refer-ring to this prior orientation.) For example, if I did not focus my eyes in a certain way as opposed to other possible ways, I would not see the stimulus as I do; yet the psychology of operant conditioning, according to Merleau-Ponty, cannot account for the way in which I must original-ly 'know how' to orient myself in this way (as it must presuppose).[43]

The simplistic billiard-ball model of causation is thus inadequate.

Reflex psychology's own data show that (1) all reflexes are to some extent *cognitively* mediated from stimulus to response (which leads to absurdity if we insist upon the *partes extra partes* conception of materiality in the context of physiology);[44] and that (2) the organism responds to its *global situation*, never to the single stimulus in itself.[45] We find therefore a circular rather than a linear causality and a structural condition in the organism which actively fights to resist a disruption of its holistic balance, equilibrium and continuity. Merleau-Ponty argues that the *partes extra partes* explanation of physiology further breaks down in light of Gestalt data which show that the functional structure of the organism (man or animal) tends to remain constant even when one of its parts is changed; the organism accomplishes this functional continuity by changing some or all of its other parts in order that the overall relation of the parts to each other remains the same.[46] In addition, Merleau-Ponty finds that it is not the stimuli in themselves that elicit the response; quite the contrary: When Pavlov attempted to condition dogs to a stimulus in itself, divorced from any intelligible or natural relevance to the response, not only did his experiments eventually fail, but the dogs became "neurotic" (Pavlov's word).[47] Gestalt experiments show that not the stimuli, but rather their *configuration* or *interrelation* elicits the response from the subject. This configuration is apprehended in terms of the *significance* of figure-ground relations. The 'stimulus' is, for the organism, the representative of a category, a generality of signification. Experiments by Ruger, for example, show that a subject conditioned to respond to a stimulus in one context may not respond to that same stimulus in another context or simply by itself.[48] Experiments by Goldstein with brain-damaged soldiers show that a lesion in a highly specific region of the brain gives rise, not to specific cognitive and behavioral impairments, but to a general "loss of abstract attitude" in all of the patient's activities. Further, the subject may be able to say a whole sentence, but not part of it; his *legato* movements remain intact while his injury renders *staccato* movements impossible.[49]

Merleau-Ponty concludes from this mass of naturalistic evidence that as an organism relates more and more consciously to its environment, the 'stimulus' increasingly assumes the role of a *sign* representing the interrelation of that stimulus to the overall environmental situation as perceived. The signification is present on a preconscious level even in the case of very primitive forms of life: A toad, for example, will wait for a highly complex configuration of stimuli before exhibiting an instinctual response. But if signification functions as a preconscious relation to the object in all conditioning phenomena, such a relation can be explained neither in terms of nerve pathways nor in terms of operant conditioning. We must assume, therefore, that consciousness—in the sense of intentionality—is always already present in the body of any organism susceptible to conditioning. There must be at least one kind of intentional consciousness which is *in the body*; Merleau-Ponty calls this prereflective form of intentionality "know-how," citing the example of a football player's subconscious orientation to the dimensions of his field.[50]

According to Merleau-Ponty, the common term underlying sensation, perception and cognitive symbolization is the motor activity of the body. When the color blue evokes my perception of it, my eye situates itself in a certain way in order to "go out to" that blue;[51] when I think or imagine the color blue, my eye prepares to go out in this same way. The relation of me to my object is thus similar to the relation of the sleeper to his slumber: I prepare for it in a way which I always already know how to do, and at some point, almost magically, I am given over to it.[52] Language, a motor activity either of the mouth or (silently) of the brain, is a voluntary movement which reminds me of its meaning and evokes in me a "kinetic melody."[53] This preconscious rootedness in the world, a preconscious which is "always already" there, is my body. "The body, in so far as it has 'behavior patterns', is that strange object which uses its own parts as a general system of symbols for the world."[54]

In sum, then, what we experience according to Merleau-Ponty is not properly the simple thing-in-itself but rather a complex interrelation of body, figure and ground. This interrelation exists before it is attended to or focused upon by reflective consciousness. Thus there must be a sort of consciousness in the body which has not attained to the status of 'reflective' consciousness, and this is what Merleau-Ponty means by 'prereflective' consciousness.

But regarding any consciousness which supposedly has not attained to the status of 'reflective' consciousness, we must ask: Is this consciousness not a form of unconscious consciousness? If so, does it not fall victim to the same valid criticism Sartre brings against all unconscious consciousness?[55] But if not—if it is on the contrary a *conscious* consciousness, then in what sense is it 'prereflective?' We cannot in our time escape this issue as easily as did Husserl, simply by distinguishing 'reflective' from 'unreflective' consciousness, for the meaning of these words has now been genuinely thrown into question by Sartre's dictum that "Every conscious existence exists as consciousness of existing."[56] The difference between seeing and being conscious of seeing no longer seems clear in light of the problem as posed by Sartre. Moreover, how is it that the body has consciousness? A good computer could perhaps perform all the functions Merleau-Ponty describes under the rubric of 'know-how'; but the primary difference between the mind and such a computer is precisely the *subjectivity* of the mind. Merleau-Ponty's description of body-consciousness does not fully account for this subjectivity which we must regard as a primary feature of consciousness if consciousness is to differ from the registering of data in a computer bank.

At this point one might have recourse to the 'life-world.' Consciousness can be preconscious from the standpoint of the individual person precisely because this consciousness is originally pre-personal. Consciousness is not merely 'in' the mind or 'in' the body, but rather in the world. Consciousness, even if it is prereflective, is already intentional and need not display the feature of 'subjectivity' since it exists in the body and in the world rather than in the reflective ego-subject of experience.

This explanation, however, also presents problems. What is the ontological status of a consciousness that is intentional even before we elevate it to the level of reflection? Can an intentional consciousness take place without my attending to it? If I attend to the way the shoe on my foot feels, for example, is the intentionality of this consciousness already there before I attend to it on a reflective level? If so, then we must account for the possibility of the paradoxical phenomenon which now emerges: 'Consciousness of which I previously was not attentively aware, but which nonetheless existed as consciousness.' In what sense can it be called 'consciousness' if I was not 'aware' of its presence?

2. Intentional objects compared with objects used as symbolizations

Husserl's stand on the question of intentionality is from the beginning already linked to the enigma of the status of prereflective consciousness. As we have seen, it becomes necessary to modify Husserl's view that attention must always be intentional in the sense of being made into an intentional object over against the present state of consciousness. The problem with such an assumption is that it entails the impossibility of attending to our own present feelings and felt meanings without changing them into mere objects of consciousness; we cannot focus upon them in their subjective being. Any consciousness upon which attention is not focused would be in this sense a prereflective consciousness; however, since Husserl says that attention is always an intentional act, it would seem to follow that any consciousness to which attention is directed is a reflected consciousness, and therefore that to become attentively aware of a consciousness which is already there is to make this consciousness into the intentional object of this attentive awareness. The inevitable conclusion, if we assume that attention must necessarily be intentional in the conventional sense, would seem to be that, insofar as I am attentively aware of any consciousness, the latter is no longer a content in consciousness at all, but becomes the object of consciousness.

This paradox would not exist if we were to remove one of two premises: (1) that prereflective consciousness is not attended to in the instant when it is prereflective; or (2) that attentive consciousness is always intentional in the sense that the thing to which we attend becomes an object external to the consciousness attending to it. Obviously, to reject premise (1) would be absurd. Whatever else may be said about the meaning of 'reflection,' the stipulation that we *attend to* the object of this reflection must certainly be included. (It would then follow that any consciousness which is not attended to is also not reflective.) To resolve the paradox, therefore, we must examine the second premise.

The idea that we cannot attend to a state of our own consciousness without reducing that consciousness to an intentional object now seems absurd. We must therefore either reject Husserl's statement that all attention is intentional, or interpret 'intentionality' in a broader sense than the mere reduction of something to an object. There are indications, in fact, that Husserl never meant intentionality in such a narrow sense. In the *Logical Investigations* he speaks extensively of meaning-intentions and meaning-fulfillments and their interrelations. This usage can be confusing in light of the fact that every meaning-fulfillment is a presentative intention.[57] In some sense, the range of objects intended in a meaning-intention must be *broader* than the more specific references in its fulfillment. But besides this difference in breadth between the meaning-intention and the meaning-fulfilling-intention, there is the vague sense of another difference, a qualitative rather than a quantitative difference.

Consider the intentionality involved in Sartre's example of looking for our friend Pierre in a crowded restaurant.[58] We may not really *see* any of the other people in the restaurant, but only see in each case whether the person we are looking at is or is not Pierre. In each case, we have made the decision in advance to classify the person we see in terms of the categories 'Pierre' and 'other people.' If asked later whether we saw a man with a long white beard, we may not recall having seen him although we may at least have seen that he was not the person we were looking for. It seems possible that we may 'see' whether or not something fits into a category without 'seeing' much else about the object or becoming attentively or reflectively conscious of seeing it at all. The intentionality at work in this category-fitting already functions even while we are merely 'looking *for*' the object and before we actually 'look *at*' it. This broader or categorial intentionality sometimes allows distortion of experience in that the categories employed may be inappropriate or too rigid, but if we had to approach the world without categorial intentions, we could never make enough inferences to organize the 'sense data' into perceptual objects. These two kinds of intentionality might also appropriately be termed 'presentative' and 'pre-presentative,' since for every presentation there is presupposed a category structure or existential *a priori* which has led to that intuition as opposed to some other intuition. The essential difference is between 'looking at' and 'looking for.'

The motivated ('looking for') dimension of consciousness limits the extent to which consciousness is intentional in the transcendent ('looking at') sense. If it is true that we to some extent selectively attend to just those intentional objects to which it is convenient for us to attend, and to some extent ignore those objects which it is convenient for us to ignore, then the motivational stance from out of which I implicitly *decide* to attend to this while ignoring that (a motivational stance partly constitutive of my category structure or existential *a priori*) must be logically prior to the decision in question. This contrast and interrelation between motivation and transcendent intuition raises the question of the eidetic psychology of attention. Is there not perhaps some relationship between the movement from 'looking for' to 'looking at' and the movement from a 'prereflective' to a 'reflective' status on the part of a consciousness? If we consider some distinctions Husserl has used in regard to this issue, we shall see that the whole idea of 'preconscious' consciousness must relate in some way to the motivational (looking for) dimension of consciousness. In particular, we must consider (1) the distinction between the cause and the intentional object of an experience and (b) the distinction between the intentional object of an experience and the symbols used to explicate that intentional experience.

(a) Husserl is careful to distinguish between the cause and the intentional object of an experience.

> [It is] absurd in principle . . . to treat an intentional as
> a causal relation, to give it the sense of an empirical,
> substantial-causal case of necessary connection . . . which
> really and psycho-physically determines my mental life.[59]

When we try to understand the 'looking for' dimension of intentional consciousness, the concept of motivation comes into play. In light of Husserl's distinction, we must be careful not to fall back into the pre-phenomenological assumption that perceived events in the world 'cause' us to be motivated in a given direction. For example, I am fired from my job. I feel angry. I go home and shout at my children. In a sense I seem to be angry with my children 'because' I was fired from the job, but the case is clearly not one of necessary connection, and least of all could it be called the 'cause' in the physical sense. Moreover, the intentional object of the anger I now feel is my children, not being fired from the job; but surely *they* are not the cause of my anger, even in a loose sense. The intentional object of an experience is always that to which I am principally attending while the experience is going on.[60] This would not necessarily be the case with the *cause* of an experience.

It may further be noted that my anger at losing my job and my anger at my children are actually only *non-independent moments* of one complex experiential whole. This is a key point. How far I must reach into various and sundry interrelating acts or partial acts which might integrally participate with the whole in question, before deciding upon the limits of a circumscription of some concrete experiential unity as a whole independent act, would be an extremely confusing question with which to deal.

(b) A second distinction we should bear in mind in relation to the intentionality of 'looking-for' is the one Husserl makes between the intentional object of an experience on the one hand (or better, the *complex* of intentional objects of an experience), and on the other hand the physical embodiments used in the *symbolization* of that experience. Husserl says, "We attend, when not distracted, to the signified rather than the signs."[61] For example, when I read about washing machines, my intentional object is washing machines, not the words on the page.

The distinction is not always as clear-cut, however, as a different example will show: My wife divorces me and I am upset. I go home and listen to Tchaikovsky's Fifth Symphony. I am still upset but I am no longer consciously thinking about my wife. As I listen, the feeling becomes more intense and becomes a purer, gut-level experience of despair. In this case, is the music the *symbol* of the despair whereas my wife divorcing me is the intentional *object* of the despair (even though I am not thinking of her at the time); or on the contrary is the *music* the intentional object, whereas the sadness is merely, as Sartre says, the "way in which" I am conscious of the symphony?[62] On this point Husserl says,

> When the facts which provoke pleasure sink into the background, are no longer apperceived as emotionally coloured, and perhaps cease to be intentional objects at all, the pleasurable excitement may linger on for a while; it may itself be felt as agreeable. Instead of representing a pleasant property of the object, it is referred merely to the feeling-subject, or is itself presented and pleases.[63]

It is thus artificial to isolate my sadness upon hearing the symphony (which seems to focus and explicate my feeling in much the same way as would verbal symbolization) from my sadness upon being left by my wife. These would seem to be moments—not pieces—of one complex and unified experiential act.

If we grant this much, it may be that there are still other variables that enter into the experiencing of the intentional object and the symbolization of the experience. For example, suppose that, shortly before my wife left me, I lost my job. This other event would also affect my experiencing of the divorce and my reaction to it in such an integral way that it would become part of the intentional object of the new experience. Furthermore, my feelings about the job may in turn have been founded on something else, which was partly founded on other experiences of other objects. Ultimately, if we pursue this line of reasoning, everything in my total past experience must be counted as a non-independent moment in the one complex intentional object of the experiencing that is going on in the exact present moment. My *Befindlichkeit* or *Stimmung* (mood, state of consciousness) at this moment reveals to me, not my relation to some specific object, but more generally and amorphously, my relation to my entire world—past, present and anticipated.

Eugene Gendlin has pointed up another relationship between the general background experiencing that is presupposed by the present experience, and the symbolization of our experiencing which takes place in the present tense.

> In speech, as in all action, there is both external observation and the felt sense of what is intended. The "feel" of what we intend to say is especially noticeable when we hear ourselves just having said something that doesn't mean what we intend. What we intend to say is not explicit until we say it.[64]

According to Gendlin, the symbols depend for their meaning on our felt experiencing of the intentional objects to which we make them 'refer.' But the experiencing, in turn, depends on our ability to symbolize it in order for the 'what' of the experience to come into focus. Because the symbol becomes more meaningful when we express and elaborate it, says Gendlin, and because the symbol helps us to focus the experience more clearly and more fully, the meaning of the experience itself becomes richer as we give it expression. More and more facets of the experience, previously unthought of, show themselves as inseparable aspects of the original experience. Multiple intentional objects of this same original experience move from a prereflective to a reflective status, so that we finally realize that all these objects were 'really' essential to the one complex intentional object of the experience to begin with.

In assessing the kind of intentionality that functions in the 'looking for' consciousness, we now encounter two new problems. (1) It is difficult to accurately specify what object is 'really' the intentional object of an experience; and (2) It is difficult to determine in many cases whether an object is the intentional object of an experience, a medium for the symbolization of the experience, or perhaps both at once. Furthermore, the words in a literary passage may symbolize an object (for example, "A stone, a leaf, an unfound door") which in turn symbolizes other felt meanings. The same duality of symbol and thing-symbolized can be found in objects in real life—for example, for Emerson, the Pen symbolized a force of social change and was also symbolized by the word 'pen.' Suppose then, in light of these problems, I now attempt to determine whether the sight of the hillside across the river is, at this moment, primarily a symbol or an intentional object. As we have seen, I cannot separate this scene from numerous other incidents associated with it that have helped to constitute its meaning to me. By Husserl's above-quoted statement about the lingering-afterward of the subjective aspect of an intention, the hill cannot simply be regarded as the intentional object of the feeling it evokes; rather, it seems to function more as a symbol to me, something which helps me to recall the developing way I have been feeling on many past occasions. But its symbolism is not clear-cut to me, involving as it does so many levels and interconnections of meanings—no more clear-cut than the symbolism of "Naked and alone we came into exile." The images point beyond themselves to many deeper underlying meanings (to me). It is artificial to separate any of them from any of the others since, as we have seen, every past experience, to the extent of its relevance, has served as a moment in the one complex 'act' under consideration. Every object is, to some extent, the intentional object of every new feeling, and to some extent the new feeling is symbolized *by* this same object.

An analysis of the intentionality of motivational *feelings* is essential to understanding the relationship between 'looking-for' and 'looking-at' consciousnesses. There is usually—perhaps always—some motivation at work in the process of attention. We cannot look *at* object **A**, for instance, *in a fully attentive sense* unless adequately motivated to look *for* object **A**; if no motivation to look for **A** is present, then some motivation to look for **B**, **C** or **D** will be present and the looking for **B**, **C** or **D** will thus distract us from fully looking at **A**. Precisely *because* we are thus distracted, **A** cannot fully be attended to and therefore remains on a 'prereflective' level. For the same reason, this prereflective consciousness remains *unsymbolized*. To symbolize a prereflective 'looking *at*' consciousness—for example, 'the way the shoe on my right foot feels at this moment'—is also to accomplish the additional purpose of symbolizing my *motivation* to attend to this phenomenon—the 'looking for' dimension of the experience. What we think *about* (looking-for) thus influences in a general way what we think to be *true or false* (looking-at). To a great extent, we see what we look for and we cannot see what our motivated category structure does not equip us to see.

If we purposely set about to attend to a prereflective content of consciousness so as to bring it into reflective awareness, the *way* we accomplish this task is by using symbols. To understand the intentionality of 'looking-for' consciousness would thus be to understand the working of symbolism and symbolization. To understand why we should be motivated to see one thing and ignore another would require ultimately that we understand how motivation relates essentially to the process of symbolizing our experience. Richard Wagner, motivated no doubt by his experience as a practicing artist, has made some valuable remarks on this subject. We shall devote some time at this point to exposing the Wagnerian view since it is so unfamiliar to most readers.

3. The role of symbolization in explicating consciousness

Richard Wagner's theory of poetry, which he developed in a series of essays,[65] shows some striking parallels with Merleau-Ponty's ideas on language. Impressed with the analogy between gesture and speech, Wagner made this remark:

> At the first beginning the formation of the mental con-
> cept of an object ran almost parallel with the subjective
> feeling of it; and the supposition that the earliest speech
> of man must have borne a great analogy with song, might
> not perhaps seem quite ridiculous.[66]

According to Wagner, the first human utterances were less words than primordially emotional songs. Such utterances would express not propositions, but passions. Their purpose would have been no more to communicate one's emotions or beliefs to others than to make them more real and more explicit for oneself. In Wagner's view, no emotion is fully present to consciousness until given some symbolic expression. Neither anger nor love becomes fully conscious until a quickening of the breath is noticed, or a cramped feeling in the chest, or butterflies in the stomach. The psychomotor symbolizations may vary, since the symbol is to some extent an arbitrarily defined place holder—the handle by which it is grabbed when interrelating it with other felt meanings. The symbol is not arbitrary, however, to the extent that in each case the physical movements and involvements with physical media such as words, pictures, and melodies serve the purpose of bringing the emotion somehow more fully into the center of our consciousness so that it can be known in more detail and intensity. When feelings are grabbed by these physically-embodied handles, then (if the person is so motivated) they can be related to each other and interrelated in complex ways. In this way, brute passions are eventually interwoven into the delicate nuances of more subtle and more representational conscious states.

Wagner also discusses the role of symbolization in combining conscious contents with each other.

> The essence of drama is knowing through feeling. . . An action which can be explained only on grounds of historic relations . . . is representable only to the understanding; not to the feeling . . . [and is representable] through appeal to the intellect's imaginative force; not through direct presentment to the feeling and its definitely seizing organs, the senses; for we saw that those senses were positively unable to take in the full extent of such an action, that in it there lay a mass of relations beyond all possibility of bringing to physical view and bound to be relegated for their comprehension, to the combining organ of thought.[67]

The function of symbolization is thus not so much to make the raw felt meanings more *immanent* as to find a way of *relating* them to each other in a way that can be expressed in one unified sweep so that the overall, complex meaning can be overviewed in one equally raw feeling. This condensation, according to Wagner, is the work proper to the poetizing intellect.[68]

> And this comprehension is ultimately enabled by the instinctive feeling—as vindicated by the understanding. The poet must take the phenomena of life and compress them from their viewless many-memberedness into a compact, easily surveyable shape. . . . The strengthening of a motive cannot therefore consist in a mere addition of lesser motives, but in the complete absorption of many motives into this one.[69]

This remark holds true not only for the symbols, but for the 'motives' in the sense of felt-meanings which these symbols symbolize as well. In this light, Wagner's way of interrelating motives, through 'foreboding and remembrance,'[70] also foreshadows Husserl's *Internal Time Consciousness* where Husserl speaks of protention and retention.[71] The essential question for our purposes is whether protention and retention reduce the retained or protended consciousness to an intentional object (when the latter is reflected upon) or whether there is not some way that a past consciousness can be carried over into a new context while remaining as immanent as it was originally. Wagner is making strides toward showing that this is indeed possible.

The moment of the first stirring of a passion, according to the Wagnerian approach, does not need to ask what it is really 'about.' It demands expression through action; through action, it explores what future experiences may have to teach. The passion makes no pretense at giving apodictic, *a priori* knowledge of its relation to the world, except in the trivial sense that my entire biography is its intentional object; it first of all *wants to explore* its possible meanings. It calls for explication, not categorization.

> But a musical motive into which the thought-filled word verse of a dramatic performer has poured itself—so to say, before our eyes—is a thing conditioned by necessity: with its return a *definite* emotion is discernibly conveyed to us, and conveyed to us through the physical agency of the orchestra, albeit now unspoken by the performer. . . . Wherefore the concurrent sounding of such a motive for us unites the conditioning, the nonpresent emotion with the emotion conditioned thereby and coming into voice at this instant. . . . A foreboding is the herald of an emotion as yet unspoken. . . . It is undefined as long as it has not been yet determined through a fitting object.[72]

Wagner's theory implies, then, that the intentional object is not given equiprimordially with the emotion, but only takes shape more and more as the situation unfolds. The kind of intentionality an emotion primarily and of itself has is thus the categorial or 'looking-for' rather than the 'looking-at' kind—in agreement with what we have found here.

Conversely, all 'looking for' or categorial intentionality appears to be essentially of a motivational nature; our consciousness in such instances is emotionally directed toward seeing or experiencing something. As we have seen, this something toward which the motivational consciousness tends is not a specific intentional object, but rather a general *class* of objects. If we want 'something sweet,' candy or cake will usually fulfill the need equally well. If we want to symbolize despair, Tchaikovsky's Fifth Symphony will do, but his Sixth will do about as well. Either symphony will serve the symbolic purpose of bringing the prereflective consciousness of despair to a reflective level. Listening to *A Love Supreme* by John Coltrane, on the other hand, may serve the purpose precisely of ensuring that the despair does *not* get symbolized and therefore remains on a prereflective level, so that we can escape, at least temporarily, the necessity for fully experiencing that particular constellation of intentional objects. In either case, the movement from prereflective to reflective consciousness does not reduce the original prereflective consciousness to an object, but rather makes it even more real from the subjective point of view. Because the motivational aspect of the 'looking for' is not intentional in the usual sense of taking a transcendent object, it motivates the increased immanent awareness of the prereflective consciousness on the same subjective level on which it originally occurred.

But although the meanings brought to light by symbolization are essentially immanent, the process of symbolization is also transendent toward the world. Symbolization is embodied symbolization, and for this reason it cannot stand away from the world as a pure and detached reflection. Merleau-Ponty shows that the very fact of symbolization, even if considered in its function of explicating private experience in the way discussed by Wagner, demands that a relation to others and to things become intelligible, for the fact of a language presupposes other people as a grounding principle of its constitution, and presupposes some sort of materiality as an array of possible embodiment, as the possible concreteness of symbols.

The body, in its role as substrate for meanings, is the prime example of the inappropriateness of a subject-object paradigm which would regard subjectivity and objectivity as separate spheres, as opposite sides of an ontological dualism; while at the same time this same phenomenon shows that the body cannot be completely reduced to the status of a functioning physical 'machine.' Naturalism has already begun to give up the project of complete objectification of the body; for the experimental approach itself leads to this rejection, as Merleau-Ponty points out. There is not enough difference between the bite of a mosquito, which I slap spontaneously, and the pinch of the experimentor, which is not a sufficient evocation of an immediate pointing response, for the 'stimulus' to stand as determinant of the response.[73] Even on this primitive level, as we have seen, the *meaning* 'insect bite' enters the picture. There must be a holistic equilibrium in terms of which *configurations* of stimuli take on meaning for the overall situation of the entire organism. Moreover, whatever causality there is must be circular, not linear. Thus the configuration of 'stimuli' ceases to be the *cause* of my behavior, and becomes its *intentional object* and/or the *symbolization* of my intentional consciousness.

But Merleau-Ponty's remarks show that this too is an oversimplification. For the cause of the brain damage in Goldstein's patients was not psychological; it was a shell splinter in the skull.[47] What kind of relationship can exist between the universe conceived as material, and the universe considered as intentional object of the 'response,' such that a cause in one universe can produce an effect in another? Merleau-Ponty's response is that there must be a kind of consciousness *in* the body, and that the body must in turn be *in* the world, in "consummate reciprocity," particularly with other people.[75] The fact of intersubjectivity, moreover, is not something to be deduced, for it is already presupposed by the fact of language, the fact that I have learned to speak. Reflection on myself, according to Merleau-Ponty, always throws me back toward other people as toward my origin. But this is only a specific case of the general rule: Reflection upon experience always reveals a store of ongoing, 'prereflective' experience. Knowledge presupposes know-how, which is in the body. Thus Sartre's dictum that seeing is no different from being conscious of seeing is true but oversimplified. I am always thrown backward in time toward a prior rootedness in the world, and that rootedness is the body. If I am to be, as Merleau-Ponty says at one point, "a consciousness, or better, an *experience*,"[76] then time is in fact always transcended—that is, I escape becoming encapsulated in one moment, and the various moments of my life are tied together into one 'self.' To say that the subject 'is' time[77] is to say that the subject is verb as opposed to thing, in the same way that, although 'walking down the street' is not a thing, this is no proof that there is no such thing as walking down the street. (Consciousness must therefore be conceived as an unfolding which need not reduce itself to an object at each reflective moment, as we discussed in more detail above.[78])

Thinking, conceived by Merleau-Ponty as dependent upon "know-how," is analogous to a psychomotor skill—the skill of retention, protention, relation, etc., which makes use of the brain in the same way that *spoken* language makes use of the mouth. The movement involved is used in somewhat the same way that I use a certain song to recall to me the way I felt on a past occasion, and to relate my present condition to that past situation. Thought 'crawls along' speech, in Merleau-Ponty's view. Speech is one of the many bodily gestures that explicate the felt meaning of my thought, my situation with respect to the world.[79] I cannot act the part of Stanley Kowalski, take up his gestures, his facial expressions and his style of speaking, without feeling his very *attitude* creep into *my* attitude; for a moment I almost *become* Stanley Kowalski. I cannot easily employ a given terminology in my speech without feeling some hint of a corresponding change in my conscious attitude. It is through really embodied languages that my bodily felt situation with respect to the world and others, and therefore my thought, are informed. The body is one pole of that experience which 'I' am, and the world and others constitute the other pole. The 'I' is the relationship.

To understand the relationship between motivational and intentional consciousness, we must ask whether there is not a relationship among conscious states within the same ego that is not only closer, but very different in kind from any relationship among consciousnesses that belong to different egos—whether such an essential difference would not stem from a fuller and different sort of transparency than can be obtained by making one state of consciousness either reflectively or prereflectively the intentional object of another. Wagner's theory that symbolization is a concrete vehicle for the unification of the immanent contents of different states of consciousness shows that consciousness is capable of such a self-transparency. If so, the phenomenon of prereflective consciousness becomes much less paradoxical. Consciousness moves from a prereflective to a reflective state only when we are motivated to carry that consciousness into the future by incorporating it with our present consciousness into a more unified meaning. This happens only when we give symbolic expression to the prereflective consciousness.

The real reason why the unity of consciousness must be a transcendental unity is that non-transcendental consciousness—consciousness encapsulated within the present moment—sees from only one perspective at a time. When many of these different perspectives are put together into one broader, more coherent perspective, the limitations of the category structure are lessened. In effect, this accomplishes the main function Husserl had assigned to the transcendental ego, but does so in a way that is to varying degrees imperfect.

But there is also an *entity* (though one whose ontological status is a complex process composed of relations among the actions of simpler entities)—i.e., the ego—which is responsible for accomplishing this effect, and without which it would not be accomplished because consciousness would continually be wandering off in unfruitful *directions*. The main point of calling this entity 'transcendental' is that its ontological status 'transcends' that of its components—the different states of consciousness in the stream of consciousness—though not in a dualistic sense. It is rather a higher-order level of *process* than the lower-level processes which constitute the elemental states of consciousness. While this process theory is not dualistic, it is not a causal epiphenomenalism or a psychophysical identity theory either.

If the additional question arises, 'If the reduction is incomplete, then does it really accomplish its purpose?'—the answer to this question is that the incomplete reduction comes equipped with a way to tell whether we are moving in the right direction *toward* a more complete reduction, and this has to do with the discussion of symbolization. The analysis of symbolization gives us a strong clue as to what we should do if we want to expect a more complete reduction to occur. This involves bringing the prereflective into reflective awareness through the symbolization that results from intersubjective dialogue, as we shall see more fully later.

4. Transition to a more detailed analysis of ego structure and ontological status

In a general way, one could perhaps guess from what has been said so far how 'unconscious' and 'prereflective' consciousness will be accounted for. The self has a great deal of leverage over its own states of consciousness, in the sense that it can bring a faint state of consciousness into sharp focus, thereby intensifying it, or it can choose to ignore or deny ('alienate') a state of consciousness, refuse to symbolize it, and therefore let it remain at a faint level until it finally ceases to exist altogether. The self can also move contents of consciousness back and forth along this dimension, from faint awareness, to intense awareness, and back to faint awareness again. The way it accomplishes this is by either symbolizing the consciousness in question, or failing to symbolize it. It may fail to symbolize a state of consciousness because it either consciously or unconsciously *chooses* not to do so, or because environmental circumstances make the physical embodiment necessary to the symbolization impossible. However, what still remains quite obscure is the answer to the ontological question as to *what* the self really is. We need to be more specific in this regard.

Therefore, let's now try to put the preceding remarks on the directionality and unity of the stream of experiences into the context of the idea that the 'I' must not be a merely *abstract* principle of unification, but must be actually experienceable, like any other consciousness. Sartre's point about the transcendental ego relies in part upon a phenomenological datum regarding the self which is essentially Cartesian in origin, but which remains convincing nonetheless, if taken separately from Descartes' other doctrines, especially his dualism. I do not experience myself as being something separate from my experiencing process as such. 'I' must 'be' my experience because if I imagine what it would be like if only my body existed, with no consciousness, such a state of affairs would be devoid of the phenomenon intended by the word 'I.' Of course, it is true, as the anti-euthenasia argument runs, that persons do in fact exist while they are not conscious—i.e., while asleep. But if a human body were devoid of consciousness, and with no possibility of ever regaining this consciousness, then no one would seriously regard such a body as a person or self. Only the potential to regain consciousness makes a sleeping body remain a person. Moreover, this potential is more than a mere logical possibility. A sleeping brain, as we have seen, functions very similarly to a waking brain, except that the synchronization of cortex and hypothalamous is missing.

The argument is often brought against this Cartesian point that a disembodied consciousness would be unimaginable. Given the inseparability of mental and physiological events, this is of course a good point. But it is not necessary for a disembodied consciousness to be imaginable in order for the definition of the 'I' as consciousness to be established—only in order to give this 'I' a dualistic interpretation. In order to establish the mere definition of the 'I' as a consciousness, it is only necessary that it be *im*possible to imagine a permanently unconscious body as being myself. This impossibility is enough to show that to be conscious is the essence of a self, or 'I.' Also, a slight modification of the Cartesian argument gets around the anti-disembodied-consciousness objection quite easily enough to establish that consciousness is not only a necessary, but also a sufficient condition for the 'I'—though, here again, Descartes' dualism must be sacrificed. Try to imagine, not your consciousness in a disembodied state, but rather your consciousness with a completely *different* body from your present one. In this case, you would still feel like the same person, even though your bodily parts had been replaced. Thus, consciousness is both necessary and sufficient to what we mean by 'I.'

Sartre's argument against the transcendental ego hinges upon such a definition of 'I.' 'I,' according to Sartre, cannot unify all states of consciousness into a coherent continuity because in this case the 'I' could not be a conscious entity. This assumes, correctly, that there is something about the meaning of 'I' which precludes its being anything other than a form of consciousness.

This definition, however, is still extremely vague. First of all, how can I specify *whose* experiencing process 'I' am without referring back to an 'I' which is already ontologically prior to those experiences themselves, ending therefore with a mere redundant circularity? This paradox forces us to admit that the 'I' is not yet adequately defined by simply referring to the experiencing process. Its meaning has merely been narrowed so as to exclude most phenomena—all, that is, except for consciousness.

A still more nagging difficulty is that, within the field of all experiences—even if these can be narrowed to include only 'my' experiences—we must still ask whether I am all of my experiences, some of them, or perhaps only one of them; or am I something which simply founds all of my experiences, something always present 'if and only if' my experiences are present, something which only unifies all of my particular experiences or determines their pattern or direction but which can still be distinguished from all of those particular experiences? Here Sartre's treatment of the transcendental ego, discussed in part A of this chapter, can help us; there we saw that consciousness and the ego cannot simply be two different things which are inseparable from each other, but rather the ego must be the totality of all consciousness looked at from a particular point of view, or else one species of consciousness, or at the very least an always-possible form of consciousness which can be actualized at any given moment.

Although we have suggested that Sartre's argument against the transcendental ego is a false alternative, it seems unavoidable nonetheless that we must approach the initial defining process from one of Sartre's two perspectives. That is, we can begin with a conception of 'I' as my experiences, and narrow the definition down until we finally end up with the particular experiences that provide the transcendental unity across the life of the delineated ego; or we can begin with a conception of 'I' as that which provides a transcendent unity across my life, and work with it until we discover that this unifier is in reality itself an experience. Theoretically, the end result should be the same either way, since the ego must meet both these qualifications. Let's begin with the assumption that 'I' have the ontological status of a form of experience (or perhaps the totality of experience—we must discover which it is), since through introspection I cannot experience myself as anything other than the experience itself.

Naturally, 'I' could probably not exist independently of 'my body.' But it does not follow that the body is partly constitutive of the 'I' in the subject-of-consciousness sense of the word. The material of which my body is composed is always changing and being replaced in the continuous bodily processes; the body's form may even be shaped by goal orientations which transcend the specific 'goal orientations' which each of the bodily cells would have if they did not cohere in the bodily unity, as Merleau-Ponty suggests. Also, I can imagine myself with another person's body, yet continuing to be myself; I cannot imagine my body with another person's mind as myself. If I were associated with a different body, or some other type of thing besides a human body, this would be to say that the *events, my* thoughts and *my* feelings, would now be executed by a different *substantive* or *substratum.* I need a substantive or substratum *of which* to be predicated, but I *am* not that substantive, any more than sound is wood when a sound wave passes through wood, or any more than this essay is the pencil that writes it or the paper on which it is written. It would be ridiculous to assume that whatever can be said of the paper can also be said of the essay, or *vice versa.* When I eat food, at what point does the food cease being food and become a part of 'me'? The only possible answer would seem to be that, strictly speaking, the food never does become a part of me; it merely becomes one of the substantives or substrata of which the pattern or process, 'I', is predicated. Like consciousness itself as seen in Chapter II, I am like the flight of a bird as opposed to the bird itself or the bird's wings or the air; I am like the transverse circular ripple emanating outward from where someone has dropped a stone into the water. (This does not mean, of course, that I am a 'pure predicate' in the universal sense of Plato, but rather that I am *this particular* happening, *this concrete* flux of a peculiar sort.)

One further implication of this conceptualization of the ego-body relation can be seen if we consider for a moment the distinction Sartre makes between two different 'bodies' that I have. There is my felt body as felt by me, 'from within,' so to speak, the 'my body for me'; and there is my body as an object of experience, interaction, scientific inquiry, etc., 'my body for others' (a distinction bearing a marked resemblance to the *Körper* and *Leib* of Husserl's *Crisis*). Clearly, when Merleau-Ponty says "I am my body," he *initially* means the former body, or something very similar, as opposed to the latter. It is true, of course, that he later equates the two bodies. But, as mentioned earlier, this equation does not render wholly intelligible *how* the objective body (the 'my body for others') can come to possess consciousness. The 'body for me' which I am is a felt body. But there is no distinction between a 'felt body' and a 'feeling of a body,' or a conglomeration of bodily feelings. There is, on the other hand, all the significative distinction in the world between a 'body which feels' and a 'feeling-process that posits and is predicated of a body,' as we have just seen. And it follows from this distinction that a felt body is not the former but the latter. It is not originarily and primarily a body; it is a feeling, or a collective integration of feelings. Thus the 'my body for me' is not literally a body at all.

If the ego has the status of a conscious process rather than a bodily structure, the next question is: *What kind* of conscious process? This question obviously presupposes that there are distinguishable kinds of conscious processes, and that the ontological interrelations among them can be understood. Here we could find ourselves diverted into a plethora of epistemological issues. But perhaps the essential point for our purposes can be established without such a digression. Schopenhauer suggests that sensations can be reduced to subjective feelings and that perceptions reduce to sensation. "What we know is not a sun and an earth, but an eye that sees a sun, a hand that feels an earth."[80] This point is debatable, yet there seems to be a certain element of truth in it, in the sense that feeling, sensation, and perception, phenomenologically speaking, all present themselves to consciousness as having an important ingredient in common with each other, while at the same time this ingredient seems to be sufficient of itself to characterize *one* of the three phenomena—feeling. Hence, in a certain sense, the other two *contain* feeling as constituent parts of them. Furthermore, the feeling element in sensation and perception is the element which is necessary and sufficient for their presence 'in' or 'to' consciousness. Thus, as we have seen, Eugene Gendlin speaks of the entire noetic-noematic complex of any given state of consciousness as a 'felt meaning.' It is by virtue of the fact that the object produces in me an *affect*, as it were, rather than merely an *effect*, that perception can be a form of consciousness. With regard to the respect in which perceptions figure as part of the 'I' (if indeed they do at all), they exist in the mode of feeling. This means that part of the ontological status, or manner of being, of perception—the relevant part—is the same as the ontological status or manner of being of feeling *simpliciter*.

We can therefore narrow the definition of 'I' a little further. Not only does it exist in the mode of consciousness, but, more specifically, in the mode of feeling. Relating the findings of this chapter to such a notion of feeling, we can now say that the self or 'I' must be a kind of consciousness which is always at least prereflectively present and available for reflection. At the same time, it must provide the unity and continuity of the stream of experience by affecting the direction of attention at each point. Its ontological status must be that of a higher-order pattern, comprised of lower-order patterns which are themselves experienceable as states of consciousness. The only kind of feeling that can possibly meet all these qualifications would have to be a type of motivational feeling. Moreover, it cannot be just any type of motivational feeling, for there are many types of motivation that would serve to cause fragmentation rather than continuity in the direction of attention. Let's turn now to explore in detail what kind of motivational consciousness this could be. Chapters IV and V will develop the theory that the motivation to 'symbolically' explicate my entire stream of consciousness—whatever particular character this consciousness may happen to have at any particular moment—is what I am.

CHAPTER IV

CONSCIOUS STRUCTURES

A. THE NON-REDUCTIVE MOTIVATIONAL STRUCTURE OF THE EGO

In Chapter II, we saw that it would be ontologically incorrect to reduce the psychic to the physical in the sense of an identity theory, although it is true that the psychic and the physical are inseparable from each other. Thus there is no harm in attempting a purely physiological description of all human behavior—even linguistic, social, and problem-solving behavior. Such a project, however, will still eventually find itself in need of some phenomenology when the time comes to correlate the physiological regularities with conscious events, as discussed in Chapter I.

A further implication of the ontological conception of consciousness as a higher-order temporal form is the inevitable untenability of still another popular form of reductionism: Drive reductionism. Drive reductionism will be taken to refer to any kind of psychological theory which asserts that all human (or any other) motivation can be ultimately reduced to, or explained in terms of, a basic need or tendency of the organism to reduce drives. Of course, *explanations* of the complex motives *in terms of* simple drives are not ordinarily as vulnerable to refutation as are *reductions* of the complex motives *to* the drives. The objections we shall present, however, are equally pertinent to the two types of theories. All drive-reduction theories, in other words, are untenable as complete motivational theories. This turns out to be true not only because of drive-reductionism's inability to account for its own empirical data, but also for purely logical and ontological reasons. Such a thing as drive-reduction exists, of course, but its explanatory power is far less than most drive theorists take it to be. Since motivation is important in our theory, we must explore this point.

A number of traditional arguments have been used to refute various hedonistic theories of motivation.[1] None of these arguments, however, are sufficient to address themselves to a more sophisticated form of hedonism, i.e., the drive-reductive theories. We must show that there are some motives which are neither for the purpose of reducing drives, nor are they reducible to or explainable in terms of drive reduction. Some psychologists might prefer to speak of such motives as 'non-reductive drives.' To do so, however, is inconsistent with the essential meaning of 'drive,' and would involve the arbitrary postulation of still another new 'drive' for every behavior in need of explanation. Finally, we shall sketch out the broad outlines of a new theory of motivation which is not drive-reductive in nature at all.

To summarize in advance the gist of our argument: Consciousness, if it is to desire anything at all, must first of all desire to continue to exist *qua* consciousness. Consciousness, however, has the ontological status of a process or pattern of change *in* a material substratum (such as the body or the brain). For consciousness to desire to continue to *be* is therefore to desire to continue to *change*; to desire a stasis would be to desire to cease to be conscious, for consciousness cannot exist as stasis. But if drive reduction were the only motivation of the organism, then the complete reduction of all drives would constitute a stasis, resulting in the non-existence of consciousness as such. The later Freud would then be confirmed in his conclusion, consistent with his initial reductionistic assumptions, that the goal of life is death.[2] The goal of consciousness would be the cessation of consciousness. This would be self-contradictory because it would entail that consciousness wants to continue to exist, but at the same time does not want to continue to exist.

1. Drive theories

'Drive' is traditionally defined by psychologists as a physiological deficit external to the nervous system which is perceived by the nervous system as noxious.[3] Here we shall use a slightly more comprehensive definition of 'drive' which, following White,[4] would also include the reductive 'instincts' (Freud's word was *"Treib"*), as well as any non-physiological deficits external to the nervous sytem, such as 'ego needs,' 'needs for security,' and other such reductive 'needs.' We shall take 'drive,' then, to include both physiological and non-physiological deficits external to the nervous system and perceived by the nervous system as noxious. Relating this definition to the terminology used by the phenomenologist Levinas, we can say that Levinas' distinction between 'need' and 'desire'[5] is virtually equivalent with the distinction between motivations that stem from 'drives' on the one hand, and on the other hand motivations which do not stem from drives. If we can show that there are motivations which are *not* reducible to 'drives,' then, such a finding will support Levinas' assumption that such a thing as 'desire,' in his special sense of 'desire,' does indeed exist as emotion which is irreducible to 'needs' or 'drives.'

Most psychological theories of motivation, and indeed all of the ones that have been fully developed as comprehensive explanations, have assumed that pleasure results from the *reduction* of such drives. That is, they side with Epicurus as against Aristippus in thinking that pleasure and pain can be situated along a continuous scale extending in a negative direction (pain) and a positive direction (pleasure). Aristippus insisted that the absence of pleasure does not constitute pain.[6] Rather, pleasure and pain constitute independent dimensions, and are not necessarily additive in the sense that the removal of X amount of pain causes X amount of pleasure. He would agree, of course, that serious pain *can* sometimes be an impediment to pleasure and *vice versa;* he would deny, however, that the absence of pain is pleasure *by definition* or *vice versa.* Pain inhibits pleasure in the way that a loud noise prevents the appreciation of music; it is not that music *is* the absence of noise, or that noise *is* the absence of music. This would also imply that, if the noise is not too loud, we can both be annoyed by the noise and appreciate the music, without the two experiences' cancelling each other out.

In addition, drive reductive theories involve an assumption which both Aristippus and Epicurus seem at times to make and at other times not to make: the assumption that organisms are motivated to *maximize* pleasure rather than merely to *optimize* it. This is an especially important point in relation to ethics because a pleasure-*optimizing* theory would leave plenty of room for a pluralistic value theory in which not only pleasure but other things as well could be considered valuable to the organism. At times, Aristippus seems to advocate an optimizing theory because he sees pleasure as midway between violent, turbulent stimulation, which is painful, and weak stimulation, which is indifferent. But this only *seems* to be an optimizing theory because, for Aristippus, the main point is that we are motivated to achieve a *moderate* intensity of stimulation and to achieve *as much of it as possible* (i.e., without moderation). Epicurus also might sometimes appear to advocate pleasure-optimizing rather than pleasure-maximizing, since to him pleasure is nothing but the complete absence of pain. But here again, this state of non-pain is to be achieved as frequently and for as long a period as possible, thus maximized.

Of course, pleasure-maximizing and pleasure-optimizing are not the only possible hedonistic positions with regard to pleasure and pain. We could also have a sliding-scale optimizing theory, where the closer we come to the optimal point, the less strongly we are motivated to come any closer; or a sliding-scale maximizing theory, where there is no definite optimal amount of pleasure, but the more pleasure we have, the less interested we are in getting still more. Also, if we regard pleasure and pain as non-additive, then we would have to speak in terms of trading a certain amount of pain for a certain amount of pleasure; we may be willing to stand in the cold to hear an outdoor concert, but not lie on nails to win the woman of our dreams, etc. The number of possible ways of combining pleasure-seeking and pain-avoidance would then be more numerous than the number of cost-benefit formulas in existence, as the reader can easily imagine for himself. There could be a maximin rule, a minimax regret rule, a maximax rule, a pessimism-optimism rule or an equiprobability rule followed by the organism with respect to all of the various pleasure/pain/maximizing/optimizing/sliding scale/fixed scale combinations possible. From this array of choices, drive theorists almost always choose without discussion the Epicurean pleasure-maximizing-pain-minimizing type of hedonism.

There is, however, one contemporary motivational theory which does call itself a 'drive' theory, yet which is not reductive in nature and which is optimizing rather than maximizing in structure. Hebb posits a drive toward an optimal 'level of arousal.'[7] For Hebb, the motivation of the organism is neither to minimize pain nor to maximize pleasure, but to maintain an optimal level of general arousal. The non-reductive motivational implications of our process-substratum model of consciousness will not be taken as contradicting Hebb's theory, because Hebb's theory in truth is neither a drive theory, nor does it demand a reductionistic interpretation. It is not a drive theory, in the true sense, because the 'deficit' which supposedly exists when the arousal level is too high or too low cannot really be characterized as 'external to the nervous system'; it is attributed primarily to the reticular activating system, which is part of the brain. Nor is the theory clearly reductionistic in nature, because too high a level of arousal would not seem to qualify as a 'deficit' in any ordinary sense. Also, the optimal-arousal theory only describes *a* motivation of the organism, not necessarily *the* motivation. Since the physiological processes described by Hebb's generalizations are really only the physiological correlates of conscious processes associated with the nervous system, it does not fit the usual drive-reduction schema in which conscious motives are merely reactions to the need for certain bio-chemical reactions to reach their completion. In Hebb's case, no 'completion' is conceivable; the motivation to maintain arousal is precisely a motivation to prevent reactions from ever reaching completion in the bio-chemical sense; this process could plausibly be viewed as the physiological correlate of the desire on the part of any given state of consciousness to continue being conscious rather than to achieve a stasis whose purpose, according to true drive theories, would be to eradicate the state of desire which motivated the organism to begin with. This is essentially why Hebb's theory is not necessarily reductionistic. In the section that follows, we shall see why a reductionistic account of the arousal theory would entail that chemical and physical reactions are the *intrinsic* values of the organism, whereas *conscious* motives are only *extrinsic* values—a notion which turns out to be logically untenable. This does not mean that voluntary goals do not have corresponding descriptions on the physiological level, but it does rule out purely hedonistic interpretations of the corresponding conscious processes, as we shall see.

Someone may object at the outset that most drive theories do not speak of 'pleasure' and 'pain' as such, but of 'positive and negative reinforcement.' In this case, 'noxious' would be construed to mean 'negatively reinforcing,' and the reduction of the noxious physiological deficit 'positively reinforcing.' But the same array of maximizing and optimizing theories and their different possible combinations and permutations would still exist in this case, only with 'positive reinforcement' substituted in place of 'pleasure.' We shall contend that there are motivations in terms of which the organism does not react to positively- or negatively-reinforcing stimuli, construed as physiological or non-physiological deficits, because the relevant behaviors are not simply reactions to stimuli at all. Rather, they are attempts on the part of the organism to exist *qua* conscious being.

Drive-reduction theories in principle cannot explain why consciousness *wants to be conscious* or *wants to continue being conscious*, because consciousness is something which in no way can be construed as external to the nervous system; thus a 'deficit' of consciousness is not external to the nervous system either. Furthermore, in wanting to continue being conscious, which means to continue changing in the form of a complex, higher-order process, consciousness wants to a certain extent the exact opposite of the stasis which would be produced by the reduction of drives. If the aim of the organism were simply to bring all of the electrons in the outer energy shells of all its atoms into the stablest possible (and lowest-energy possible) combinations, it could do so quite easily; the result, however, as Freud points out, would be death.

2. Attempts to accommodate discrepant data

Most psychologists are well aware that a substantial amount of evidence has accumulated which cannot easily be accommodated to drive reductionism. Yet, so deeply ingrained in our common sense is the notion that all behavior must be oriented toward some sort of 'happiness' or 'pleasure' that none of the three most common responses to the discrepant data really reject drive reductionism at all. (1) Many theorists simply add a new 'drive' to the list in order to account for any behavior which is discovered not to be motivated by the drives we already know about, until we end up with literally thousands of drives—one for each behavior in need of explanation.[8] (2) Other psychologists avoid the issue altogether by taking refuge in a supposedly atheoretical, pure behaviorism whose only purpose would be to describe regularities in behavior, not to subsume the various facts within a comprehensive theory. But, far from giving up the drive-reductionistic presupposition, pure behaviorisms still insist that 'positive and negative reinforcement' are the essential determinants of the frequency of any given behavior.[9] (3) Still others posit 'non-reductive drives' of some sort, such as an 'instinct to mastery,' a 'drive toward competency,' a 'need for optimal arousal,' etc., interpreting an organism's failure in these regards as still another type of 'pain' or 'unhappiness,' and supposing that the organism's ultimate *purpose* in maintaining optimal arousal or in achieving competency is to better enable the organism to reduce those drives which *are* reductive in nature, thus achieving some sort of 'happiness,' construed as the ultimate goal of conscious existence.[10]

Without going into laborious detail, let's quickly review some of the empirical data that seem to contradict the assumption that motivation is essentially of a reductionistic nature. Dashiell, in 1925, and Nissen, in 1930, found that a rat will cross an electrified grid to gain the privilege of exploring new territory.[11] Later, Wolfe and Kaplon found that chickens prefer grain which requires them to expend effort to consume, as opposed to grain that could have been rapidly consumed, even though both consisted of the same absolute amount of food. (Chickens would rather peck than eat.)[12] Sheffield and Roby conducted a series of experiments which seemed to imply that animals eat more for the taste of the food than for need reduction.[13] Berlyne then found that learning reinforced only by the so-called 'exploratory drives' is resistant to extinction and shows quick recovery after extinction.[14] Sheffield, *et. al.,* and Kagan found that sexual excitation is reinforcing for rats even where ejaculation is not permitted.[15] Butler, in a well-known study, found that monkeys can solve complex discrimination problems for the reinforcement of being allowed to look out the window.[16] Similarly, Montgomery found that monkeys will press a bar for the sake of visual exploration.[17] Kagan and Berkun then discovered that rats will run on a treadmill for the sole reinforcement of being allowed to press a bar. (This study also points to the difficulties involved in distinguishing what constitutes a 'consummatory' response, which distinction is vital to reinforcement theory.)[18] Harlow's famous studies showed that monkeys will solve a hasp problem for the sake of solving it.[19] Welker discovered that subjects seem to prefer certain types of visual objects (those which are more complex) when presented in pairs.[20] Morgan, in a controversial finding, showed that there is a different 'hunger' for each type of nutritional food value, and that these hungers are relatively independent of each other. (It was this type of finding which led drive theorists to begin proliferating 'drives' to such an extent that it seemed as though there must almost be a different drive to account for every type of behavior.)[21] Rosvold then showed that there are many different brain centers for any given drive. Finally, Woodworth showed that some concept of exploration is presupposed by the existence of any 'operant level,' which in turn is presupposed by any behavioristic reinforcement theory.[22]

The real problem posed by these data is not that no viable cause-and-effect mechanism can be conceived on a physiological level which would be capable of explaining the phenomena of non-reductive motivations. On the contrary, given the inseparability of conscious and physiological events, it would be strange indeed if events which have a conscious meaning were not also capable of a physiological description. It is entirely possible that some such physiological theory as Hebb's concept of optimal arousal could constitute an adequate causal account for the non-reductive behaviors just listed. It could be that the organism's tendency to maintain an optimal level of physiological arousal causes it to prefer more complex stimuli, to explore its environment for no purpose other than exploring it, and to prefer pecking over eating. The real problem, however, comes in conceiving the psychological correlates of these physiological events. For when psychologists attempt to conceive the psychological correlates of the physiologically non-reductive tendencies (to call these tendencies 'drives' would be misleading, since there is no deficit to be reduced), they seem predisposed to continue construing them in a reductive fashion. Optimal arousal, or its conscious counterpart, is inevitably assumed to amount to some sort of pleasure, and deviation from optimal arousal is construed as a corresponding sort of pain. The organism's motivation, described in terms of consciousness, would then become simply to maximize all forms of pleasure (including optimal arousal) and to minimize all forms of pain (including deviation from optimal arousal), in spite of the fact that the 'pain' which results from deficits of general arousal (boredom, for example) is not physically localizable, concretely describable, or conceivably quantifiable. That such a psychological interpretation of the physiological phenomenon of arousal is mistaken is easily seen when we realize that the organism will maintain arousal at the expense of pain or at the sacrifice of pleasure, and will do this, not for the sake of some greater ulterior reward, but for the sake of arousal itself.

The question can meaningfully be asked, 'Why does the organism prefer optimal arousal over the maximization of (other forms of) pleasure or the minimization of pain?' If physiological arousal itself is interpreted as corresponding on the conscious level with just another type of pleasure to be maximized, this question in principle can never be answered. The meaning of 'pleasure' and 'pain' must again be thrown into question; it is difficult to see what consciously experienceable quality the 'pleasure' of a chocolate milk shake and the 'pleasure' of optimal general arousal could have in common with each other, since arousal itself is a precondition for experiencing the pleasure of the milk shake or any other pleasure or pain on a conscious basis. The maintenance of optimal arousal is something the organism can be observed to tend to do regardless of whether doing so leads to the gratification of any deficit and regardless of whether it brings pleasure or pain. To conceive the tendency toward optimal arousal in pleasure-maximizing-pain-minimizing terms is a confused attempt to use concepts which are applicable only to the reductive drives in attempting to conceptualize an essentially non-reductive tendency.

The confusion involved in this kind of psychological interpretation of the physiological phenomena is essentially the same as the error in the traditional argument for hedonism which maintains that (1) anything we do by choice is by definition something we want to do; (2) anything we want to do is by definition something which gives us pleasure; therefore, (3) anything we do by choice is something that brings us pleasure. The fallacy, as pointed out very clearly by J.C. Gosling,[23] is that an equivocation is involved in the use of the word 'want.' In statement (1), 'want' means whatever I choose to do; in (2) it means whatever causes me to have a certain conscious experience which I enjoy having and which must be defined ostensively. Obviously, these two senses of the word 'want' do not always coincide; Oedipus chose to discover the truth about his past, knowing (or at least strongly suspecting) that it probably would not bring him much enjoyment. To assume that whatever consciousness wants to achieve is pleasure (or happiness) by definition is to make an unwitting *philosophical* presupposition, and an erroneous one at that. And for just this type of reason, if it makes sense to ask *why* consciousness *wants* to maintain a certain degree or intensity *of* consciousness *per se* (not just in order to produce pleasure), such a question cannot be answered by empirical means at all. It requires philosophical clarification.

Consider, for example, White's attempt to answer it by positing a general 'drive toward competency.'[24] As White admits, this theory stretches the meaning of 'drive' so far that no 'physiological deficit external to the nervous system' need figure into it, and the theory is frankly a mere description of a type of behavior rather than an explanation. But the central problem with the theory is not noticed by White: The concept of a drive toward competency is circular. White defines competency as "an organism's capacity to interact effectively with its environment."[25] But if we ask what 'effectively' means, the answer must obviously be 'in such a way as to enable the organism to attain its ends.' What, then, *are* its ends? Either to reduce its *other* drives which *are* reductive in nature, in which case we are back where we started (with the non-reductive behaviors being reduced to means toward reductive ends); or to attain 'competency' itself, in which case we have merely gone in a vacuous circle, for we still don't know what competency means. Even the attempt to posit non-reductive drives leads to tautologous circularity and to a redundancy which is at best useless, at worst misleading in that it encourages us to think of such non-reductive desires as the desire to develop our cognitive abilities, for example, as just other needs to be reduced. Thus the goal of conscious existence still appears as a kind of pleasure or happiness to be achieved ('happiness' on the problematic model of 'mental pleasure'). The structure of the organism's value priorities and the relationships between its intrinsic and extrinsic values still have not been elucidated.

A still more serious confusion which often exists in reductionistic thinking is to speak as though intrinsic values for the organism could only exist on a physiological level, whereas only extrinsic values could exist on the conscious level. My desire for a milk shake becomes an extrinsic valuation whose purpose is to serve as a means toward the end of re-establishing certain chemical equilibria in the body. The problem here is that the motivation on the part of consciousness to exist *qua* consciousness while maintaining these equilibria cannot be understood in these terms. This confusion is clearly evident in the work of Freud, to choose one example among many. Freud labels the conscious activities of the nervous system the'ego' and the drives (physiological deficits external to the nervous system) the 'id.' From the system based on this opposition, it follows that the id is unconscious and the ego conscious (or partly so). One must thus perceive one's emotions as forces that drive one from behind, in much the same way that one perceives external phenomena. The real emotions themselves are unconscious; they are defined as non-conscious entities; only the objectifying perception of what they are is conscious. Since the driving emotions are physiological phenomena, and therefore not conscious in themselves, the relation between the emotion and the subject's perception of it is the same as the relation between the Kantian thing-in-itself and its outward appearance as a phenomenon. I can never really know what it is that I feel simply by feeling it. My ego (which is my conscious being) can only learn what my id really feels and 'adjust' itself accordingly. In principle, the ego still cannot *feel* the feeling—only the id can do this—but rather the ego must content itself with merely *seeing what these feelings are* and dealing *with* them 'realistically.' On the drive-reductionistic view, especially when this particular confusion is involved, there can be no such thing as a conscious emotion. Man is necessarily separated from his feelings, *by the way in which the terms are defined.* He controls them or is controlled by them. In any case, he is at war with them. This model of man as a sort of steam engine thus trades in the problem of repression or unconscious consciousness (which it succeeds in explaining after a fashion) for the contrary problem—*how is conscious consciousness possible* in the case of emotions? Whatever values we consciously experience are only extrinsic values; the intrinsic values are physiological processes the value of which cannot be directly experienced or even posited by consciousness. It becomes what Hegel called a night in which all cows are black.

One further example may help point us in the direction of a correct understanding of the conscious correlates of non-reductive physiological phenomena. It is sometimes asked why the infants in Spitz's marasmus studies die from a lack of cuddling, fondling, etc., even though the traditionally accepted physiological drives (deficits external to the nervous system) are satisfied.[26] One explanation—the most common one—is to posit as an *ad hoc* hypothesis a new physiological drive with some such description as a 'need for cuddling.' If such a need really existed, however, then it would be difficult to explain why *adults* do *not* die of marasmus. To explain away this fact, it would be necessary to posit that adults are capable of developing 'substitutes' for fondling, in some sense. Some psychologists speak of 'strokes' in a metaphorical sense, as though expressions of social approval were somehow substitute ways of gratifying the physiological need for physical contact. (How a social relation can ever be made to satisfy a physiological drive or need would have to remain an unanswered question. The notion that social reinforcers are secondary reinforcers, even if tenable, would not be an adequate explanation here; if a *primary* reinforcer, such as food, cannot substitute for maternal affection, then why should friendship and other such *secondary* reinforcers serve any better?) Besides piling *ad hoc* hypothesis upon *ad hoc* hypothesis, this theory would also involve the essential unclarity of any theory which tries to regard one need as a substitute for another. Thomas Wolfe, for example, regarded sexual desire as a substitute for the need for maternal affection; but there is no more reason to assume this than to assume that maternal affection is a substitute for sex, or that both sex and maternal affection are substitutes for some more basic, underlying need, perhaps of a general and unspecified nature. The question remains, then, if a given need is basic enough that its non-fulfillment leads to death, how the fulfillment of some *other* need (whether basic or derivative) can serve well enough to prevent the organism's death. Would it not be more likely that the two needs are substitutable for each other because they are two different means of satisfying a still more basic need whose nature we have not yet understood?

3. An alternative hypothesis

Perhaps in the case of many of these discrepant data a better explanation can be derived from the direct analysis of consciousness as such. Consciousness seeks not only the gratification of negative needs (deficits) by means of reduction of the deficits, but demands also that there be values of a positive nature. Consciousness itself, of course, is valued by consciousness in its own right, provided that the consciousness in question is not the mere consciousness of pain; if this were not true, it would not be logically possible for consciousness to desire pleasure (i.e., the consciousness of pleasure) or any other conscious experience. But consciousness must be symbolized in order to continue to exist, and the only means available to the neonate for the symbolization of non-negative states of consciousness is through physical contact with the mother (or some other person). This interaction with the primordial other enables non-negative states of consciousness to occur. Apparently, the presence of such non-negative states of consciousness is necessary in order for the neonate to be motivated to maintain an energy level high enough to discharge the perfunctory activities of eating and drinking. Without the possibility of such non-negative consciousness (which, because of the necessity for symbolization-through-embodied-activity, cannot simply occur in an environmental vacuum), the child literally is not interested enough in continuing to exist to motivate the needed effort. Thus marasmus is preventable in infancy only by introducing a mother-figure. In adulthood, or even in slightly later childhood, marasmus is not an issue because other methods are available of accomplishing this symbolizing function.

The simple desire on the part of consciousness to continue to be conscious—which entails the necessity of symbolizing the consciousness through physical activities usually structured in terms of interaction with other conscious beings—is at least equiprimordial with the reductive needs, if not even more basic than they are. Social activities such as symbolization (through speech, play, etc.) cannot be derived from reductive drives by means of secondary-reinforcement kinds of explanations (although being linked with reductive contingencies may strengthen them) because the two types of motivation are equiprimordial with each other.

How important are the non-reductive motives in relation to the hedonistic ones? Obviously, if non-reductive motives exist at all, then there can be no *fixed* proportion between their importance and that of the others. Instead, the non-reductive motives will themselves determine the relative importance of the two types of motives by arranging the conditioning contingencies in such a way as to habituate the organism to either a large amount of pleasure of a given type or a small amount, as deemed desirable by the non-reductive motives themselves. Nothing about this is mysterious or opposed to traditional learning theory (of the Hull-Spence type, for example). 'Contingency management' (i.e., arranging the reinforcement contingencies of one's own life so as to cultivate favorable desires, such as a desire to study, and eliminate un-favorable desires, such as the desire to smoke) is a frequently used form of behavior modification. If contingency management is used by the organism merely to obtain a greater long-term pleasure by curtailing short-term ones, then there is nothing non-hedonic about the operation. And if there were no motivational consciousness which did not by necessity seek pleasure as its ultimate goal, then it would be impossible for the organism to set any limits to its own ultimate desire for pleasure; for no hedonistic motivation could choose against the eventual maximization of pleasure, though errors might of course be committed in the 'hedonic calculations' toward this end. But a non-hedonistic motive can choose in such a way as to set up its environment so that the reinforcement contingencies which determine some of the habits of the organism are arranged for the purpose of fostering even *stoic* habits, if that is what is desired by the non-reductive drives. The non-reductive drives thus have the power, within broad limits, to determine the extent to which the organism seeks the indulgence of its reductive drives and hedonistic desires. Of course, there is generally no reason why they should *oppose* the seeking of a certain amount of pleasure, as long as pleasure-seeking goals do not obstruct the non-hedonistic ones. The point is simply that we condition ourselves, again within limits, to have the particular desires we end up having and to require the particular amount of gratification we end up requiring. As the homespun sage Chester said in the TV western "Gunsmoke," when offered a free banana, "I don't want to cultivate an appetite I can't afford." When pleasure-seeking activities become so prominent as to impede the goal of maintaining consciousness at the desired level of intensity, the organism can't afford them.

At least two kinds of activities are motivated not by reductive needs, but by a desire on the part of consciousness to be conscious. One of these activities, symbolization, was discussed in Chapter III. Consciousness, desiring to continue being conscious, is motivated to do the kinds of things that are necessary in order to symbolize itself. As discussed more fully elsewhere, this class of activities includes a wide range of art forms, language functions, and—perhaps most important—human interrelationships of an empathic kind. Certain structures of dialogue serve the symbolizing functions better than others. We shall elaborate more fully on the specific character of these preferable structures in the next chapter.

A second type of activity motivated by the desire to be conscious is the desire to find or create value in life. To see why this is true, imagine what it would feel like to have reached the ultimate conclusion that 'nothing matters'—the conclusion Sartre is often thought to have reached at the end of *Being and Nothingness* when he says "It makes no difference whether I become a leader of nations or get drunk alone." Even the person who reaches a genuinely nihilistic conclusion regarding value issues, feeling that none of the things that he once valued and none of the things he sees his peers valuing 'matter' any longer, that their supposed value is only illusory—even such a nihilist experiences such a state of affairs as a kind of 'disillusionment.' That is, although he feels that nothing matters, he would prefer that something *did* matter. Within this preference that something did matter (though as it happens for the moment nothing does) is harbored the most basic of all values—the value which consciousness places on *there being* something that matters. This fact is not only phenomenologically accessible through the experience of disillusionment, but is also an ontologically necessary dimension of consciousness. If at any given time I value any object or state of affairs, it is logically presupposed that I want to value something-or-other; I want there to be value. For, if I did not value anything at all, then I could not enjoy or appreciate the experiencing of the particular thing in question—it would be indifferent to me. Thus, if I value anything in particular, I must first of all attribute value to the state of affairs such that anything is valuable to me in the first place. Such a state of affairs necessarily includes, as a precondition to the experience of value, a condition of the psyche such that the psyche is able to find or create some value or other, even if only the value of the search for value itself. In short, the value of finding or creating value has priority over any particular value which is found or created. Since valuing anything necessarily has an emotional component (a positive feeling toward that which is valued), this point also implies that whether or not I feel any emotions at all (and to what extent I feel emotions) has priority over any particular emotion that I feel.

If I were to be faced with a state of affairs in which the indulging of some particular desire were to reduce the intensity of the emotional life in general, then, from the authentic perspective, it would be self-defeating to indulge the desire—for example, if I were to commit myself to living the life of an automaton in order to make more money. There are obviously ethical implications here, though it would take us too far afield to pursue them in detail. The main point, for present purposes, is that consciousness is motivated not only to be conscious, but to be a valuational and emotional consciousness, to experience a certain amount of emotion. Moreover, since the being of consciousness is the kind of thing which requires effort to sustain, consciousness would not continue to exist if it were not motivated to exert this effort. Consciousness cannot progress without a motivational-emotional dimension's being present at each step which serves to motivate the *direction* of the unfolding of consciousness in terms of selective attention and focusing.

These two types of conscious activities—symbolization and the act of valuing that there be value—are interrelated. What consciousness wants, when it wants there to be value, is that its emotional intensity be facilitated at some optimal level, independently of whether the specific emotions involved happen to be pleasant or unpleasant in nature. (Consciousness of course also seeks some amount of pleasure, as discussed above, but that is beside the point here.) This means, then, that consciousness desires the symbolization of itself in its emotional dimension; for as discussed in Chapter III, the symbolization of a consciousness tends to intensify the consciousness or at least to allow it to continue existing at its present or a comparable level of intensity (though the *what*-content of the consciousness necessarily changes somewhat in the process), and this is as true of the emotional dimension of consciousness as any other. In fact, since the emotional dimension is presupposed by the existence of consciousness as such in the first place, then merely by desiring the symbolization of consciousness *per se*, consciousness will necessarily and automatically also accomplish in the process the symbolization of the emotional dimension of itself as well. For example, when I use the process of symbolization to help me remember a name, I also symbolize in the same action the value to me of remembering the name in the first place, just as by acting to help the cause of the poor I symbolize at the same time my empathy with the plight of the poor. To symbolize a consciousness is inherently to symbolize the *value* of the consciousness. It follows that the most basic emotion, without which none of the others would continue to exist at the conscious level, is the desire to symbolize my own consciousness by means of action in the world.

Within this broad class of conscious aims which need not be gratifying in the sense of pleasure, there therefore also exists a sub-class of gratifying feelings whose gratifying character does not depend upon the previous existence of painful or ungratifying feelings whose 'reduction' would constitute pleasure. In this sense, Aristippus is closer to the truth than Epicurus. Pleasure and pain are not additive with respect to each other. The being-conscious of consciousness is valued by consciousness for its own sake. Activities which are necessary in order to maintain a certain degree of consciousness on the part of the conscious being (speech, play, social interaction, even the pecking of chickens which is preferred over eating on their part) are motivated by the desire to be conscious *per se*, not by the reductive needs. For the adult, fulfilling work—as the outgrowth of play—might well be included in the class of symbolizing activities whose purpose is simply the being-fully-conscious of consciousness. Evidently, some problem-solving behavior could be included here as well, since the solving of problems is one method available to consciousness of being fully conscious.

4. Importance of non-reductive motives for the existence and structure of consciousness as such

The important point as far as the transcendent unity and continuity of consciousness is concerned is that it is precisely those motives which are non-reductive that constitute the self as a unified unfolding across various momentary states. For the non-reductive motives do not desire to see realized any objective state of affairs in the world *per se*, or in the body *per se*. What they want is that a certain state of affairs exist *in consciousness*—not a state of pleasure (at least not primarily this), but simply a state of complete existence. The continuation of the full existence of consciousness is not automatic, as it would be with a stone, but requires a peculiar and complex kind of effort on the part of consciousness. Since the ontological status of consciousness is change (i.e., a pattern or process), then if one given state of consciousness should attempt to prolong itself into the future *without changing*, the result would be that it would cease to be an instance of consciousness at all. For consciousness to continue to be entails that it stop being precisely what it is, and change into something else, in accordance with a certain temporal structure and rhythm, at each new instant. Also, in the case of an entity like consciousness, existence is a matter of degrees; even if consciousness succeeds in changing enough, and in the right direction, to continue being, there is still the danger that it will exist to a smaller extent, that the quality of its experiencing will be less intense than it is motivated to be. Thus it could be said to 'stagnate' in such instances.

In order to avoid such stagnation, consciousness must strive to bring about a certain kind of relationship between one state of consciousness and the next. But in order to accomplish this, symbolization of the original state is necessary. The symbolization of one state of consciousness enables it to continue existing as consciousness by changing it into still another state of consciousness. For the same reason (if for no other), consciousness cannot exist without positing value.

To understand how this process serves to facilitate the pattern of selective attention which gives the stream of attention-progressions its direction and unique character, it is also necessary to see how the elements of cognition themselves fit together to form the attention-progression. This will be the subject of the next part.

1. Four basic elements of consciousness

A priori, there are at least four capacities of consciousness the failure of any one of which could allow such phenomena as self-alienation to occur, and without which no self would be possible at the conscious level. The first and most obvious of these capabilities is the experiential *direction of attention*, in an active sense. To what objects of perception does the person initially place himself in such a position as to be exposed? Where does he look, to what parts of a situation does he pay the most attention? All these questions direct themselves to an attentional mechanism which is already presupposed by the fact that I am now being experientially affected by certain things while ignoring others—a mechanism which logically precedes any particular experiences, but which also presupposes on its own part a stream of past experiences which has led up to the implicit decision to attend to one thing rather than another.

To recognize the importance of the simple direction of attention in lending a certain overall pattern to the flow of experiences, we need only consider those instances in which our attempts to control the direction of attention fail. Often, trying to control our own selective attention can be like trying to purposely 'be spontaneous.' When we force ourselves to go against its course, we immediately recognize that even the way in which we go against its original pattern was decided by it itself in its preconscious immediate past, and that even our realization of this fact could not have taken place without its active participation. In such instances, it seems to be one step further back, necessarily just beyond reach. Such experiences highlight the importance of paying attention to something-or-other as an action which is necessary to the occurrence of any consciousness. Projective techniques of psychologists, though extremely inaccurate instruments whose meaning is also extremely fuzzy, are attempts on the part of psychologists to study a subject's peculiar habits of attention-direction in order to learn something about his general personality structure. The mere passive failure to be in the habit of actively directing one's attention in certain ways as opposed to others, and the complex patterns of neurosis and even normal confusion that can result, would almost seem capable of assuming by itself the central role in the understanding of many self-alienating forms of selective consciousness. In fact, some psychologists, such as Meldman,[27] have attempted to make attention the leading concept in the nosology of psychiatric disorders. Thus the attentional 'mechanism' alluded to by so many psychologists, far from being a vacuous concept, could make a fertile object of phenomenological investigation.

But such an investigation could scarcely get off the ground before it became evident that a second mental capacity is integrally interrelated with attention—*memory*. Like the attention mechanism, remembering is an active rather than a passive activity. It seems tautologous that any activity is active rather than passive, but in this case the tautology is not vacuous; for memory is the kind of capacity about which one may well wonder, not how it can fail to function, but how it can function as well as it does.

The reason the attention mechanism could not function without the aid of some rudimentary form of memory is a purely *a priori* one. Without the ability to remember, I could not extend the paying-of-attention-to-something in *time*, which in turn is a necessary form without which no sensibility whatever would be possible. I would forget from moment to moment what it was I had been attending to. Thus memory is an *a priori* necessity not only for the most complex mental operations, but also for the most basic, the raw feeling which cannot take place without taking place through time. Of course, this does not mean that memory is nothing more than continued-attention; it would be absurd to say that to remember an event from 1960 requires that I have been attending to it since 1960. What it means, however, is that attention would be impossible without some memory, of a very rudimentary form at least.

The working of memory in turn presupposes the presence of a third capacity, which we shall call cognitive *'synthesis.'* The activity of the memory may be compared to a relay race in which, if thought is to be carried into the future, the agent that carried it in the past must first be brought into conjunction with the agent that will carry it in the immediate future. Any time two activities of the intellect are related to each other in any such way as this, it is evident that there has been need of some transcendent function in the sense that something must have been able to do more than simply attend first to the first idea and then to the second; it must have been able to attend to *both* ideas simultaneously, so to speak, or within the same 'span of vision.' Admittedly, this is a rough and metaphorical characterization of what happens; one can see it more clearly by simply focusing upon its occurrence in one's own conscious progressions. But such is what is meant by the role of the synthetic function of consciousness in the present sense of the word 'synthesis'—i.e., the principle which allows two ideas to be attended to *jointly*, before which no relations between the ideas could possibly be established or even posited by consciousness. Synthesis is as necessary to things in space (figure-ground) as in time (remembering, continuing-to-attend, reasoning, being reminded of things, discovering, etc.). Merely thinking first, 'God is omnipotent,' and then 'There is evil,' leads nowhere without the synthetic capacity's first conjoining the two items (along with the meaning of their terms) into one object of attention in order for the *fourth* capacity here proposed, the *analytic* capacity, to see what relations can be established between them. In the meantime, the attention-direction, the memory, and the synthetic process must all continue actively functioning in such a way as to extend the two ideas, 'God is omnipotent,' and 'There is evil,' long enough in *time* that any conclusions or problems which the juxtaposition of the two premises might entail may be allowed to emerge in the form of a more unified expression of some of the ideas contained in the pair of ideas viewed as a whole.

If this capability to synthesize should fail, the two ideas would become 'dissociated' and the person would be allowed to escape (from the already-entailed but experientially unexplicated conclusions) into some 'normal' or 'abnormal' form of self-alienation. He would still be as free as anyone to think sometimes 'God is omnipotent,' and at other times 'There is evil,' but when he found himself venturing too close to conjoining the two ideas, he might learn to avoid the resultant pain (the anxiety aroused by the issue) by ceasing at the crucial moment to think one or both of the premises—not by ceasing to admit their veracity, but simply by ceasing at the appropriate times to grant them any conscious status whatever. If someone resorted to such a 'defense' too frequently, it is conceivable that he might break down the *general* habit of synthesizing in the appropriate kinds of instances, in which case the as yet unclearly conceived phenomenon of 'psychological disturbance' might result. It is easy to see the similarity between the process just described and many of the attentional patterns of 'hysterics' and 'obsessives' as described by Eysenck and many others.

The slightest upset of any one of these four capacities in any situation can cause reverberations throughout the entire interlocking web of functions and bounce back to again re-upset the originally malfunctioning capacity, forming vicious circles and spirals within the attention progression. Also, if the 'self' (a concept to be further clarified) already wants or expects (intends) to see something other than that which is really there, then the necessity of all these repeated, complex, creative and highly active 'operations upon' the thing—hence also voluntative and time-taking operations—which are constitutively necessary to the act of perceiving what is there, can facilitate either a convenient escape from or an involuntary loss of the apprehension of the truth. (Hence also the possible alienation of one voluntative intention from another, where intention **B**, which may have followed from intention **A**, now doubles back to contradict **A**.) This might also suggest an explanation for how I can perceive something just enough to realize that I do not want to perceive it and thus end up not perceiving it, as when I am so disconcerted at being sexually propositioned by a strange woman that my mind fails to cognize the meaning of what she is saying even though the meaning is perfectly explicit. The phenomenon of purposely failing to perceive something may seem more paradoxical than it really is if we do not take into consideration how many active processes are involved in the most simple cognition, and that, as John Turk Saunders aptly pointed out, any cognition can be present to a greater or lesser *extent*, so that 'marginal' apperceptions can be fleetingly present to a tiny extent and then purposely be relegated to unconsciousness.[28]

2. The productive and receptive styles of attention progression

The 'productive' and 'receptive' styles of attention progression, as we shall call them, are higher-order predicates than the four conscious functions just described (attention, memory, synthesis and analysis). The productive and receptive styles are not simply two additional functions to be added to the others in a list. Rather, the productive style is a way of patterning or interrelating the four simpler functions across time, so as to coordinate them into the unity and continuity of a meaningful, directed, and purposeful progression. The receptive style is another way. The two styles are not mutually exclusive; both function in every normal consciousness, alternatively and in patterns which emerge as third-order predicates.

The 'productive' function of the consciousness-progression is what we shall term the tendency to draw out implications from felt meanings already contained or entailed in previous ideational or emotional material—for example, deducing a conclusion from premises which are already 'there' in the field of consciousness. In this productive mode of progression, there is a sequential connection between ideas; one idea feels as though it 'comes out of' its predecessor and is significantly interrelated with it, not necessarily in a formally logical way, but in some sense having terms in common between the thoughts such that the one determines the other, that the latter is an unfolding of the former or in some way follows from or is relevant to the former. From the standpoint of the four basic elements of cognition without which self-alienation would occur, the productive style utilizes analysis and synthesis, but de-emphasizes simple attention to that which is external to present consciousness, and also de-emphasizes the memory of past acts of simple attention to objects which were at the time external to previous consciousness. In other words, the productive function is only capable of pursuing in sequential fashion a certain line of thought or emotion, divorced from all other facts, ideas or feelings, and disregarding considerations of the relevance or importance of pursuing that particular train of thought further. When the productive style has pushed one topic of attention so far that nothing more can come out of it, only the receptive style can then step in and take over to introduce new material into the progression. Left to itself, the productive capacity alone would merely revert to a previous stage of the progression and become repetitive, as in a repetition compulsion.

Husserl refers to the productive capacity in his First Logical Investigation when he says,

> If **A** summons **B** into consciousness, we are not merely simultaneously or successively conscious of both **A** and **B**, but we usually *feel* their connection forcing itself upon us, a connection in which the one points to the other and seems to belong to it. To turn mere coexistence into mutual pertinence, or more precisely, to build cases of the former into intentional unities of things which seem mutually pertinent, is the constant result of associative functioning. All unity of experience, all empirical unity, whether of a thing, an event or of the order and relation of things, becomes a phenomenal unity through the felt mutual belongingness of the sides and parts that can be made to stand out as units in the apparent object before us. . . . [In this way] an object or state of affairs not merely recalls another, and so points to it, but also provides evidence for the latter, fosters the presumption that it like-

wise exists, and makes us immediately feel this in the manner described above.[29]

Thus still another way of distinguishing the productive style is to note
that, wherever it is operative, the *order* of the thoughts cannot be reversed
without destroying some of their meaning.

The 'receptive' function, by contrast, often characterizes the manic
and the hysteric, relying as it does on simple perceptual attention and
on merely associative memory. After spending perhaps fifteen to thirty
seconds on a given train of thought, the subject's attention will skip to
something irrelevant; his stream of consciousness, if it is filled with too
many receptive moments, may become a disconnected hodgepodge of
unrelated thoughts. The receptive function, nonetheless, is one necessary
component of the normal operation of consciousness. Although relying
too heavily upon it to the exclusion of the productive function or in inappropriate contexts leads to hysteria, a strong and persistent contact
with it is essential because it allows the person to be receptive to newness
of experience, to stimuli coming in from the outside. On the other hand,
too many new stimuli (whether coming in through perception or through
associative memory) can block the flow of sequential explication and
drawing-out of the deeper or more far-reaching, subtle and significant
implications from the experiential material that has already been
encountered.

The 'obsessive' thought pattern could thus be viewed as overly productive from past ideas (so that he runs out of new material and becomes
repetitive and inert); his attention pattern is not receptive enough toward
encounters with the outside (notably with other people). The hysteric,
by contrast, is so receptive that he becomes flighty and cannot take the
time to think through the real meaning of stimuli, but simply always
accepts almost unquestioningly and passively the first datum that happens to come to mind. Both the obsessive and the hysteric tend to be
indiscriminate about *what* they attend to, each in his own way; yet, in
another sense, each carefully censors what he will and will not allow
himself to attend to.

In both instances, the question is essentially one regarding *value* structures. For, in both instances, the question that is being ignored is: What
is *worth* spending this particular period of time paying attention to?
Neither the obsessive nor the hysterical way of thinking is able to make
a good decision in this regard at most junctures. This would suggest that

the implicit decision, whether to use the productive or the receptive style at any given moment, cannot be made within the productive or receptive styles themselves, but requires still some other style.

Clinical-psychological folklore has it that hysteria is flight 'from' reality while obsession is flight 'into' reality, or into a segment of reality in order to escape other segments. If Otto Rank were to think in these terms, he might postulate that the 'artistic' (or 'healthy' person, in his sense) would be the one who was able to interrelate the productive and the receptive capacities so as to bring each into play where most appropriate. An obviously important question which remains is: In concrete terms, *how* can this be accomplished?

It is interesting and suggestive to contrast these notions, rooted as they are in the phenomenology of consciousness, against Eysenck's orthogonal dimensions of personality, 'extraversion-introversion' being one dimension, the other a physiologically-based 'anxiety' (elsewhere called 'emotionality' and 'neuroticism' interchangeably by Eysenck). Eysenck correlates these dimensions with the various psychopathic disturbances as indicated by the following graph.

The horizontal dimension is defined by Eysenck's Extraversion scale, and the vertical dimension by a Neurotic Anxiety scale.[30] An alternative and perhaps contrary schematization, using the terms defined in this section, would substitute 'receptive' in place of 'extraversion,' and 'productive' in place of introversion. It is conceivable that productive and receptive patterns could be observed by means of analysis of the subject's language. Developing such a procedure, of course, would be an ambitious project and certainly beyond our scope here. Needless to say, Eysenck's notion of Anxiety/Neuroticism/Emotionality is quite confused, as are so many 'personality factors' defined in purely factor-analytic fashion, and we shall not attempt to discuss it here.[30]

3. The creative component of cognition

We have seen that the four basic functions of cognition stand in need of some transcendent function in order for their actions to be coordinated into a working whole—a need also displayed by the productive and receptive functions. Yet any such transcendent function and its nature would also have to have been predetermined already by the prior working of the four basic components of past cognitive activity. These four, of course, would have to have already been transcendently coordinated by an even more prior function which in turn was determined by another previous fourfold. No matter how far back we trace any stream of consciousness, we find still another such fourfold. Therefore, whatever the nature of any transcendent governor of all these fourfolds might prove to be, its power will always have been vested in it at the instigation of the four basic components. Like any chosen governor, on the other hand, the transcendent function—however abstract or relational may be its ontological status—does wield some fleeting moment of partial autonomy. This must be the case, for the nature of the interaction between the productive and receptive styles has proven to be no mere chance phenomenon, but a purposive means willfully directed toward certain ends. (This relative autonomy on the part of the transcendent function, of course, would not contradict the possibility of a complete determinism in human nature, as I have discussed elsewhere. Whether the transcendent function is autonomous with respect to other functions has nothing to do with whether some ultimate factors or other have caused it to be the way it is.)[31] Without such a relative autonomy of the transcendent function, there could be little unity, coherence or direction in the stream of consciousness. How are we to account for this transcendent function? Is the transcendent function equivalent with the self? Ontologically speaking, *what* is it? Can the transcendent continuity *be* at the same time a concretely experienceable feeling, as Chapter III suggested it must be in order to be a transcendental 'I'?

The only concrete feeling which can both (a) actually exist in any specific moment of time (and indeed in every specific moment) and at the same time (b) provide the transcendent unity and direction of consciousness—which can make the decision, for example, whether to selectively attend to this or that—is the concrete emotional feeling of wanting there to be value in life, which, as we have seen, is more fundamental than any particular value that might be posited. The desire for there to be value, as felt in a specific context, pushes the elements of consciousness which happen to be present at that moment in the direction of more adequate symbolization of themselves, which in turn *changes* them into the desired future state of consciousness, thus allowing consciousness to continue existing at the desired level of intensity by means of the necessary amount of *change* (and the right structure of change). Change, we should recall, is the ontological status of consciousness. This desire for just the appropriate direction of change-through-symbolization is not in any way equivalent with any of the four basic elements of cognition, nor with the productive or receptive styles. On the other hand, it could not possibly occur without a previous creative working-together of the productive and receptive styles, and thus also of the four more basic components. For this reason, it will be termed the 'creative' component of cognition. It is also 'creative' in the sense that it, and only it, is capable of creating value for the stream of consciousness, and of making the value-priority decisions which ideally should govern the direction of attention at each instant. The creative component of cognition motivates the direction of consciousness, thus providing its unity; it is always present (though continually changing); and it is the only state of consciousness which, according to the requirements of Chapter III, 'I'—in the sense of a limited transcendental ego—can possibly be. And because it motivates the symbolization of consciousness, which intensifies consciousness, and thus counteracts repression and denial, leading to greater authenticity (i.e., self-honesty), it does indeed perform the essential function that a transcendental ego is supposed to perform: By motivating authenticity, it questions its own prejudices and presuppositions, which is the essence of a phenomenological reduction, however limited and incomplete.

It is easy to imagine examples of the working of this nonreductive motivation whose aim is not the occurrence of any objective state of affairs in the world, but rather the occurrence of some subjective state of affairs within consciousness. Consider for example the case of the 'henpecking wife'. (To avoid sexism, we could also imagine a parallel analysis of wife-beating husbands.) If we were to assume that every emotion has some object over against consciousness as its intentional object, then we would have to assume also that the henpecking wife has been provoked into anger because of some objective event which has occurred, and that there is in turn some objective situation the attainment of which would quell her hostility, thus producing a conscious state of 'satisfaction.' But this is not the case with the henpecking wife. There is no objective state of affairs which could be arranged by the husband or anyone else which would be capable of subduing her wrath. If she says that she is angry because her husband has failed to wash the dishes, this does not mean that she would not be angry if he had washed the dishes; it means simply that, if he had washed the dishes, she would be angry about something else instead. Recalling our analysis of symbols and intentional objects in Chapter III, then, it is more appropriate to say that the henpecking wife initially feels a negative emotion and then, in order to experience this state of consciousness more fully, she looks around in her environment for some situation which might serve as an opportunity to symbolize this negative emotion. In this way, she maintains an optimal level of intensity in her stream of consciousness, although the consciousness is not pleasurable for her but, quite the contrary, is altogether unpleasant. It is also obvious, therefore, that she is more interested in producing a certain intensity of consciousness in herself than she is in whether or not the consciousness so produced is pleasant or unpleasant. She does this, again, by finding in the world an opportunity to symbolize the unpleasant consciousness which she already feels to some extent, thus intensifying it. But the supposed 'object' of her wrath is not *really* the intentional object of the emotion; it is only a symbolization of it.

How prevalent is this kind of structure of emotional life? It would be mistaken to regard it as a mere oddity, a pecularity of certain eccentric individuals such as the 'henpecking wife' or the 'wife-beating husband.' For the structure we are talking about here is the most basic structure of motivation—the motivation on the part of consciousness to *be* consciousness, even at the sacrifice of dull pleasures which would not serve to maintain the intensity of conscious life. How often the object of an emotion is at least to a considerable extent a mere symbolization rather than an intentional object proper of the emotion, would depend in turn upon whether the emotion in question is a non-reductive one.

Henpecking, of course, does not serve its symbolizing purpose well, because it does not serve the symbolizing purpose well enough to make the person aware of the initial negative state of consciousness. It is an unsuccessful attempt at symbolization. A more fruitful attempt might be to listen to Tchaikovsky's Sixth Symphony, or to read *les Miserables*, or to take her husband to a marriage counsellor, where the real emotions which actually exist could be symbolized without the necessity of pretending that they are different from what they really are.

If what we have said so far about the non-reductive nature of the creative component of cognition is true, then we must conclude that the non-reductive emotional motivation which is always present in consciousness—whose purpose is to seek symbolization of the corresponding conscious state as a whole, so as to allow consciousness to continue changing, and thus to continue existing—always seeks, not some objective state of affairs in the world, but rather a state of affairs in the world which would facilitate symbolization. And this is why emotional relationships with other conscious beings are so important to the very being of consciousness. Interpersonal relationships, as we shall see more fully in the next chapter, are structured in such a way that they are ideal vehicles (or *can* be ideal vehicles) for the symbolization of emotion. Not *only* interpersonal relationships serve this purpose, of course; art, sports, and even philosophy can serve a similar purpose. Even sitting alone and thinking can serve it—although one is in a sense relating to other people even in this case because the language in which one thinks has been learned from other people. Even political activity, as a symbolization of one's feelings toward mankind as a whole, can serve the symbolizing motivation.

It would also follow that we are often mistaken when we think that we desire to see an objective state of affairs actualized in the world for its own sake or for the sake of 'pleasure' or 'happiness.' Motivational theories which attempt to reduce everything to hedonic and drive-reductive motives are systematically mistaken in this regard. Also, since there are a variety of different ways to symbolize any given state of consciousness, there is no one objective occurrence which is absolutely indispensable to the 'well-being' of consciousness in this respect. The non-reductive motives are quite different from the reductive ones in this sense. The avoidance of excruciating pain is absolutely essential to the well-being of consciousness with regard to pleasure-pain. But no given objective state of affairs is strictly necessary as far as non-reductive motivational consciousness is concerned, as long as *some* opportunity for symbolization remains open.

Now let's proceed, in the next and final chapter, to put together all that we have learned about the relationship between consciousness, the self (which is the same as the creative component of cognition), and the non-reductive motivation which in each instant of the stream of consciousness is the directionality which makes possible a self, in order to construct an overall picture of the structure of consciousness as it unfolds in the pattern of a transcendental ego. We shall find that the ego may be more or less transcendental, depending upon the extent to which consciousness succeeds in finding symbolic expression for itself.

CHAPTER V

THE DIRECTED ATTENTION PROGRESSION

We have determined that 'I' am a particular species of consciousness—the motivation to focus, intensify and explicate felt meanings. We have also seen that I am not equivalent with all my states of consciousness, but only with those constitutive of the creative component of cognition, which is the source of this motivational feeling and consequently the source of the direction of the stream of consciousness in terms of the selective attention process. The creative component is the preconscious, categorially intentional (but not presentatively intentional) and value-positing dimension of consciousness; it determines in part what I see by motivating where I look at each instant; it is thus the transcendental ego.

The existence of a creative component in cognition allows the more basic functions not merely to occur at random, but to work together in such patterns as to move toward a goal. This kind of goal-orientation, in turn, facilitates not merely deductive reasoning, but creatively deductive reasoning. For example, it enables the reasoning mathematician to sense the shortest route to the desired conclusion. From any set of premises, an infinite number of conclusions can be deduced with validity—hence the frustrating experience of so many math students, of continuing indefinitely with a valid chain of inferences without ever reaching the needed conclusion. Of all the possible inferences we could make at a given juncture, we must decide *which one* to make. It is true, of course, that computers are able to make analogous 'decisions' without any creative component. But if given the task of evaluating a real-life argument, the work of a computer would be similar to that of the beginning logic student who is incapable of distinguishing the crucial issue at stake in the reasoning from the many trivial problems which could perhaps be eliminated given enough time. And this is just where computers need the help of human beings; no computer has a sense of the value of one correct criticism as opposed to another. We cannot give a computer an invalid argument from a logic text and ask, "Would it be worth your time to clean up the reasoning in this argument so as to preserve its essential conclusion?" A computer has no sense of how to avoid 'irrelevant objections.' Given the value of computer time, it would be prohibitively expensive to allow the computer to designate how its own time is to be used in such cases. In human thought, the rhetorical devise of irrelevant objection highlights the failure of the creative component of cognition: The irrelevant line of reasoning may not be invalid at all, yet it is a poor choice of *direction* as far as the real issue of the argument is concerned. Similarly, the participants in a discussion may both fail ever to zero in on the crucial or decisive point simply because they both continue reasoning along lines that, while perhaps valid, miss the crucial point. The ability to avoid this outcome is a function, not of the analytic or synthetic elements of cognition, but of the creative component. Hobbes may have had some such state of affairs in mind when he spoke of a distinction between reason and wit, defining the latter as the ability which allows a dog to catch a rabbit. Perhaps Schopenhauer also was thinking along these lines when he said, in his usual arrogant style, "Of inference all are capable; of judgment, only a few."[1]

From any proposition, then, a variety of other propositions can be deduced, but in practice we always deduce just one at a time. In general, from any moment-actual in the temporal flux of consciousness, we can progress on solid grounds of some kind (reasonable or emotional) to any one of an infinite number of possible subsequent moment-actuals, but, again, in practice we always progress to just one. If we construct a schematic diagram of the possibilities present to just one such progression, what we have looks like the trunk of a tree branching out into its limbs. And for each of these latter possible moment-actuals, we find an infinite number of branches emanating from it—only one of which, however, can actually be chosen as the second progression in the series. The branches lead to the stems, the stems to the twigs, and so on indefinitely. Of course, certain possibilities will always be excluded by forces exterior to the subject's own faculty of decision, so that the number of choices at each instant becomes finite rather than infinite, and the matrix of choices available to any given individual at any time takes on a unique shape. Nonetheless, an implicit choice is made as soon as the subject elects to attend to this rather than that, to be productive rather than receptive, logical rather than emotional or merely associative, etc. As we have seen, such a choice cannot be assumed to be arbitrary, even in the case of the most extreme imaginable hysteric. Let's refer to this complex network of possible attention progressions as the total 'attentional matrix' from which the subject chooses a stream of consciousness.

It should be noted in passing at this point that, even if we could know with precision what state of consciousness another person is experiencing, this knowledge would not be sufficient to tell us anything about what kind of person he is. We would also have to know something about the range of choices previously available to the person, from which he chose the state of consciousness in question. But even this would not be enough, unless we could understand the person's reason for making the particular decision in question. This, however, cannot be inferred, simply because any given effect may have had a variety of possible causes; thus, given any decision, it is conceivable that there could have been an infinite variety of possible motivations underlying it.

More reliable information could be obtained if we could observe the person in the process of performing a certain special kind of conscious process. This special process takes place whenever a person returns to a branch on the tree that he had previously progressed from, in order to try out a new direction, or in order to repudiate the choices he has made and to choose instead a different branch, or in order to get the overall picture in his own mind of where he is in relation to where he has come from and what his original purpose was of going in that particular direction—whenever, in general, the topic of his present attention (its 'intentional object') is the whole chain of unfolding or exploring mental processes that have led him to where he is in his attentional matrix. In this kind of 'reflective' process, it is as though the person made a note to himself regarding the 'road not taken' in the temporal sequence, and placed this note in a conspicuous place in the *spacial* world (through embodied symbolization) where he could be sure to see the note later so as to be able to see the relation of the road taken to those not taken. Symbolic activities thus facilitate the attempt of consciousness to double back on itself in this way. A given verbal expression or a piece of music, for example, may remind us of how we felt or what we thought on a past occasion by, in a certain sense, enabling us to relive the earlier progression in its subjective or noetic dimension.

The apparent exception to the rule that physical symbols are needed in order for consciousness to unfold and thus occur turns out on closer inspection not to be an exception at all. Someone may suppose that it is possible to remember information previously encountered and to bring into play the logical implications of such information in a new context without the aid of physical symbols, but merely by using *mental* symbols. Such a supposition forgets, however, that mental and physical events are inseparable and therefore that for every mental symbolization there is also a symbolizing *action* at the *physical* level, even if only in the brain. Moreover, the ability to accomplish symbolization activities in the brain alone is derivative in nature; we first learn to use external symbols, such as sounds that we enact with the mouth or numerals that we write or read, and then only later learn to short-cut the process by transferring the process into the brain. In some areas, such a transfer of symbolic operations completely into the brain is virtually impossible. Without such *external* forms of symbolization as art, music, drama, and talking to other people, a person's emotional life, for example, would remain quite impoverished. And even in those instances where we *can* accomplish the needed conscious progressions without external physical symbols—as when someone is able to play a game of chess purely in his mind—we should note that even this person could accomplish his purpose *still more easily* if he did use external symbolic actions such as actually moving the pieces on an actual board. In sum, then, the difference between accomplishing a conscious progression by manipulating external objects which function as symbols, and accomplishing a conscious progression by manipulating the physical material in the brain is a difference of degree, not of essence.

In the special case of reflection mentioned above, the symbol or symbolic activity serves what might be called a stabilizing function. It enables us to wander off in some possible direction of our attentional matrix in full confidence that our symbolic referent will enable us to return to the same spot if the need should arise. It lends stability to the overall progression and ensures that the progression will not continually run off in haphazard and 'irrelevant' directions, never able by its own choice to return. Without such stabilization, consciousness could never maintain the level of intensity which it at each moment desires.

The most common type of stabilizer is the other person. To realize why this is so, we should recall a comment of Husserl on the way in which the meanings of words (and the concepts for which they stand) become sedimented in consciousness. Husserl emphasizes in the *Logical Investigations* that an entire sentence is not necessarily required in order to convey meaning. A word can convey meaning because it embodies a concept; the concept itself in turn presupposes the truth of certain propositions. Thus these other propositions are in a sense contained in the word. When words' meanings become sedimented, however, we forget many of the presuppositions they entail unless something unusual happens to call our attention to the sedimented presuppositions.[2] When our attention is indeed called to the sedimented presuppositions, this in effect causes our stream of consciousness to double back to reconsider or, in a sense, to 'relive' the particular moment of our attentional matrix at which those presuppositions originally occurred. (In such instances, we may also find that the making of the presupposition originally occurred on an unconscious or semi-conscious level, as when a skilled rhetorician gets us to make a presupposition which we remain unaware of making.)

In a dialogical situation with another person with whom we have established empathy, there is a marked tendency for this kind of stabilization to occur when needed because each person is trying to understand the other's meaning and to get the other to understand one's own meaning. Even if the other person does not question my usage of a word or concept, the fact that I am looking at the word or concept from the other's point of view, in order to determine whether he can understand it, causes me to question its sedimented meanings, thus leading me back to the logical or emotional process whereby the term acquired its implied presuppositions. I then find myself fully and explicitly enacting conscious processes which previously were only incompletely, implicitly or 'preconsciously' enacted. In effect, I make the unconscious conscious because of the stabilizing effect of the other person's presence. This does not happen in all relationships between persons, of course. Obviously, no re-examination of sedimented meanings occurs as a result of the relationship between a thief and his victim. It occurs only when empathy is brought to bear in the interest of communication. Only empathic relationships serve the symbolizing and stabilizing functions in this respect. Dialogue is thus the paradigmatic symbolic action which serves to help consciousness to continue being conscious, which in turn is the most fundamental motivation of consciousness. Many other forms of symbolization, of course, serve the same purpose: the arts, political action, philosophy, moral action, etc. Thus consciousness feels numerous preferences as to how states of affairs in the objective world should be arranged—not for drive-reductive purposes, but simply to facilitate symbolization.

We have now laid the groundwork for the final step of our discussion, which is to show why it is that the transcendental ego exists to a great extent when consciousness and the external world interrelate in such ways as to facilitate symbolization, but exists only to a lesser extent when this relationship is such as to block symbolization.

1. The symbolized attention progression

Chapter III showed that there are two kinds of intentionality—categorial and presentative. Categorial intention means deciding what I am going to look *for*, prior to the act of looking-at. Presentative intention means looking *at* the object as something which is actually there in consciousness (whether or not between brackets). Looking-at presupposes having looked-for, but the reverse is not necessarily true. This assymetry in the necessary-and-sufficient relations between looking-for and looking-at suggests an order of priority between the two in terms of the way consciousness is built up from its basic components.

Not every state of consciousness is both categorially and presentatively intentional, i.e., both a looking-for and a looking-at. For example, some emotions, when conceived in their essential noetic purity, and when analysed in detail, entail no particular noema; they entail only a looking-for, not a looking-at. In answer to the objection that I would have to have looked *at* the object, in my imagination at least, before I could know what to look for, the reply can be given that an emotion only very *broadly* circumscribes certain vague attributes of whatever class of phenomena might satisfactorily serve its ends (especially where these ends are of a symbolizing nature, as they always at least partly are). Also, as we saw in Chapter III, emotions do not generally intend specific objects (except in the trivial sense that every event in my past history is part of the whole intentional object of any feeling I might have); it intends rather a future *mood*. That is, it hopes to actualize some future conscious state, rather than to actualize some future state of affairs in the world. An aesthetic object, for example, in order to be viewed and valued as such by consciousness, must have an explicating and symbolizing function.

Strangely enough, then, emotions do not directly value objective states of affairs in the world. The worldly object or state of affairs has only extrinsic value; it is in some pursued conscious phenomenon, which the object is needed to help along, that the intrinsic value is to be found. I only *seem* to perceive my desires as desiring states of affairs in the world because there is usually some state of affairs in the world that will be required (because of its symbolizing and actualizing function) if it is to be possible for me to feel a mood of the class which my original passion is intending. For example, I cannot fully feel that which Tchaikovsky's Fifth Symphony symbolizes for me unless I actually listen to the symphony.

This *mood*, which is intended by the passion, need not necessarily intend anything on its own part (except in the trivial sense mentioned above). In principle, it is possible for a mood to be neither a looking-*for* anything, nor a looking *at* anything. (It is true that it must be *accompanied by* symbolization; but, as pointed out earlier, there is a great difference between a symbol and an intentional object.) Rather than looking at some transcendent intentional object (i.e., an object over against itself), the mood is simply a *feeling of* that very feeling itself, which entails no externality; the externality only stems from an accompanying state of consciousness. And there is no need to call this kind of mood 'reflexive,' since it does not go 'outside' itself and then circle *back* to view itself, but merely remains within itself, sensing itself as an immanent and purely subjective affective tone (a quality with an intensive quantity). A passion, moreover, differs from a mood only in that the passion is that specific type of mood which also intends (i.e., looks for but not at) some other (future) mood.

Therefore, in terms of intentionality, three primary kinds of consciousness can be distinguished that make up the building blocks for the entire stream. First there is the *mood*, which feels itself as quality but neither looks for nor looks at any transcendent object; second, the *passion*, which both feels itself as quality and in that feeling feels itself as looking for some further (future, transcendent) mood; finally, there is the *presentative intention*, which feels itself as quality and in that feeling feels itself as looking *at* some transcendent object. Examples of this last type of consciousness would include memory, which feels itself as looking *at* a past consciousness; perception, which feels itself as looking at an external object; and synthesis, which looks at two past consciousnesses at the same time. Examples of combinations of the three types of consciousness would include deduction, which looks at the felt relationship between two past consciousnesses having been linked by synthesis, but also looks *for* a more unified statement of a newly-focused aspect of the relationship; and imagination, which feels itself as looking at an imaginary object inasmuch that its consciousness of the precise characteristics of this object is vaguely sketched in, but as looking for an actually existing object to the extent that the image may be of an object imagined as if it were real, as in Kant's imaginary hundred dollars.

The mistaken interpretation of passions as intending *specific* moods—and, still worse, specific things or states of affairs—can give rise to a complete hedonism which serves only to block empathy with other people and therefore block needed symbolization and lead to de-stabilization of the conscious progressions which need to be explicated. In its most basic role as the desire to be conscious, passion intends mood, but no *specific* mood; on the contrary, it only broadly circumscribes specifications as to what kinds of moods will and will not do. For example, the mood must be such that the part it plays makes the overall progression of moods across time have variety, intensity, and not an excessive amount of pain, and the passion also intends that there should be *some* mood.

The observations so far noted can be synthesized in terms of the attentional matrix as an array of possible states of consciousness. At any given moment along the flow, there is a finite number of these possibilities that will be feasible given my situation in the world. Of these many possible states of consciousness, at each moment only one can be chosen (or a very few—for the sake of simplicity, let's speak as though only one could be chosen). This choice is made on the basis of the directedness of each *previous* branch of the matrix. We shall therefore call each branch that is actually taken a 'vector,' because it has both a direction and an intensity or magnitude. The sequence of vectors chosen as consciousness progresses through the attentional matrix would appear diagramatically as follows:

Because each vector, however, is both a passion and a mood (the passion constitutes its directedness and the intensity of this direction; the mood is its felt affective quality and the intensity of this quality), we should change the above notation to show that each vector is two-dimensional rather than one dimensional. On one axis there is the directedness of the passion; on the other, there is the felt quality and magnitude of the mood. To represent this situation, let's make each vector into a triangle.

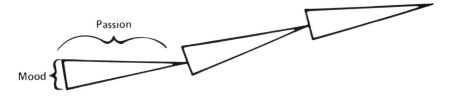

We can conceive of the triangle also as being polarized: At one pole is the mood, at the other the passion (and they gradually fade into each other).

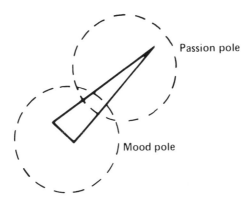

The region where the two poles overlap represents the area in which I can be conscious of the unity of both in one stroke. These poles are actually more like force fields, which sometimes theoretically extend far outward from their nuclei, but which in practice are only appreciable within a certain area. This means that to some minuscule extent I would always be conscious of both poles, even if I were living mostly in one or the other; but the consciousness of one pole might be negligible, while at the same time having the capability of being focused and therefore intensified to the extent of becoming noticeable.

We must finally make still another modification. We noted above that a passion intends not an object, but a future mood, or a complex of several future moods. We shall represent this aspect of motivation graphically by directing each vector not at some static moment where it ends and the next one begins; rather, let's aim it *at* the *next mood*.

It thus chooses the next mood to actualize not on the basis of some objective considerations or other, but merely according to the immanent quality of the felt meaning of that mood.

Thus each mood, since it has been authentically precipitated by a preceding passion, has within itself a passionate element which intends a future mood; and the future mood which this passion intends is itself an impassioned mood, intending a still further mood. This last is true because the underlying passion for being conscious (thus experiencing still further passions) intends only the kinds of moods that are passionately involved in an unfolding creative project whose aim is to maintain, explicate and carry forward the permanent state of change which is consciousness itself, whose continuing to exist always implies changing into something different from what it already is.

It can now be seen how *presentative intentions* function in the successful progression. We noted above that in order for the progression to succeed, it is necessary that it be symbolized concretely; and that if concrete practical dealings in the world of means and ends are involved, the relation of means to end (and the end intended is always an emotional value) must at the same time assume the relation of symbol to symbolized. Thus at any moment in the flow of consciousness, an intended concrete situation in the world will be implicated; the ways in which this situation is perceived, and which aspects will be focused upon, will be chosen for their symbolic value—that is, for their effectiveness in helping to explicate and focus felt meanings. The addition of this symbolic function of transcendent or presentative experience yields a picture of the way consciousness unfolds which is more true to life:

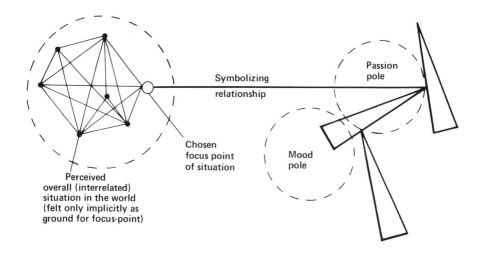

But we must add to this picture the point previously noted, that everything in my past experience is part of the whole intentional object of my present experience. This means not only every past aspect of my perceived-overall-situation, as is indicated by the interrelated network of points in the diagram (some of these points are there in the present tense, some in the past), but also every subjectively felt mood and passion in my past. In fact, the past objective situation is only retained by means of the felt continuity in the stream of moods and passions. Some of the unfocused aspects of the situation thus refer me backward to the past moods and passions, and this is the symbolizing or explicating function of the unfocused aspects (i.e., those that were focused in the past but have now receded into the ground for the present figure). These past concrete perceptions help my moods and passions to transcend their temporal encapsulation and allow their overall relationship to be felt. This felt overall relationship in the course of moods and passions is the transcendental ego, or creative component of cognition. Its continuity carries over from the past and is partly governed by the situation (which at the same time is partly chosen by a past passion). It is accomplished by means of vectorial explication, and is essential to stabilization, which occurs when the situation has to a sufficient extent been chosen for its meaningful symbolizing-explicating value.

At the next moment in time, when new situation-aspects are perceived, these new aspects do not merely *replace* the old aspects; they are *added to* the old aspects, and to some extent they cause the old aspects to be seen *better*, because within a broadened perspective. (We speak here of the optimally successful attention-progression, not of those that become blocked, distorted or deflected, and hence alienated.) The perceived situation thus expands, and the network of felt references to past moods and passions becomes more complex, but at the same time clearer because seen within a more comprehensive horizon. This continuous revising influence further facilitates the peculiar process of perpetual change which is necessary to the continued existence of consciousness. At this new moment, then, the old focus-point—along with the moods and passions it implicates—recedes into the perceived overall situation and becomes ground for the new focus point.

This increased clarity in the network of felt references to past moods and passions makes possible that particular type of consciousness capable of remembering and synthesizing felt meanings, therefore capable of knowing how I got where I am in the matrix and why—the process referred to earlier as stabilization.

We have attempted to represent the way in which the process of explication functions in every attention-progression, though usually the subject of the progression does not to a very great extent focus on this process. Most of us, in fact, in our everyday activities focus primarily on the present transcendent object that is perceived only at the point where one passion leaves off and the next mood begins. There is no reason to suppose that living predominantly in this transcendent attitude should block the flow of connections just described; in fact, such an attitude would, on the contrary, appear necessary to the transcendental ego's self-explication. What, then, does block this flow, and how does such a blockage lead to alienation? That will be the subject of the next section.

In connection with the general theory of motivation elaborated here, it might be charged that a kind of egoism is at work—that according to this theory, it would be impossible for anyone to value anything other than his own consciousness, except as an extrinsic means toward the end of explicating his own consciousness. But such an implication, it might be argued, would be patently absurd, because it is a fact that some of us do value the well-being of future generations, which cannot possibly affect our future consciousness in any way whatever, since we will be dead at the time. The answer to this objection, however, is that, in valuing the well-being of future generations, we empathize with mankind considered as an abstraction. And this is something that we must do to the extent that we wish to exist as human beings at all. If we did not empathize with the general form of mankind, we would correspondingly lack the ability to empathize with particular human beings, as discussed more fully elsewhere.[3]

2. The blocked attention progression: totalization and alienation

By describing the 'successful' attention progression, we have described the non-self-alienated progression, or at least the one which is not extremely self-alienated. The successful progression ideally escapes alienation from itself precisely because it is *not* the most successful one from a drive-reductionistic viewpoint; that is, it is not essentially the one most conducive to happiness or contentment. It is, one might say, the most honest or authentic way, even in cases where dishonesty would serve the interest of happiness better than honesty. If happiness has any empirically definable meaning at all, then one must admit that the person who consoles himself that 'the grapes were sour' is happier than the one who storms away cursing his lack of a stepladder. But, for our purposes here, the latter exemplifies the more successful attention progression because, being the more self-honest, it allows a greater degree of being-conscious with the ontological status that belongs to consciousness. The slave who spits in his master's face—or even imagines himself doing so—may well be more fully conscious in the long run than the happy but servile slave, precisely on account of experiencing his lot for what it really is. Moreover, he is then free to move beyond these feelings to others, whereas experiences which are purposely blocked out of consciousness for purposes of self-deception are prone to return to block the conscious progression itself, as we shall see.

We noted earlier that intersubjectivity can be the most helpful of all art forms in terms of explicating moods and passions. For the purposes of human emotions, dialogue is perhaps the most appropriate of all symbolic concretizing functions, primarily because dialogue has the capacity to unfold in patterns that correspond to the step-by-step progressions of passions and moods. It must of course be conceded that dialogue always makes use of one of the other forms of symbolization, such as music, speech or visual representation. That dialogue should utilize the other arts for its concretizing functions only further shows that dialogue is an extremely complex art form which is capable of being sensitive to the most subtle nuances of the progressions. But the superiority of intersubjectivity as art, in this sense, perhaps lies most of all in the ability of another consciousness to adapt his concretizing patterns of response to the consciousness that the speaker has previously expressed—the flexibility of the form, which allows it to continually maintain relevance in improvisatory fashion.

In dialogue, the feeling is always at least partly felt (usually in its mood pole) before it is given symbolic expression. Once it is expressed (in terms that are defined universally—i.e., in terms of respects in which things can be similar or different), then the universalizing interpersonal field of possible perspectives reacts in terms of the mood which has now been expressed. The possibility of a broadened perspective first facilitates a more transcendent attitude toward the feeling, in this way bringing it home with clearer focus and thus more intense immanent awareness; the mood is then felt also in its non-reductive passion dimension, and this passion motivates the next mood, which is again symbolized and carried forward in the same way. For this reason, intersubjectivity is potentially the most concretizing of all forms of symbolization. Attempting to live my own conscious progressions without authentic discourse with other people would be more difficult than trying to play a game of chess without the board—though, as we have seen, it is theoretically possible; it seems, furthermore, that anyone who can play without a board can play better with one.

Of course, it does not follow from this argument that a person should spend all or even most of his time attempting to interact with other people. On the contrary, it is vital that there always be a moment in the process when one is freed from the structure of interaction. This freely imaginative phase in the flux allows the immanence and feltness of the felt meaning to be pursued in its own self-directed rhythm and pattern. After the feeling has been expressed, transcended, focused more clearly and intensified, then the person must return into himself to experience undistractedly the immanent felt quality and the motivated directedness of the now-progressing experience. Also, the realm of dialogical concretizing functions need not be limited to speech. Any *action* which is relevant to an interpersonal sphere—and to some extent a merely imagined action—can be a symbolic expression of one's felt meanings and can thus achieve the transcending function of discourse with others.

Not only is a dialogical structure of symbolization helpful in the unfolding of conscious progressions; this unfolding could not possibly take place without such a structure. (Of course, one can, and typically does, engage in dialogue with oneself, but this type of dialogue alone is not enough for some purposes, because it is not concretizing enough. Eventually, I must go back out into the world.) The progressions could not move forward without a dialogical structure because the later steps in the progression will be unforeseen in their fullness, thus the matrix of symbols needs to readjust its game plans at every juncture. If the first step is not answered with an appropriate readjustment, the second step will never be felt fully enough to achieve symbolization, and the progression will come to a halt.

When conscious progressions are continually and consistently thwarted in this way, the eventual result is a de-intensification of feeling, a breaking up of parenthetical structures, a blocking of vectors, and finally a substantial loss of transcendental ego. At this point, the person's creative project may well be abandoned or forgotten. He 'adjusts' to the immediate situation and becomes self-deceptive, by way of defense against the ensuing meaninglessness of the resulting substitute states of consciousness (since he is no longer able to generate non-reductive meanings).

Perhaps the classic illustration would be the army sergeant whose frustration at having been the object of the wrath of the officers above him 'causes' him, in some sense, to behave in a violent or aggressive way toward his men: His men are the intentional object of his anger, in the Husserlian theoretical framework, since they are that to which he is attending in the anger; but they are not the cause of the anger, although he thinks that they are. Thus, either it is possible for his consciousness to have an intentional object of which he is unaware, thinking that the intentional object is something other than what it is—in which case phenomenological reflection is confronted with a serious problem in determining what the intentional object of an experience is, so that the problem of self-alienation contaminates the description of the phenomenon (and therefore the true essence involved may be interpreted wrongly or in such a way as to be biased in favor of prejudices or linguistic confusions of which one is unaware)—; or else knowing that the men in his charge are the intentional object of his experience (of anger) does not really penetrate to the essence of the experience, which involves also some relation to the officers who provoked it in a manner of which the sergeant is incapable, in his present condition, of becoming aware. The sergeant's anger 'at' the officers, of which he is unaware, and his anger at his men, must therefore be non-independent moments of one complex experiential totality. A further problem then becomes one of deciding where to draw the line between one simple act and another, so that the relations of founding and founded acts can then be considered. Either of these alternative approaches to the problem, however, involves in some way dealing with the problem of self-alienation as a propaedeutic to phenomenological description, the authentic performance of the phenomenological reduction, and the intuition of essence.

The acuteness of the problem can be focused still more sharply if we consider Husserl's distinction between the intentional object of an experience and the symbolization of the experience, as discussed in Chapter III. For Husserl, there is a clear distinction between the symbols that are used to call forth an experience, such as the words on a page, and the intentional object of the experience, which is the state of affairs symbolized by the words. If the sergeant's subordinates are regarded as offering him the opportunity to symbolize his feeling of anger at the officers—or, to use a simpler example, if instead of taking out his aggression on his men, he goes and gets drunk in a place where music is played and comes to experience what would seem to be an aesthetic appreciation of the music, then he is immediately attending to the music being played, not to the feelings which the music symbolizes for him (as one of its properties), and the intentional object of the feelings is seemingly absent from his consciousness altogether, since he is not thinking about it at the moment. Hence the importance of the transcendental ego, which alone can render possible a cross-temporal unity in which it is discoverable which objects are the intentional objects of which experiences. In this sense, the relation between the problem of the transcendental ego and that of self-alienation becomes clear. If the sergeant is to discover what the intentional object is of the experience he is having with the help of the symbolization provided by the music, he may need to find that many other past experiences go together to make up the one complex intentional referent of a founded act which at first appears quite simple. The question then arises, is it possible that the meaning of a larger number of experiences than one might suppose is acquired through the symbolizing properties of those experiences, and even primarily through these properties, i.e., through their ability to symbolize other experiences to which one is not primarily attending at the moment?

Ultimately, it may turn out that the sergeant would not have had that particular reaction to the wrath of the officers, were it not for other past experiences which constituted his modes of experiencing in such a way as to motivate that reaction. Thus the officers' hostile acts would be neither the whole cause nor the whole intentional object of the sergeant's experience. There is the possibility that, ultimately, as Chapter III suggested, everything in the sergeant's past experience must be included as a non-independent moment in the one complex intentional object of the present experience. The present experience would then reveal to him, not his relation to some specific object, but more generally and problematically, his relation to his entire world, past, present and anticipated. But to the extent that a transcendental ego unifies various experiences and incorporates them into a picture of their proper intentional interrelations, experiences and objects must be chosen which are capable of facilitating such an accomplishment. For example, the decision to read Husserl is itself such a choice. Moreover, and perhaps more importantly, a way of ordering and interrelating experiences must in each case be chosen on similar grounds—otherwise it would remain dubious, to the subject of the authentic phenomenological reduction, which intentional objects are the objects of which experiences, which are primarily symbols, etc. Such a choice could only be the work of a transcendental ego, of sorts, and could be present only to the extent that some such ego exists.

A situation which diverts or thwarts the authentically motivated progression of attention can be called a 'totalizing' situation. An arbitrarily imposed schedule of activities, for example, can be a totalizing experience. The reason for this effect is that each moment in the stream of consciousness takes on its meaning in relation to past and future moments. The meaning of the twentieth move in a game of chess can only be felt if I am able to carry over from the previous moves a feeling for their rationale and implications. Constant or extended interruptions can disrupt this feeling. There is an analogous aspect in real life. Suppose we represent the successive points in time in the stream of consciousness by means of a row of dots (below). To the extent that these moments are meaningful, they refer forward and backward in terms of the structure of the progression that is being pursued:

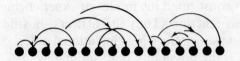

To the extent that such relations are chopped off by an arbitrarily imposed sequence of non-symbolizing and therefore nonauthentically-motivated activities, the result is a decrease in the meaning not only of the whole progression, but also of each moment individually:

The crossed-out areas above might represent time consumed in a meaningless, monotonous work activity; the times between these areas, with their limited interrelations of meanings, might correspond to some short-term 'recreational' activity or 'outside interest.'

Probably a more common case is the configuration of the work-play split, belonging, for example, to the person who lives two separate lives—one at work and the second at home or in his 'off' hours:

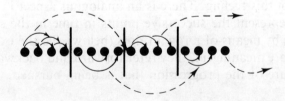

This pattern is more hopeful, because it shows that man is at least to some extent capable of overcoming the totalizing effects of the arbitrary chopping-up of his time (although the dotted line represents a less complete relation than the solid line). But it also reveals one of the more harmful effects of the reductionistic orientation toward life. Life in more complex forms of civilization can be so often geared toward mechanical needs to the exclusion of human needs, that the schism and conflict between the two tends to be taken for granted. For similar reasons, there is usually a relation of radical irrelevance between 'working' hours and 'off' hours.

When what I must do for a livelihood, because of the way in which social institutions are ordered, is irrelevant to my values and to my 'real life,' then arises the problem of 'grasping,' or what the Buddhists call *trishna*. A situation arises where there are two distinctly compartmentalized species of time: work-time and play-time. The object then becomes to minimize the one and to maximize the other. Everything is in this way simplified for the worker, and he is absolved of any responsibility except to do his job obediently. He is then left with one ready-made aim of life and with one ready-made means toward this end: Minimize work, maximize fun; "grab for all the gusto you can get." But then everything comes to seem boring, and life becomes a 'drag' (i.e. the felt progression of time drags, will not move forward; nothing really matters). At the same time that this oversimplification is taking place, the interpersonal network becomes so complex that few if any of the people involved can do anything to affect it or change it. Means and ends are split from their primal unity and lose any sense of direction or motion.

This paradox leads to a circle. The work-play dichotomy itself, which oversimplifies, both causes and is caused by the very desire to simplify everything. For example, the idea of attending school for a certain number of years and then 'graduating,' with fanfare and a mood of finality—is motivated by a desire to get the learning process out of the way and have nothing more to do with it, except in special cases where one's work necessitates it. Since school—learning—fits neither into the category of work nor into that of play, it is worked into the schema on the pretense that its primary function is preparation for work. Indeed, the students have been taught long before graduation—perhaps inadvertantly—to make the association 'work = thinking = unpleasant,' and the implicit converse, 'fun = not-thinking = not doing anything useful or constructive.' But work itself, which is usually thought of as being unpleasant simply because it is work, is in fact unpleasant for a different reason—because it is never 'my' work, but rather the boss's work or the teacher's work; freedom, in such a case, almost by definition becomes 'goofing off' or 'consuming,' because there are only short minutes or hours of freedom—never enough to establish the momentum and direction for an interesting creative project to develop (a project which in its usefulness might more resemble a new form of 'work' than 'recreation'). Picture someone who runs his own electronics shop, or a jazz musician eager to perfect and expand his technique—the rare, romantic enthusiast who often shows up in detective novels, who 'lives and breathes' his work; whereas the electronics worker on the assembly line for the purpose of making money for his corporation, or the musician condemned to perpetual 'top forty' music, may well say that he can only 'breathe' when the work day is over. Such overgeneralization of the phenomena into the categories of 'work' and 'play' constitutes a constriction of the existential *a priori* which will take on immense importance for the way in which the transcendental ego functions, especially with regard to its alienation from itself.

The parenthetical pattern of the person who leads a double life sheds light on an interesting aspect of self-alienation. The same ability which frees man from being imprisoned in the present moment by making transcendent unity possible, also gives him the choice to wall off one part of his consciousness from another part, so that the two never confront each other. I might be a priest during my working hours and a mad rapist at night. In a less extreme case, I might simply act according to presuppositions which are mutually contradictory because of the experienced mutual irrelevance of the two levels of conscious progression.

When totalization assumes the form of an interpersonal situation, such a situation can be conceived as interpersonal alienation. When one's authentic conscious progressions are alienated from one's interpersonal context, the tendency is to feel 'superfluous' or *'de trop.'* The authentic progressions are unable to find symbolization, whereas the totalizing community continually encourages other conscious progressions—ones that are alien from one's authentic direction—and continually offers opportunities for the alien thought patterns to be symbolized. The resulting *self*-alienation, which ends in inauthenticity and/or loss of intensity and focus of felt meanings, can then be conceived as 'dehumanization.'

It was in essentially these terms that Marx originally introduced the terms 'alienation' and 'dehumanization' in the *1844 Manuscripts,* where he states that "The demand to renounce illusions about one's situation is a demand to renounce a situation that required illusions."[4] Marx implies here that, in the capitalist society, the workers cannot be really conscious of their historical situation (as ironically exemplified by instances of workers beating up and harassing distributors of leftist pamphlets). They cannot be historically conscious, according to Marx, *because* the system by which the worker is victimized dehumanizes him to such an extent that his consciousness is no longer capable of being an authentic and full self-consciousness. The concrete actuality of competition against other workers has more reality for him than the remote possibility of an egalitarian society with full employment. As to the way in which this process comes about, Marx expands on a Hegelian theme. Spirit or Mind, finding it necessary to know itself by objectifying itself through creative, self-expressive production, cannot know itself by creating a product which symbolizes nothing in relation to the worker's own motives and purposes in life.

For example, after spending eight hours printing sixty boxes of identical computer cards, I shut down my press, pick up one of the cards—and there is the imprint of my labor; there is *me* objectified, because there is where my consciousness has been occupied for the past eight hours. The card's absurdity is the mirror of my absurdity. I, in turn, am only the mirror of its absurdity. If I have been objectifying myself in the physical movements of running a printing press which prints only card after identical card all day, without this activity's resulting from authentic motives (e.g., that I am proving my worth to society, or that I own the printing company myself), then the question arises: What kind of symbolizing function is this activity capable of assuming? How broad is the range of possible selves capable of being symbolized (or 'objectified') by this activity, and are *any* of these possible selves authentic possibilities for me?

Thus an equilibrium obtains between arrays of available symbols (activities in the world that I can use to define myself) and the range of possible thoughts and feelings that can maintain themselves within such a structure: (1) A state of consciousness must be concretely symbolized in the world before it can be fully experienced and carried forward. (2) If the consciousness is not concretized in this way, it will die out, thus reducing the extent to which I am a conscious existent. (3) If the activity in which I am engaged and the values which I am motivated to pursue are not capable of assuming the relation of symbol to symbolized, then either I must desist in doing the activity, or I must desist in having the value or consciousness which fails to get symbolized and objectified as a result of the activity. (4) If I cannot or will not desist in the activity and therefore must desist in having the state of consciousness or value direction, then either I must lose part of my conscious being, or I must try to deceive myself into having feelings that *are* capable of being symbolized by the activity which I must perform. If the action cannot be forged to fit the motivation, then the motivation will be forged to fit the action. For this reason, the factory foreman, like Sartre's cafe waiter, finds it difficult to play his role for a number of years without effectually *becoming* the role.

With regard to the means of production, it is important to avoid overstating the case here. It still may be wholly possible for someone to perform even the most meaningless task without being dehumanized, provided certain conditions are met. Our earlier conclusions regarding the requirements of symbolization do not imply that no one can be conscious if there is *anything* in his environment that does not further symbolization; they imply, rather, that no one can be conscious, in the sense of a transcendental ego, if there is *nothing* in his environment that furthers symbolization. If condition **A** tends to block symbolization, while condition **B** tends to further it, the question is whether **A** outweighs **B** in importance or *vice versa*. Practically speaking, if the actual work itself is completely meaningless, the crucial variable becomes to what extent the concomitant *social* relations are also meaningless. Only if there is authentic intersubjectivity among the workers, and/or some intense emotional situation outside the job, can consciousness override and overpower (i.e., succeed in ignoring) the totalizing and dehumanizing social and physical conditions on the job. If the worker's consciousness can override these conditions, then it will become possible for self-alienation to be avoided, and eventually for historical self-consciousness to develop. The point, however, is that the brain and body alone cannot carry forward the symbolizing functions indefinitely without help. Thinking with one's brain alone is only a temporary measure used to fill in the gaps between other, more concrete symbolisms. Eventually, the realm of interpersonal relations, political action, etc., must come into play.

For these reasons, if we reflect upon the problems considered thus far, their circular nature becomes increasingly impressive. To what extent does self-alienation, in the guise of self-deceptive social myths, *purposely* strive to protect itself from the truth by reproducing itself in the future and in other consciousnesses so as to escape the challenge of authentic intersubjectivity? To what extent does an alienated *status quo* tend to align itself in such a way as to actively resist the overcoming of alienation? If we are to try to find our way out of self-alienation, it might be helpful to consider the circular *system* of which our own self-alienation is only a moment or phase. Such a social and political investigation, however, would take us too far afield from the original purpose of the present study, which is to analyse the interrelations of the material realm, consciousness, the self, and self-alienation.

One further issue must be addressed. Since the theory of consciousness and epistemology interrelate with each other, we should now examine the ways in which the theory of consciousness posed here interrelates with epistemology. What are its epistemological assumptions and implications?

3. Epistemological ramifications

We noted at the outset that the theory of consciousness tends to form a circle with the epistemology we use to study it. Our response to this dilemma was to proceed on the basis of as few epistemological assumptions as possible—fewer, it seemed, than the champion of "presuppositionlessness" himself. Husserl supposed that our experiencing of a subjective datum within the phenomenological reduction reveals the intentional object of the experience; we rejected this assumption, allowing that subjective distortions due to limited and biased category structures may actually lead to an incorrect assessment of what the intentional object of an experience is.

But now let's see how epistemological considerations are affected by the theory of consciousness itself. It becomes evident that the fundamental assumption that consciousness exists or occurs leads to a grounding for the applicability of logic to things in themselves. And this same fundamental assumption, together with logic and with the process-substratum theory, leads to a refutation of idealism and to the conclusion that we empircally experience things in themselves, though imperfectly.

(a) **The applicability of logic.** It is with deceptive simplicity that Aristotle specifies the principle of noncontradiction as "that which anyone who knows anything knows." It may well be that anyone who can claim to know anything must admit that if I believe propositions **A** and **B** both to be true, and if **A** and **B** contradict each other, then the conjunction of the propositions must be wrong. But even in such a clear-cut case as this, the tendency is to overlook the fact that there is something even more certain and apodictic—to the subject of the judgment—than the truth or falsity of the propositions: The one thing the subject knows with total indubitability is the *fact that* he is conscious of believing such-and-such to be the case. This consciousness may even present the beliefs as being different from what they really are; but the fact that the consciousness *is there* is more indubitable than any conclusions about whether that which the consciousness seems to present is really true—more indubitable because necessarily prior and more immediate. Somewhere in the act of feeling itself lies an immediate awareness so self-evident that it takes a special, unaccustomed act of reflection to focus on it. Like an overused word, its meaning is furthest from us because closest to us.

When my eyes feel the presence of a tree, it may or may not be true that there is really a tree there, or that my representation of the tree is accurate to the *n*th significant figure; but the fact that my eyes *feel* the presence of an alleged tree (whether the feeling is justified by external reality or not) is more indubitable than the universal and necessary applicability of logic either to phenomena or to noumena. There are always feeling-data the existence of which I can know with apodicticity, regardless of whatever else I may doubt and regardless of what I may doubt about their nature or ontological status. These must not by any means, however, be confused with the concept 'sense data,' which refers to sensations in their representational aspect. By the feeling intended here is meant my subjectively felt sense of the meaning of the subjective experience, as well as my subjective belief that it is a representation (i.e., that there is really a tree out there in time and space). It is the existence and the particular quality of the feeling which is certain, not its representational aspect.

But these feelings are in themselves *noumena*, in the Kantian sense, because of the necessity and indubitability of my subjective sensing of them. They are not merely important in that they attempt to provide me with a means of knowing the outer world—e.g., the supposed tree—although they often do that too. But they are also important in that they *are* part of the world: Namely, they are that part of the world which I myself comprise, recalling the definition of 'I' outlined earlier. And because of the peculiar coincidence of reality and subjectivity in feeling, feelings constitute a portion of reality that is known with more certainty than anything else could possibly be, although the statements I make *about* them may well be false, and although they may not 'mean' or 'be about' what I think they are about. (The problem with this type of knowledge is never that it asserts too much, but rather that it asserts less than I tend to think it asserts. For example, it is strictly improper to say "I feel that you are totalizing me." The feeling *simpliciter* does not posit that there is a person out there causing me to feel a certain way; this is added in judgment by thought. The more concise statement would be "I feel totalized," and when I state it in this way—provided I have defined 'totalized' experientially and only experientially—there can be no doubt about it, although it is highly dubious whether the person out there is doing some activity which I would like to label 'totalizing.') Perhaps I cannot know that sweetness is an essential or primary—or even secondary—'property' of sugar; yet I can know what the experience feels like with reference to which I have defined what I mean by the term 'sweet' to myself. I may even forget what the feeling felt like; but in the instant when I feel it, there can be no doubt as to its being the subjective quality. It is not 'what' I feel, but only 'how' I feel that the feeling presents to me.

Thus there is a synthetic claim, or a set of synthetic claims, that is more dependable than even any analytic claim could ever be: That I am conscious, that I feel and experience in a subjective sensing of something (I am not yet sure what). I know this could be no illusion, because to experience an illusion is just as much to experience as to experience a reality. If I dream that I dream, the process of dreaming about dreaming is something that is *really* taking place.

Husserl correctly insisted that the principle of identity, or non-contradiction (being two sides of the same coin), flows from this sensing. When a composer attempts to capture in music the mood of a certain moment, he knows that there is only one set of tonal relationships capable of doing the job precisely. And in knowing this, he knows that the feeling (and its corresponding symbolization) has its own identity and structure, distinguishable in specifiable ways from numerous other possible feelings, whose symbolization would be correspondingly different. Thus the principle of identity—that something which is, is, for the moment at least, identical with itself and numerically different from that which is numerically different from it—this principle is applicable to feelings (or Gendlin's 'felt meanings'), which are noumena in the Kantian sense (not to imply that Kant would agree that they are noumena). This principle of identity as intended here is not to be confused with a merely semantic principle of identity which would maintain that a symbol has the same meaning if it recurs in a different context. The logical principle claims the identity of the referent only *in the given circumstances,* not necessarily if the circumstances should change.

But the *necessary* applicability of logic to this one class of noumena (at least) cannot be something we conclude by inductive or probabilistic psychological expectations that the future will be like the past. Then it would not be necessary or dependable. What makes it seem so dependable? Once we have reflected on the fact that we feel tired, for example, then we have already said to ourselves (perhaps not in explicit symbols) that we are tired; and if we say it over and over however many times, we know by the intentionality of what we mean that we have added nothing to the original statement. On the other hand, when we say that we feel both tired and not-tired at the same time and in the same respect, then when we honestly consider what we have said, we notice that it is not only false, but in fact both subjectively and objectively meaningless. With regard to what we *mean* by what we are saying, reflection reveals that it is impossible to meaningfully formulate a truly self-contradictory assertion. This is the principle of noncontradiction, which turns out to be nothing but a restatement in other words of the principle of identity. But what is the basis for asserting the *necessity* of the applicability of the principle of identity? Is it a logical or an epistemological assumption? And if it is either, then do we not either assume a great deal, or else fall into the epistemological circularity for which Kant and others have been criticized, basing logic on our epistemology while at the same time basing epistemology on our logic and its applicability to noumena?

The principle of identity (hence also the principle of noncontradiction) says that if we say something a thousand times, we have said no more than if we had said it just once. This, according to some, is dependable precisely because it asserts nothing about the original proposition except what was already contained in that proposition; it is merely a symbolic device for further clarifying the same meaning intention. And this would seem to be an appropriate characterization. But it is not entirely clear that this has not already entailed a number of logical steps in the very demonstration of logic's applicability.

In a strange way, this mutual dependence of logic and epistemology brings us to the heart of the mind-body problem, transposed into an epistemological problem. How can it be possible that an embodied mind, which functions supposedly in accordance with physico-chemical principles, also does not deviate from the rules of logic in the actual content of its conscious productions? When I perform a syllogism, I am not aware of obeying chemical laws; my sole reason for affirming the conclusion seems to me to be its objective truth and validity. It seems absurd to suggest that if that thought pattern did not happen to accord with such-and-such causal physical events, then there would be different logical rules. If the premise **A** impels me toward conclusion **B**, is it the fact that logic demands that I think **B** that is responsible for my concluding it, or is it that a chemical event, **a**, corresponding to the idea '**A**' happens simultaneously to have caused, through natural laws, the chemical event **b**, which happens to then cause me to think the idea '**B**'? Would it not be the most amazing coincidence if both the causality of the chemical transformation and that of the objective and valid logical entailment always happen to coincide? As Husserl asks in the *Logical Investigations*, what is the relation between the subjectivity of knowing and the objectivity of the content known? Some have attempted to explain away the dilemma by relativizing truth into an objective psychological event; but this begs the question and discounts what we actually intend or mean when we utter a logical statement. Others have taken the opposite alternative and divorced the mind from the body, making it a special type of substance which is not bound to any material; this is not only unintelligible on the grounds of the very logic that was meant to be preserved, but it is inconsistent with some parts of what we can only assume to be fairly reliable sensory experience. An interesting suggestion would be the one implied by Darwin, whose theory would suggest that it is indeed a remarkable coincidence that truth and neurophysiology happen to be constituted in such a way as frequently to coincide; but, like so many other remarkable biological coincidences, if it had not happened to evolve that way, the species would not have survived long enough for us to talk about it. This notion might to some extent calm our wonder, but it does not give us much understanding. It does not help clarify the epistemological basis for assuming that logic is applicable only to the realm of phenomena, or that it extends to noumena, or has applicability delineated in some other way.

It is commonly accepted that a computer works by the laws of physics, but computes mathematical truths. This fact does not surprise anyone any more than the discovery that building blocks or beads on an abacus invariably conform to mathematical principles. For it is the very fact that the parts of an abacus *conform* to mathematical truths which in itself constitutes the ability to 'assert' them. We can view the constitution of our ability to do the same in an analogous way. If one bead of an abacus combined with another did not equal two beads *in fact*, then the abacus would not tell us, out of its situated point of view, that one plus one is two. The human brain is more complex than an abacus, but its main essential difference is that it renders possible a *subjectivity* which *feels* the effects of the operations performed. It *is* not this subjectivity, but it renders it possible in the sense that it provides a concretely embodied system of materiality which subjectivity uses for symbolic purposes, while at the same time being nothing but a predicate *of* the interaction of the material with other material, etc.

But this analogy does not make clear, granting that I can *use* logic in particular cases, how I can *know* that this logic I am using is an avenue toward necessary and universal truth, without which, as Husserl says, it would not be logic at all. Again we must ask, what actually goes on that gives us intuitive, direct awareness of the apodicticity of logic?

By feeling the fact that I exist, I know—no logical steps involved—that whatever is other than me, if there is anything other than me at all, must *be* other than me; I feel my own consciousness (my being) as a discrete meaning. (That it is impossible to draw a precise line where 'I' leave off and 'the world' begins, is irrelevant. It is impossible to draw a precise line between red and blue on a spectrum, but this does not mean red is not different from blue.) But already packed into the meaning that something could be other than me is the subordinate meaning that it would *be*. This constitutes direct awareness that if anything other than me is, it is other than me; and simultaneously included in the meaning of 'being other than me' is 'being.' This is the way I immediately apprehend the core of the phenomenon that Parminides pointed to in the 'that which is, is' (leaving aside his denial of change). In the same direct way, I know that that which is not, is not. It is the irreducible meaning of being a part of whatever is that presents to me this fact about what is. There is no logical step involved in such a demonstration; it is merely a description of the way I know that that which is, is. But 'that which is, is' is essentially what logic says. The rest is a working out of a system of synonymous terms.

It is in this way that, when we say that logic holds for felt meanings, then since the world of phenomena is a felt world, we have already included our sensing of the world in those felt meanings for which logic holds. Logic then holds for phenomena as well. It is now clear how upside-down it would be to say that logic holds for phenomena but not for noumena. Indeed, the only thing that allows us to assert that it does hold for phenomena is that we already know that it holds for certain noumena—our feelings—and, by contrast, to whatever noumena are other than me, possible or actual.

(b) **The process-substratum theory negates solipsism.** It is interesting to note that, if we accept as premises (1) that logic is applicable, (2) that consciousness occurs, and (3) that consciousness has the ontological status of a pattern of change or process, then it can be deduced that solipsism and extreme subjective idealisms are untenable. By this we do not mean the kind of solipsism which says merely 'I am the only conscious being,' but rather the more extreme form of subjective idealism which says, in effect, 'It is impossible for me to know that there are any beings of any kind other than myself,' i.e., 'The world is my idea.' It is sufficient to point out several odd claims that would be entailed in a systematically solipsistic philosophy.

We saw in Chapter III that the term 'I' must be viewed as referring to my experiences, or at least to some of my experiences; it has the ontological status of a kind of experiencing process, as opposed to a physical thing. For, if I omit all aspects of my self concept besides my feelings, I find that my self concept remains; whereas, if I omit my experiencing while leaving all other aspects of my 'self' intact, nothing remains which could conceivably be called an 'I.' Experiencing is thus both necessary and sufficient as a defining quality of what I am, given certain qualifications discussed in Chapter III. This concept of the self, if correct, suggests that at least one inconceivable claim is implied by any solipsism: There exist changes (experiencing, sensing, thinking—in short, my self) but at the same time there exists nothing *which* changes, i.e., no substratum for the change. When I say 'I am the only thing there is,' I am asserting that my experiences (which are only changes) are the only things there are. Such a viewpoint would be logically similar to the position that there is such a thing as walking down the street, but that there are no such things as streets or feet. This conception of the nature of mental processes would not allow for the existence of any entities whereof my experiencing can be predicated. Nor can it be argued that the experiences simply are predicated of 'me,' since I myself *am* nothing but a constellation of the events in question; such a position would fall back into the concept of myself as a thing rather than a process. (It is not necessary to take any stand here on the dubious issue of 'substances,' as discussed in Chapter II. Whether the things of which my experiencing is predicated are substances or not is beside the point. Whether there are indeed any basic substances at all is beside the point.)

But an interesting possibility still remains. The solipsist could postulate the existence of just enough stuff for his experiences to be predicated of—for example, his own body (how much material that would take, exactly, would be difficult to resolve)—while still denying that anything besides just this much exists. This possibility raises the further question: Did the stuff of which my experiences are predicated exist before the experiences began to happen, or did it just come into being at the same instant that the experiences began to be predicated of it? And by the same token, if my experiences should stop happening (if for example I should die, or if I go to sleep at night), would the stuff remain, or would it suddenly disappear? The former alternative would seem tantamount to a denial of solipsism and an admission that at some time something did or does exist without the subject's awareness. The latter alternative is conceivable (though strangely *ad hoc*, besides entailing not only that something can come from nothing, but that something can continually pass back and forth into nothingness); however, it is subject to further problems.

One difficulty can be stated in the following way: I have had experiences during or after which I thought of myself as being somehow a different person from the one I had been previously. To a lesser extent, I am different now from the way I was yesterday, because yesterday I was watching a movie while today I am engaged in a different activity—remembering that I watched a movie yesterday, for example. However, the only evidence I now have that I (or some version of me of which the present 'I' is a slight modification) ever did watch a movie is that the present 'I' remembers it that way. Hence the feeling of watching-a-movie is not present to me now (as I engage in the activity of remembering it) as the same subjective experience that it was yesterday; I can only remember that experience as an *object* of my present experience. So is the solipsist to accept the existence of that person who yesterday sat watching a movie (or thinking he was watching a movie)? Or am I to say that he did not exist since nothing but *my subjective consciousness* exists (perhaps plus whatever material that consciousness is to be predicated of), and that therefore, as an *object* rather than *subject* (in my memory), the 'I' of yesterday never really existed, but only the one present 'I' exists? To put the question more decisively, if I kept *changing*, however slightly, from time to time, at what point would I cease to be 'me'? If someone shows me a baby picture of myself, am I to maintain that the baby never really existed since only 'I,' in terms of my present experiences, can really exist? If not, then at what point am I to say that I (and thus the whole illusory world) began to exist, and before which no events really happened but I now merely trick myself into thinking that they happened? Was the baby's consciousness enough like mine that I can say he was really the same as me and thus really existed rather than being just another of my present illusions? If so, then what about the fetus? Or the ovum?

But experiencing *is* a kind of change. Therefore, to the extent that I—as process of experiencing—exist at all, I have to have been born out of a (real) world that already existed. True solipsism, however, is compelled to assert that experience must take place without any time having elapsed from the beginning of the experience to the end, since by the time I had completed the process of experiencing one of my illusions, the beginning of that experience would already be nothing but an *object* for the immediately present subject. But every experience, no matter how spontaneous, must, like every good tragedy, have a beginning, a middle, and an end. The concept of an event or occurrence implies extension in time. Not even an illusion or self-deception could happen without some time elapsing during the happening of it. (This is true, that is, in the sense of 'time' which would define it simply in terms of change.)

The only sensible alternative to this consequence would be for the solipsist to say 'To the extent that my past selves were similar to my present self, they (and the stuff of which they were predicated) existed; to the extent that they differed from my present self, they did not exist.' But existence *simpliciter* (as opposed to existence *qua* such-and-such type of thing) is like pregnancy: There are no 'extents' involved.

(c) **Intersubjectivity.** Once it is granted that my consciousness exists, and that the stuff of which it is predicated exists (whatever system of physics one chooses as a description of the properties of this stuff), it also becomes apparent that consciousness has the capability of perceiving a wide range of things in the material world essentially as they really are. The reason for this is that we know that other people (to greater and lesser extents) perceive our states of consciousness as they really are. And the feeling dimensions of these states of consciousness are noumena, i.e., things whose existence is absolutely unquestionable to the subject of experience. But the most common way other people use to perceive our feelings is to listen to our speech; and speech is a system of physical phenomena—sounds made with the mouth or writing on a page. So it can easily be deduced that, if I express my feelings through speech, and other people more or less accurately perceive my feelings by perceiving a system of physical things (my speech), then they must also be perceiving the physical things more or less accurately. And if people can perceive my feelings (which I know are real) only to the extent that they can perceive the physical world (whose reality subjective idealists question), then the existence of the physical world becomes at least as certain as the existence of my feelings—whose existence is absolutely certain. So not only does logic apply to noumena as well as to phenomena, but we also perceive noumena with our senses—though of course our perception may be more or less inaccurate. The world we perceive is therefore, at least in its broad general outlines, the real (noumenal) world in this sense.

Of course, someone may object that I cannot be certain that others perceive my feelings for what they are, because I must first assume that my perception of the other person is accurate before I can conclude anything about his perception of me. The answer to this objection involves the way in which I am able to teach another person to communicate in a language I understand, and to continually increase the level of communication as measured by the language I receive back from him. For example, I may commit a logical error of which I remain unaware until the other person points it out to me. And even if the other person is not a conscious being after all, but only a cleverly programmed computer, the fact remains that the computer is accurately assessing my states of consciousness (which are noumena) by listening to the pattern of my speech in the physical world (which must therefore also be noumenal) The computer (or person) then perceives other aspects of the material world with the same perceptual apparatus, which then can legitimately be assumed to operate just as accurately as when it was perceiving my states of consciousness. Thus the physical objects it perceives with this perceptual apparatus must be assumed to be equally real or noumenal. It is also true that I may systematically and unconsciously deceive myself, inventing the other person's verbal responses to delude myself that the other person understands me. But this can happen only to the extent that my consciousness itself is self-alienated.

Suppose an observer, S., is attempting to perceive my feelings as I apodictically know them to be in themselves, and that I am attempting to ascertain (apodictically) whether to some extent his intuitive experience of my communication corresponds to the true state of affairs that I am trying to get across. Because there is something in the world other than me, I of course already know from the beginning that there is something out there. The question is, what? When I direct my attention out there, I perceive whatever is there with a greater or lesser degree of accuracy, with a greater or lesser degree of warpedness and subjective filteredness. The question now is, how much of the perception is misperception and how much is true perception of the genuine noumena that the feelings underlying S's perceptions (of my communications) *actually are*? (I know there has to be *some* amount of truth in my perception, for it tells me that there is *something there,* and as we just established above, at least this much is correct.)

What will be going on in this hypothetical transaction is then in effect that on the basis of the refutation of solipsism I assume, and also perceive, there is something there in that relation to me in which I rightly or wrongly imagine a *person* to be. I ask myself whether this something is really a person, and whether or to what extent I know this person as he really is, noumenally. Then, in a language which I understand inside me and which I have no reason to assume that S. understands, I throw at him several series of messages.

(i) In the *first series*, assuming that the content of the messages purports to be my own feelings which I am trying to communicate, I apply the following interpretation of the interaction. It is evident to begin with that the degree of my comprehension of him or of any message he might throw at me will have to be less than or equal to the degree to which he speaks a language which I can understand; and this can be no greater than the degree of accuracy of his comprehension of the sense of the messages I have been aiming at him. Now it can similarly be assumed that the degree of this accuracy of S's comprehension fo the sense of the message I am trying to impress upon him will have to be less thanor equal to the degree to which my message was directed toward S. in a language that he can understand or learn to understand; otherwise, there is little hope that he will know what I am saying and that my noumenal reality is being laid bare for him.

But in turn, we can also say that the degree to which my message *is* directed to S. in a language he can understand can be no greater than the degree to which I perceive S. as he really is, or correctly assume that he is of such-and-such character, shares certain items of cultural attitude, belief and knowledge, etc., at least insofar as these things pertain to his ability to understand my language and that which is communicated in the language. It follows from the chain of inequalities set up in this way that the degree of my comprehension of the sense of his messages is less than or equal to the accuracy of my perception or presumption of who the person S. really is in himself (noumenally). This means that, to the extent that personalities are misperceived, the communications will talk past each other and make no mutual sense (assuming, that is, as in the present case, that the content of the communication is my states of consciousness which I am trying to get the other person to understand).

(ii) I now proceed to the *second* series of messages, which are to be built on the foundation of the first. In each of these new messages, I add something in each case, no matter how slightly, to what I said to S. in the first series. And, however small a percentage of this he picks up, it *adds* some amount to his perception, and therefore, by the chain of inequalities set up above, adds to my subsequent comprehension of his response. In this way, if I continue, I know that my understanding of how much he perceives is in fact increasing. I thus become familiar with the amount of comprehension which I have added, and I know that at least this amount is in fact understood. I then repeat the whole process over and over, each time taking note of the increase in my comprehension of his response and of the particular content of the perception which gave rise to this increase. My perception of the accuracy of his perception therefore increases in accuracy and sooner or later must begin to approach a fairly good approximation of what really is the case.

Proportionally to this increase in my perception of the accuracy of his perceptions, what is presupposed as necessary ground by it, *via* the chain of inequalities, is that *his* perceptions of *me* have increased and are now approximating what I know apodictically to be what I am in myself, really. We have thus reached the point of transition from my metaphysical knowledge of myself, to someone else's metaphysical knowledge of me through empirical intuition, through the senses.

We now have several facts at our disposal. We know by *reductio ad absurdum* (from (b) above) that the idea that nothing can be independent of my subjective modes of knowing it is an exaggeration of the limitations of human perception. We also saw that we can know apodictically, completely, and exactly, certain momentary feelings, with the qualifications mentioned in that discussion—an instance of certain knowledge that turns out to be by no means vacuous.

This last claim has the interesting consequence that, if experiences are noumena, then *time* cannot be viewed as *merely* a subjective form of sensibility, although many temporal relations may vary considerably from subject to subject. But the really-real, the thing-in-itself, is extended in time; for we have direct and indubitable knowledge that our feelings—these really-real entities with which we are acquainted—*are* extended in time. Of course, this does not necessarily mean 'time' either in the Newtonian or in the Einsteinian conceptualization, or in any particular sense of relations among measured-off units. It simply means that, where time is defined in terms of the fact that there is change, there must be time because the one thing we are acquainted with completely, our experiencing, is nothing but change.

But if there is change, then *something* must change. Thus there is space—again, not necessarily in any particular conceptualization in terms of empirical or quasi-empirical properties, etc.; but, where space is defined in terms of the fact that there are some things (and these need not necessarily be attributed with any particular quasi-empirical properties either, such as 'substance'), then there must be space—not as a condition for the possibility of the validity of an experience that may or may not be valid, but a *real* space as a condition for the possibility of *real* experience.

Does this mean, then, that we should attach absolute credibility to empirical experience? And does it mean, further, that we should attach absolute credibility to objectivistic psychology, whose purpose is to perceive the subject-made-object as precisely as possible? The inaccuracies inherent in the hypothetico-deductive method discussed in Chapter I, especially as they apply to psychology, would seem to indicate not. While it is true that another person's consciousness and character can be inferred with some degree of verisimilitude, it is also true that we often misperceive character, even in the continuing two-way interaction. And, as we have seen, it is the continuing two-way interaction that allows us to validate most fully our perception of another person, or to formulate a more correct perception. In the simple, one-way perception, there is a whole plethora of things that can go wrong.

One problem is that, to the extent that a perception is based on inferences (as it always is in objectifying psychology), we must infer from an *effect* (our perception of physical things that we can actually see) to its supposed *cause* (the conscious phenomena we are trying to study). But everyone is aware that any given effect may have been brought about by any number of possible causes. So it would be necessary, strictly speaking, to control for all possible causes for an effect before reaching a conclusion about the true cause. And this problem opens the way to all the biases and distortions peculiar to the use of hypothetico-deductive reasoning in psychology, as Chapter I suggested.

What we must conclude, then, is that, while the general *modes* of human experience are not completely twisted out of shape, as the subjective idealist would have it, neither can we usually have much certainty in our perception of the mechanisms of particular things, and still less when it comes to particular people. We can make hypotheses, rule out certain explanations as extremely unlikely, validate theories with statistical correlations, etc. But in the realm of psychology especially, we should maintain a generous degree of respect for all the errors and distortions to which this method of investigation is always prone, even under the best of circumstances.

On the other hand, the more we contrive ways to use the other person's *subjectivity* as it interacts with our own, the more chance we have to acheive understanding. For, as the above analysis just suggested, it is in the give-and-take of the two-way interaction that messages are continually modified, communication increases, and, based on the increase in communication, we validate the amount of improvement in our understanding of the other person's consciousness. At the same time, however, the same process continually reminds us that our understanding is far from complete, and we are continually surprised by the necessity to revise it.

In sum, what must be said about the epistemological presuppositions and implications of this theory of consciousness is this:A minimum of presuppositions are made without any more ultimate foundation than themselves: (1) That consciousness exists and is delimitable from that which is delimitable from it (the principles of identity and non-contradiction as applied to states of consciousness). (2) That the subjectively felt quality of a state of consciousness is known to the immediate consciousness itself even though (a) my states of consciousness may not be completely transparent to *me* (since 'I' cannot be assumed to be numerically equivalent with each of my states of consciousness); (b) the state of consciousness may be remembered incorrectly at a later time; (c) the *object* of the state of consciousness (either the intentional object or the real object) cannot be assumed to be what the consciousness seems to think it is; (d) statements made reflectively *about* the subjectively felt quality of a state of consciousness cannot be assumed accurate *ipso facto*. From these minimal presuppositions, it follows that (3) Logic is applicable to noumena (including consciousness itself). These basic assumptions, it must be confessed, are conjoined with (4) a kind of coherence analysis of the realm of all theories of consciousness, in which logic is used to eliminate alternative theories, leaving the process-substratum approach as the only one that seems to make sense of the data. The process-substratum theory then implies that the physical realm, which serves as substratum for consciousness, must really exist, though no specific theory of the meaning of physical concepts such as 'matter' and 'energy' need be involved, and no concept of 'substances' or 'ultimate substratum' is used. It would be difficult to imagine how a viable theory of consciousness could be based on fewer epistemological presuppositions than the ones listed here.

The very distinction between 'analytic' and 'synthetic' statements reflects the uncomfortable epistemological position in which philosophy in general has tended to find itself. Analytic claims, traditionally considered the proper domain of philosophy, are always true by definition. They are truisms, trivialities, tautologies, statements that are so utterly obvious, at least theoretically, that they should hardly need saying at all. They can hardly even be called statements, for they express nothing but what was contained in the definitions of the relevant terms, which is to assert little that is more substantial than simply their sense in relation to each other. On the other hand, synthetic claims are equally uninteresting. They are just a matter of looking to see, of reading numbers from meters, etc. Although they may often prove useful, they are not considered the concern of philosophy and are relegated to the methods of the natural sciences. They concern what man can do (hence the expressions 'operational definition' and 'experimental operation') but not what he is, or what he should do, and perhaps not even what the world is. What, then, is philosophy? A collection of truisms? Perhaps even if philosophy is no more than this, it does have a certain therapeutic value, since sharpening and learning to apply the analytic tools does in some ways expose and help to counteract many of the self-alienating thought patterns most of us were innocently forced into during the most helpless years of our childhood. This in itself might be valuable if we could decide on some grounds or other what 'valuable' means—still another instance where the alternatives of 'analytic' and 'synthetic' knowledge seem to offer little resolution.

The crux of this problem (neglecting for the moment the possibility of phenomenological reflection) would therefore appear to be that anything we can possibly say that means anything will inevitably fall into one or more of three difficulties: It may be true by definition—an empty tautology devoid of any substantial content, hence trivial and of interest to nobody; or it may have empirical content at the expense of falling into epistemological prejudice, losing any possible grounding in apodicticity, necessity or relation to the entire world order, and becoming contingent, subjective, relativistic, mutable, probabilistic, etc.; or, finally, it may be wrong. (Even the assertion just made, by the way, is obviously trivial, although when we view it phenomenologically we see that it expresses an essential impossibility.)

Kant was seriously troubled by this stifling and embarrassing problem, and attempted to answer it with his Copernican shift toward according the subjectivity itself with certain qualities which in turn entail certain necessities and regularities in the experienced world of phenomena (but not necessarily in the true world of noumena). Yet examination of the basic steps of Kant's reasoning reveals that the whole of his own argument can escape the dilemma only by recourse to circularity (a circularity which he seems partly to recognize in the introduction to the *Critique of Pure Reason*): namely, there is a mutual dependence of his logic and his epistemology upon each other. The question must arise as to which is the assumption and which the conclusion. Kant sees man's categories as categories of reason; it is natural that he should see them this way since, if he is looking at man from this perspective, the *validity* of these categories is presupposed—or else Kant would not be seeing man's modes of experiencing for what they really are. (This circularity in Kant's thought is discussed in more detail in Heidegger's *What is a Thing*,[5] especially pp. 148-153, 209-211, 223-224. Heidegger's *Kant and the Problem of Metaphysics*[6] and pp. 114-118 of Husserl's *Crisis*[7] also shed interesting light on this issue.)

It may well be, therefore, that the present essay—which deals in a way with the problem of the circularity of epistemology itself—is plagued by an even more stringent set of prolegomena than the ones Kant set forth. Kant shows how it might be possible—perhaps even inevitable—that there be such animals as necessary, *a priori* synthetic truths. But he does not appear to succeed in establishing a method of knowing with apodicticity what any of these truths are, even in the realm of epistemology. In general, it becomes evident that I cannot base an adherence to the universal applicability of a logic (to either phenomena or to noumena) upon any epistemological system which in turn has already been based upon logic in the first place. And in deriving his epistemology, Kant takes many logical steps. It is obvious that logic is not really one of the principles that turn out to be universal (with respect to phenomena) as a result of Kant's analysis, because that analysis is, precisely, an analysis; and as such it presupposes the principle of noncontradiction.

Logic and epistemology are in this respect a circular system that can only be gotten into by a leap—or at least which stands in need of some other method of being gotten into. It would appear that, as Kant's paradigm case illustrates, an epistemology can only be justified by logic, whereas a logic can only be justified by an epistemology. Where does the circle begin? Most philosophies have taken logic as the starting point and proceeded toward epistemology. Then some have gone back and justified logic in terms of their epistemologies, in the same breath with other universal principles, such as causality.

But what about the alternatives to Kant's approach proposed by modern positivist and empiricist philosophies, which choose to base epistemology on a logical formalism?

The original motivation for the linguistic approach to philosophy was an authentic one. Hume noted that the reason he could not understand many philosophers who talked about 'the Absolute' and 'the Real' was that they themselves did not know what they meant. He thus resolved to deal only with what he could know and explicitly understand.[8] A.J. Ayer furthered the cause by declaring that any statement for which no method of determining its truth or falsity is provided, is meaningless and not worthy of philosophical consideration.[9] This class of statements, of course, included ontology, religion, metaphysics and aesthetics.

At this point, it might well be that philosophy has worked its way out of a job, for all that remains of philosophy after such a strict dismemberment as this is epistemology—and if we accept as our epistemology Ayer's "criterion of verifiability", only empirical science remains.

Ayer's criteria, however, have been torn apart and rejected by Hempel and other recent philosophers of science and logicians. Indeed, it has been demonstrated that it is impossible in general to formulate consistent empiricist criteria for truth or adequate knowledge, or even for the meaning of words, which would both include and exclude all the classes of statements which they should. We have discussed the literature demonstrating this impossibility elsewhere (see Introduction, note 3).

These criticisms of the positivist, empiricist, and linguistic criteria for meaning raise the same question that was left unanswered in the discussions of Kant: Is there a difference between the meaning (to me) of a thing-in-itself and the meaning (to me) of my subjective impression or opinion of the thing as it presents itself as phenomenon? Can I honestly reduce the former to the latter? Can the subject's modes of experiencing—including even the most sophisticated methods of scientific experimentation—be simply *defined* as access to the truth? How am I to ascertain the relation between them? We can ask these questions the same of phenomenology as of neo-Kantianism and naturalism. Kant made no attempt at answering them. Both phenomenalists and phenomenologists, in different ways, ultimately hope to answer them by calling upon us to perform some sort of 'reflection,' hoping thereby to arrive at the 'pure data of consciousness.'

This concept of "conscious data" is problematic in several respects, as to some extent we have already hinted. Price has successfully clarified it up to a point, leaving several unanswered questions. In his book *Perception*,[10] Price insists that natural science cannot answer the epistemological questions about perception. The idea that the world which I perceive is related to the "scientific" world of protons and electrons as appearance to reality is based on a fallacy, according to Price, and would destroy the very premise on which science itself depends. Physiology says that when I look at a tomato, light rays emanate from the object and impinge on my retina, and that this stimulates the optic nerve, which in turn causes a change in the optic centers in the brain, etc. But this explanation is based on constructs which stem in turn from perceptions of the same kind as my looking at the tomato. The question Price asks is: When I see a tomato, how much is there that I can doubt? I can doubt whether it is a tomato that I am seeing, and not a cleverly painted piece of wax. I can doubt whether there is any material in the thing there at all. But one thing, he says, is indubitable: There exists a red patch of a round and bulgy shape, standing out against a background of other color-patches, and this whole field of colors is directly given to my consciousness. In this way, he articulates the now-familiar concept of 'sensa' or 'sense data.'

Price then answers several objections. One is what he calls the *'a priori* thesis,' which protests on the ground that in perception we are actively thinking—judging and classifying—and it is impossible to do less than this. But Price says simply that this is irrelevant, because it only might show that nothing stands *merely* in the relation of givenness to the mind without also standing in other relations, but it does not suggest that nothing is given at all. And the 'empirical thesis' (either in the form of subjective idealism or as rationalistic idealism), which says that the world is entirely constructed by 'thought' or 'mind,' is refuted on the grounds that association (in the sense of thought) is a relation and implies that there are two terms to be associated with each other; and the presence of two things that are to be associated cannot be further explained by recourse to the concept of association. Whatever is associated must first be given or rest on the given.

Price then goes on to consider what concepts would be added to that of a sense-datum if someone wanted to call it a substance, or a material object, or an impression, or an innate idea, etc., and concludes that these all depend upon further claims about the relation between sense-data and external 'reality.' He therefore concludes that sense-data, in their most basic conceptualization and in the sense in which they are 'given,' are not substances, but events or occurrences.

This is an interesting conclusion, and one whose implications can be better seen if we approach the problem from a slightly different angle. For although this way of thinking stems from a phenomenalism which in the light of Husserl's analyses is an oversimplification, there is still much that can be learned from its study. Gestalt psychology, as was seen earlier, suggests that what is perceived is the *relation* between the parts of a whole phenomenon, not the parts themselves. With the exception of the one possible case of direct reflection on a sense-datum, Gestalt's point here is not at all inconsistent with what Price says, since he calls thought an association. But as Sartre and Merleau-Ponty stress, vision, taken in the most immediate way, already opens onto a world of intended things, not mere qualities, and qualities themselves have part of their meaning in terms of relations. Only in theory can I reflect on these sensa that somehow prior to my awareness get translated into intended objects. Least of all can I become conscious of this supposedly cognitive process of translation itself. How is it possible, then, that I see relations among parts I cannot see, and that I am conscious of complex predications upon simple sense data without being conscious of the sense data themselves?

This is perhaps the most enlightening form of the problem of unconscious consciousness, for it poses the question in a way that hints at the direction of an answer: What must the ontological status of consciousness be if it is to be consciousness of a process without first being consciousness of the things which are in process? Similarly, what must the ontological status of this consciousness be if it is to be consciousness of relations without first being consciousness of the things which are in relation? In short, what must the ontological status of this consciousness be if it is to be capable of such operations as a prereflective thetic consciousness of which the consciousness is unaware, but which affects and is affected by *reflective* thetic consciousness of which this same consciousness *is* aware?

For more cogent elucidation of this question, we must turn to phenomenology, because phenomenology confronts consciousness *as* consciousness rather than attempting to explain it as a thing-like mechanism. Other arguments cited in earlier chapters also show that any acceptable treatment of 'reflection' would have to be phenomenological.

When we turn to the phenomenological treatments of the issue, we find a disconcerting paradox. There seem essentially to be two alternative approaches within the context of a constitutive intentional phenomenology; one approach taking Heidegger as its leading figure, the other Husserl. But the seemingly valid Heideggerian criticism of Husserl proposed by Kockelmans and others appears to be only an *instance* of what Husserlians sometimes criticize Heidegger for;[11] and the Husserlian critique of Heidegger seems only an instance of what Heidegger criticizes Husserl for. Each criticism seems devastating from within its own perspective, but devastated from the contrary perspective.

Husserl deems it possible, by means of the reduction, to abstain from being interested in questions of 'reality' [*realität*] in the field of objects. But if we take the Heideggerian perspective, we see that a consciousness *seen while performing the epoché* is not a true picture of a consciousness which for ontological reasons must be presumed to be always already concernfully related to a real world. As Merleau-Ponty also points out, a true epoché while taking consciousness itself as the object is impossible.[12] That world which, in A.W. Watts' terms, man was born *out of* rather than merely *into*[13] could not have been a mere intentional object of consciousness, and therefore it cannot be related to as merely intentional by a consciousness which is already born with consciousness *of* this birth-out-of-the-world. One might even go a step further to argue that preconsciousness, or at least consciousness of others, precedes self-consciousness both developmentally and logically. And Husserl would not contradict this. But he would also argue at this point that, although the world out of which I was born was not as such a mere intentional object, and does not even present itself intentionally as having been only this, it is still true that *I can only know it as such*; the world *as perceived* of necessity can be nothing other than a system of intentional objects.

Husserl, as we saw earlier, says that when I intend the world, I intend it *as* real; perception does not posit the world as imaginary. Thus, either (1) consciousness is authentically interested in the world as a system of intended objects, disregarding whether these intentions correspond to some objective reality, in which case there is no difference between being interested in an object 'as if it were real' and being interested in it 'as if it were only imagined'—which Sartre has shown on Husserlian grounds would be absurd;[14] or (2) consciousness is also interested in the reality of certain objects—in which case there will be no counter to Lukacs' argument: that after a phenomenological description of the essential structure of the object as intended has been completed, then the time comes to move outside the brackets and talk about whether the essence *as perceived* really has anything to do with anything real on the side of the object.[15] But any such discussion of a real world, aside from the fact that consciousness can regard its intentional object as if it were something real, seems to lie outside the self-imposed limits of the phenomenological reduction. Heidegger, on the contrary, can speak of the reality Lukacs insists upon, by analysing the ontological relatedness consciousness must bear in its being to this reality.

On the other hand, Heidegger, who takes the contrary position, runs into the contrary problems. Heidegger transcends the problem of appearances and realities by showing that man is always already in-the-world (i.e., a real world). But then the *appearance*, that there seems to be a problem of appearances and realities, would appear to become a deceptive appearance, in which case there would still indeed be such a problem. Someone will respond that Heidegger's position is that deceptive appearance is only one of the ways man relates to a real world which he still primordially but non-thetically understands in this relatedness. Nonetheless, from the viewpoint of *conscious* consciousness, the deceptive appearance continues to cover over reality; and Heidegger's own results, obtained by phenomenologically apprehending eidetic essences involved in the meaning of consciousness-in-the-world (if we interpret *Dasein* as having consciousness as one of its more prominent features), reveal that this consciousness, because it is in the world, must confront the world through existential *a priori* which have already been conditioned by realistic or self-alienated encounters with the world in the past. Man thus comes to know himself by studying his past with a view to uprooting his prejudices. But as Calvin Schragg asks,[16] how can man see his prejudices *as* prejudices if he looks at them already in a prejudiced manner? How, in fact, can Heidegger determine what man's essential categories or existential *a priori* are, if Heidegger himself provides himself with no method of knowing whether he can only look at man as influenced by the categories through which *he* is looking?

Either way we approach the problem, it seems that man can only know his intentionalities by perceiving them through intentionalities, and then not only does he fail to know himself or his prejudices and self-deceptions; but in fact he is now *two* steps removed from the truth.

It would be hopeless at this point to appeal to the life-world. If a reflective experience is perspectively impoverished, a prereflective experience is going to be even more so. If I cannot decide whether it is my children I am really angry with, or whether I am merely frustrated with my day at the office, then I will certainly be no *more* enlightened if I simply *live in* the supposed anger-at-my-children.

The epistemological deck is thus badly stacked against any genuine approach to the problem of self-alienation. I have no criteria for determining whether I know something, or even whether my intentional categories are meaningful or meaningless. And I cannot 'correct' my experience by reflecting on the distorting aspects of the intentionalities involved. In no sense can I rely on my own intentional experiences until after I have discovered a method for avoiding self-alienation and therefore self-deception. This means that the discovery of such a method will have to do without the help of any particular intentional experiences. We have to find a way of focusing on experience *without regard to any particular intentional objects* and *without the mediation of reflection through intentional perspectives*. The first step in this process would seem to be devising a general ontology of consciousness based on as few epistemological and ontological presuppositions as possible. That is what the present study has attempted to do.

4. Conclusion

We are now in a position to state with some certainty several ontological conclusions about consciousness and its relation to physiology and to the self. We have seen that conscious events are not *caused* by their corresponding physiological events because it would be impossible in principle to establish any directionality for such a relation; to introduce a manipulation into the pattern which is consciousness would necessarily be *ipso facto* to change the corresponding physiological correlates in the process. This does not mean that consciousness has no causes (that would be a different question); it means simply that a given conscious event is not caused by the corresponding neurophysiological event which is inseparable from it in the sense of being necessary and sufficient for it.

At the same time, parallelism, interactionism, and the identity theory fail to characterize the relationship between consciousness and physiology adequately. Parallelism and interactionism become untenable because of internal difficulties, whereas identity theory fails to recognize and account for the fact that phenomenological reflection upon a given conscious event and objective observations of the same conscious event can never even in principle yield precisely the same kind of information, although there is no need to suppose in this connection that phenomenological data are incorrigible. Identity theory also fails to recognize that the localizability of higher-order patterns is a different kind of localizability from that of lower-order forms, and that causal explanations for higher-order forms require additional explanations beyond those which would suffice to account for the lower-order processes that 'compose' the higher-order ones. In terms of its observability, its localizability, and the kind of causal explanation it would require, then, consciousness has properties that are not precisely matched by its physiological correlates. This means that, from an ontological perspective, only the process-substratum model is capable of making the interrelation between consciousness and physiology intelligible.

A possible epistemological implication of this point should be mentioned which was not pursued here because it was beyond our scope: If consciousness must exist in the form of a process which takes the physical as its substratum, then time must have *actuality* in some sense, as the dimension of reality in terms of which processes, by definition, are different from their substrata. Thus time must have more than a merely subjective being and should not be conceived as *merely* a subjective mode of apperception. There would remain, of course, a distinction among the three types of time: (1) phenomenological time; (2) objective time as a way of measuring objective occurrences; (3) time as it 'actually' is, the interaction between which and phenomenological time produces objective time. If a process *actually* differs from its substratum, it must do so in terms of an *actual* time. This difference is then perceived by us in terms of both objective and phenomenological time, depending upon which perspective we take on the observation.

With regard to the enigmatic nature of the various forms of 'unconscious consciousness' (prereflective consciousness, etc.), we have seen that the explanation must be framed in terms of the structure of the self. One state of consciousness may be alienated or opaque in relation to another because the transcendental unity of consciousness is not automatic, but is a difficult task which the self must accomplish. The relevance of selective attention and inattention, in terms of categorial or 'looking for' intentionality, led us to an investigation of the immediate and on-going motivation to direct attention at each moment as the explanation for preconscious and unreflective conscious phenomena.

The ontological status of the self consists in being both a concretely-experienceable mode of consciousness and a unifying and directing principle which provides the continuity and structure of the ego, enabling the latter to become transcendental, to some extent, by escaping its encapsulation in the present conscious state. Both the saliency of certain objective ways of organizing experience and the process of selective attention provide unity in the stream of consciousness, but only the consciousness which motivates selective attention in the interest of the self-explication of consciousness is the 'self.' This consciousness is the non-reductive value which consciousness places on there being further or additional consciousness, which in turn motivates the creative component of cognition—the only component that can be concretely felt, yet serves as the transcendental unifier which makes possible creative reasoning and the avoidance of diversion into irrelevant sequences of reasoning. It is the creative component, operating often on a prereflective level, which decides at each instant what will be thought *about*, and which of the four more basic functions of consciousness will be applied to it, in which order of sequence and in which style of attention progression (productive or receptive)—ultimately influencing what kinds of theses will be thought to be true or false by the ego. The more transcendental unity there is in the functioning of the ego, the less alienated are its various states of consciousness from each other, thus the more adequate the category system and the less consequent distortion of reality. The creative component of cognition, which is the self, motivates this transcendental unity because it insists upon the continuation of the conscious process through self-explicating symbolic activities.

It is the opportunity to symbolize each moment in the stream of consciousness that determines whether this self-explicating process will be possible or not. Social systems are organized so as to facilitate the symbolization of certain forms of consciousness while preventing the symbolization of others. In this way, to a greater or lesser extent, societies are able to create, if they choose to do so, people who for the most part share the beliefs that the society needs for them to have. The more self-alienated the members of a society become, the more they will attempt to protect their own self-alienating ideologies by structuring the social system so as to control consciousness in this way, thus avoiding the loss of cherished distortions and misperceptions, functioning as sedimented and prereflective presuppositions, which support the self-alienated category structure. This process, however, would be the subject of another study, perhaps more sociological than philosophical in nature.

Ralph D. Ellis
Clark College
Atlanta, Georgia 30314

NOTES

INTRODUCTION

[1]William James, "Does 'Consciousness' Exist?" John McDermott, ed., *The Writings of William James* (New York: Random House, 1968), 169-70.

[2]Richard Rorty, "Mind-Body Identity, Privacy, and Categories," *Review of Metaphysics,* 19, 24-54.

[3]R.D. Ellis, "Phenomenology and the Empiricist Criteria for Meaning," *Philosophy Today*, 24, 146-152.

[4]Alvin Goldman, "The Compatibility of Mechanism and Purpose," *Philosophical Review*, 78, 468-82.

[5]See Chapter II, notes 2, 4, 5, 7, 11, 12, 16, 20, 21, 24 and passim.

[6]Maurice Merleau-Ponty, *The Structure of Behavior*, A. Fisher trans. (Boston: Beacon, 1967).

[7]Merleau-Ponty discusses these problems in *The Phenomenology of Perception*, Colin Smith trans. (New York: Humanities Press, 1962).

[8]Karl Popper and John Eccles, *The Self and Its Brain* (Berlin: Springer-Verlag, 1977), 1-60 and passim.

[9]E.g., H.G. Godamer, *Truth and Method* (New York: Seabury, 1975); Don Ihde, *Hermaneutic Phenomenology* (Evanston: Northwestern University Press, 1971).

[10]Ludwig Landgrebe, *Major Problems In Contemporary Philosophy* (New York: Ungar, 1966).

[11]Ellis, "Phenomenology and the Empiricist Criteria for Meaning."

[12]See Chapter II.

[13]Donald Kiesler, "Some Myths of Psychotherapy Research and the Search for a Paradigm," *Psychological Bulletin*, 65, 110-36; see also note 4, Chapter IV.

[14]Godamer; Ihde.

[15] R.D. Ellis, "Existentialism and the Demonstrability of Ethical Theories," *Journal of Value Inquiry*, 16, 165-75.

[16] Edmund Husserl, *Ideas*, W.R. Boyce Gibson, trans. (London: Collier, 1969), 101-43.

[17] Husserl, 180-88.

[18] Maurice Merleau-Ponty, *The Primacy of Perception*, J. Edie, ed. (Evanston, Northwestern University Press, 1964), 75.

[19] Jacob Needleman, *Being in the World* (New York: Harper & Row, 1968).

[20] J.S. Bruner, *Contemporary Approaches to Cognition* (Cambridge: Harvard University Press, 1961).

[21] D.P. Ausubel, *The Psychology of Meaningful Verbal Learning* (New York: Grune & Stratton, 1963).

[22] Ernst Cassirer, *Einstein's Theory of Relativity*, W. Swabey and M. Swabey, trans. (New York: Dover, 1953).

[23] Wolfgang Kohler, *Gestalt Psychology* (New York: Liveright, 1929); K. Koffka, *The Principles of Gestalt Psychology* (New York: Harcourt, Brace & World, 1935).

[24] Jean Paul Sartre, *Being and Nothingness* (New York: Washington Square Press, 1966).

[25] Sartre, *The Transcendence of the Ego*, F. Williams and R. Kirkpatrick trans. (New York: Noonday, 1957).

[26] See Chapter III.

[27] For elaboration of this point, see Eugene Gendlin, *Experiencing and the Creation of Meaning* (Toronto: Collier-Macmillan, 1962).

[28] Merleau-Ponty, *The Structure of Behavior*.

[29] Aron Gurwitsch, *The Field of Consciousness* (Pittsburgh: Duquesne University Press, 1964), 17-36.

[30] David Jones, "Emergent Properties, Persons and the Mind-Body Problem," *Southern Journal of Philosophy*, 10, 423-433.

[31]Jones, Robert Coburn, "Persons and Psychological Concepts," *American Philosophical Quarterly*, 4, 208-221; Roderick Chisholm, *The First Person* (University of Minnesota Press, 1981); Robert Nozick, *Philosophical Explanations* (Cambridge: Harvard University Press, 1981); see also Sydney Shoemaker, "Persons and Their Pasts," *American Philosophical Quarterly*, 7, 269-85; Wolfe Mays, "Persons and Self-Reference," *Journal of the British Society for Phenomenology*, 1, 55-56.

[32]R.D. Ellis, "Agent Causation, Chance and Determinism," *Philosophical Inquiry*, 5, 29-42.

CHAPTER I

[1]Paul Feyerabend, "Materialism and the Mind-Body Problem," *Review of Metaphysics*, 17, 49-66.

[2]D.M. Armstrong, "Is Introspective Knowledge Incorrigible?," *Philosophical Review*, 72, 418-19.

[3]Richard Rorty, "Mind-Body Identity, Privacy, and Categories."

[4]For example, Guy Lafrancois, *Psychological Theories and Human Learning* (Belmont: Wadsworth, 1972); F. Kanfer and A. Goldstein, *Helping People Change* (New York: Pergamon, 1980); Kiesler; it is also noteworthy that Melvin Marx, writing in Encyclopedia Britannica's 1980 *Science and the Future* yearbook, cites the resurgence of introspective investigations as the year's most important event in the field of psychology (382-85).

[5]J.B. Watson, *Behaviorism* (2nd ed.) (Chicago: University of Chicago Press, 1930); "Psychology as the Behaviorist Views It," *Psychological Review* (1913), 20, 157-158.

[6]Husserl, *Phänomenologische Psychologie* (Den Haag: Nijhoff, 1962), passim., see especially pp. 35-41; Amedeo Giorgi, "Phenomenology and Experimental Psychology," *Duquesne Studies in Phenomenological Psychology* (Pittsburgh: Duquesne University Press, 1971), I, 6-29; H. Spiegelberg, *The Phenomenological Movement* (The Hague: Nijhoff, 1960); Needleman; D.P. Schultz, "The Human Subject in Psychological Research," *Psychological Bulletin*, 63, 358-72; Merleau-Ponty, *The Phenomenology of Perception; The Primacy of Perception; The Structure of Behavior*.

[7]Carl Rogers, "A Theory of Therapy, Personality, and Interpersonal Relationships as Developed in Client-centered Framework," in S. Koch, ed., Psychology: A Study of a Science, III (New York: McGraw-Hill, 1959); Abraham Maslow, *Motivation and Personality* (New York: Harper and Row, 1954).

[8]Husserl, *Phänomenologische Psychologie*, 35-41.

[9]Merleau-Ponty, *Phenomenology of Perception*, vii-xxi; Sartre, *Transcendence of the Ego*; see also infra., Chapter III.

[10]Merleau-Ponty, *Phenomenology of Perception*, 434-456; A. Manser, *Sartre: A Philosophic Study* (New York: Oxford University Press, 1966), 164, D. Tulloch, "Sartrian Existentialism," *Philosophical Quarterly*, 2, 31-52; M. Kaye, *Morals and Commitment* (London: Covent Garden, 1971), to mention only a few.

[11]Thomas Kuhn, *The Structure of Scientific Revolutions* (Chicago: University of Chicago Press, 1962).

[12]Kuhn.

[13]Needleman, 9-46.

[14]Hans J. Eysenck, *The Dynamics of Anxiety and Hysteria* (New York: Praeger, 1957).

[15]Henri Poincare, *Mathematics and Science* (New York: Dover, 1963).

[16]Merleau-Ponty, *The Structure of Behavior*, 10-93 and passim; Kurt Goldstein, *The Organism* (New York: American Books, 1938); Aron Gurwitsch, *The Field of Consciousness* (Pittsburgh; Duquesne University Press, 1964).

[17]Maslow, 27-30, 35-38.

[18]Carl Hempel, *Philosophy of Natural Science* (Princeton: Englewood Cliffs, 1966), 40-45.

[19]Eysenck.

[20]K.W. and J.T. Spence, "Relation of Eyelid Conditioning to Manifest Anxiety, Extraversion and Rigidity," *Journal of Abnormal and Social Psychology* (1964), 68, 144-49.

[21]R.B. Catell, *The 16 Personality Factor Questionnaire*, Inst. Pers. and Abil. Test, 1950.

[22]Cattell.

[23]Eysenck.

[24]Spence.

[25]Giorgi, 13-15.

[26]Giorgi, 10.

[27]Giorgi, 9.

[28]Schultz, 227.

[29]R.D. Laing, *Self and Others* (New York: Pantheon, 1969).

[30]Jean-Paul Sartre, *Psychology of the Imagination* (New York: Washington Square Press, 1966).

[31]Merleau-Ponty, "The Child's Relations With Others," *The Primacy of Perception*, 96-155.

[32]Sartre, *Sketch for a Theory of the Emotions* (London: Metheun, 1971).

[33]See note 6.

[34]Merleau-Ponty, *The Primacy of Perception*, 75.

[35]Laing, 32.

[36]Eric Berne, *Games People Play* (New York: Grove Press, 1967).

[37]Georg Lukacs, "Existentialism or Marxism," G. Novack, ed., *Existentialism versus Marxism* (New York: Delta Press, 1966).

CHAPTER II

[1]U.T. Place, "Is Consciousness a Brain Process?" *British Journal of Psychology*, 47, 44-50.

[2]Richard Brandt and Jaegwon Kim, "The Logic of Identity Theory," *Journal of Philosophy*, 64, 515-37.

[3]Merleau-Ponty, *The Structure of Behavior*.

[4]Wilfrid Sellars, "The Identity Approach to the Mind-Body Problem," *Review of Metaphysics*, 18, 430-51.

[5]Thomas Nagel, "Physicalism," *Philosophical Review*, 74, 339-56.

[6]Isaac Asimov, *The Human Brain* (New York: Mentor, 1965), 193ff.

[7]Norman Malcolm, "Scientific Materialism and the Identity Theory," *Dialogue*, 3, 115-25.

[8]Merleau-Ponty, 46ff.

[9]Merleau-Ponty, 40ff.

[20]Merleau-Ponty, 38ff.

[11]Donald Davidson, "Actions, Reasons, and Causes," *Journal of Philosophy*, 60, 686.

[12]Goldman, *A Theory of Human Action* (Englewood Cliffs; Prentice-Hall, 1970), 4.

[13]J.L. Mackie, *The Cement of the Universe* (Oxford: Oxford University Press, 1974), 160-92.

[14]Goldman, 6-8.

[15]Nagel.

[16]John O'Connor, ed., *Modern Materialism: Readings on Mind-Body Identity* (New York: Harcourt, Brace & World, 1969), 15-17.

[17]P.F. Strawson, "Persons," H. Feigl et. al., eds., *Minnesota Studies in the Philosophy of Science*, vol. II (Minneapolis: University of Minnesota Press, 1958).

[18]Bernard Williams, *Problems of the Self* (London: Cambridge University Press, 1983).

[19]Davidson; see also Davidson's "Mental Events," L. Foster and J.W. Swanson, eds., *Experience and Theory* (Amherst: University of Massachusetts Press, 1970).

[20]Norman Malcolm, "Explaining Behavior," *Philosophical Review*, 76, 97-104.

[21]Stephen Noren, "Anomolous Monism, Events and 'The Mental'," *Philosophy and Phenomenological Research*, 40, 64-74.

[22]Gilbert Ryle, *The Concept of Mind* (New York: Barnes and Noble, 1949), 32ff.

[23]Ludwig Feuerbach, *Principles of the Philosophy of the Future* (Indianapolis: Bobbs-Merrill, 1966), 47.

[24]Vivian Weil, "Intentional and Mechanistic Explanation," *Philosophy and Phenomenological Research*, 40, 459-73.

[25]Richard Taylor, "Fatalism," *Philosophical Review*, 71, 56-66; see also S.M. Cahn, *Fate, Logic and Time* (New Haven: Yale, 1967).

[26]Mackie.

[27]Goldman, "The Compatibility of Mechanism and Purpose."

[28]Malcolm, "Scientific Materialism and the Identity Theory."

[29]Michael Simon, "Action and Dialectics," *Philosophy and Phenomenological Research*, 39, 468-9.

[30]Goldstein.

[31]Sartre, *Sketch for a Theory of the Emotions* (London: Methuen, 1962).

[32]Weil, 466.

[33]Goldstein.

[34]William James, "Does 'Consciousness' Exist?"

CHAPTER III

[1]Williams, 16.

[2]Williams, 9-18.

[3]Williams, 3.

[4]Sartre, *The Psychology of the Imagination* (New York: Washington Square Press, 1968).

[5]Williams, 14.

[6]Williams, 14.

[7]D. Kretch, *et. al.,* "Relations between Brain Chemistry and Problem-Solving among Rats," *Journal of Comparative and Physiological Psychology*, 53, 509-19.

[8]Sartre, *The Transcendence of the Ego.*

[9]Sartre, *Being and Nothingness*, Hazel Barnes, trans. (New York: Washington Square Press, 1966).

[10]Husserl, *Ideas*, 102, where he says, "It is from out these centres of experience *(Erlebnisse)* themselves that through the adoption of the new standpoint the new domain emerges. . . . The phenomenological *epoché* renders 'pure' consciousness accessible to us."

[11]Husserl, *Ideas*, 102-3.

[12]Husserl, *Ideas*, 307.

[13]Husserl, *Ideas*, 307.

[14]Sartre, *The Transcendence of the Ego*, 52; Eugen Fink, "Die Phänomenologische Philosophie Edmund Husserls In Der Gegenwärtigen Kritik," *Kantstudien*, 38, 356ff.

[15]Contrary to Sartre's statement (*The Transcendence of Ego*, 88) that "The ego is a noematic rather than a noetic unity. A tree or a chair exist no differently."

[16]Sartre, *The Transcendence of the Ego*, 69.

[17]Ludwig Landgrebe, *Major Problems In Contemporary Philosophy* (New York: Ungar, 1966).

[18]Gerd Brand, "Intentionality, Reduction, and Intentional Analysis in Husserl's Later Manuscripts" in J. Kockelmans, ed., *Phenomenology* (Garden City: Doubleday, 1967), 197-217.

[19]Merleau-Ponty, *Phenomenology of Perception*, Introduction.

[20]Merleau-Ponty, *Primacy of Perception*, 75.

[21]As Kuhn suggests.

[22]Husserl, *The Crisis of European Sciences*, D. Carr, trans. (Evanston: Northwestern, 1970), 182.

[23]Knut Erik Tranoy, "The Foundations of Cognitive Activity," *Inquiry*, 1976, 131-50, points out that the values and priorities of the scientific and academic communities determine what kinds of research will be considered important, and therefore carried out. Thus the value-determined direction of thought indirectly limits its *content*.

[24]Needleman, *Being in the World*, develops the idea that quasi-Kantian category structures can limit what we see by limiting the preconceptual categories in terms of which we thematize our perceptions, and that there can be such category structures which differ in individuals, and which change.

[25]Husserl, *Crisis*, 186.

[26]Husserl, *Ideas*, 157, where he refers to a "fundamentally different ego for each separate stream of consciousness."

[27]Erwin W. Straus, "Aesthesiology and Hallucinations," in Rollo May, ed., *Existence* (New York: Basic Books, 1958), 139-169.

[28]Husserl, *Logical Investigations*, J.N. Findlay, trans. (New York: Humanities Press, 1970), II, 541-2.

[29]Husserl, *Ideas*, 214-15.

[31]Husserl, *Logical Investigations*, II, 584-5.

[32]Husserl, *The Phenomenology of Internal Time-Consciousness* (Bloomington: Indiana University Press, 1966), 110.

[33]Sartre, *Sketch of a Theory of Emotions*, 56.

[34]Husserl, *Ideas*, 108-9.

[35]Gurwitsch, *The Field of Consciousness*, 17-36.

[36]Gurwitsch, 31.

[37]Gurwitsch, 32.

[38]Gurwitsch, 29.

[39]Merleau-Ponty, *Phenomenology of Perception*.

[40]Sartre, *Being and Nothingness*, 93-95.

[41]Husserl, *Crisis*, 182.

[42]Husserl, *Ideas*, 307.

[43]Merleau-Ponty, *The Structure of Behavior*, 10-93.

[44]*Structure of Behavior*, 27-28.

[45]*Structure of Behavior*, 25.

[46]*Structure of Behavior*, 47.

[47]I.P. Pavlov, *Leçons sur l'activité du cortex cérébral* (Paris: Legrand, 1929) 12-13, cited in *Structure of Behavior*, 123.

[48]*Structure of Behavior*, 103.

[49]Goldstein, 168.

[50]Merleau-Ponty, *Phenomenology of Perception*, 137ff.

[51]*Phenomenology of Perception*, 210.

[52]*Phenomenology of Perception*, 211.

[53]*Phenomenology of Perception*, 145.

[54]*Phenomenology of Perception*, 237.

[55]Sartre, *Being and Nothingness*, 86-116.

[56]*Being and Nothingness*, 13.

[57]Husserl, *Logical Investigations*, II, 570ff.

[58]*Being and Nothingness*, 40-42.

[59]*Logical Investigations*, II, 572.

[60]*Logical Investigations*, II, 585.

[61]*Logical Investigations*, II, 582.

[62]Sartre, *Sketch of a Theory of Emotions*, 57.

[63]*Logical Investigations*, II, 574-5.

[64]Gendlin, *Experiencing and the Creation of Meaning*, 69-70. Gendlin's conclusion here is similar to that of Ernst Cassirer, *An Essay on Man* (New Haven: Yale University Press, 1944), although the reasoning is somewhat different. Cassirer defines man as the *animal symbolicum* (p. 26) because of the universality of this function in man; Gendlin's analysis is based upon phenomenological reflection upon the role of symbolization in the act of focusing and explicating felt meanings.

[65]H. Ashton Ellis, ed., Richard Wagner, *Wagner on Music and Drama* (New York: Dutton, 1964).

[66]Wagner, "The Origins of Modern Opera, Drama and Music," in Ellis, p. 153.

[67]Wagner, "The Artwork of the Future," in Ellis, 188-9.

[68]Wagner, "The Artwork of the Future," 191.

[69]Wagner, "The Artwork of the Future," 194.

[70]Wagner, "The Artwork of the Future," 222ff.

[71]Husserl, *The Phenomenology of Internal Time-Consciousness*, 110ff.

[72]Wagner, "The Artwork of the Future," 222-3.

[73]Merleau-Ponty, *Phenomenology of Perception*, 123.

[74]Goldstein.

[75]Merleau-Ponty, *Phenomenology of Perception*, 354.

[76]*Phenomenology of Perception*, 96.

[77]*Phenomenology of Perception*, 422.

[78]See Chapter 3, part A.

[79]Merleau-Ponty, *Signs*, J. Wild, ed. (Evanston: Northwestern University Press, 1964) seems to be the most complete exposition of this point.

[80]Arthur Schopenhauer, *The World as Will and Idea* (New York: Philosophical Library, 1965).

CHAPTER IV

[1] J.C. Gosling has pulled together these arguments in an excellent way in *Pleasure and Desire* (Oxford: Clarendon, 1969).

[2] Sigmund Freud, *Beyond the Pleasure Principle*, J. Strachey, trans. (New York: Bantum, 1959).

[3] Robert White, "Motivation Reconsidered," *Psychological Review*, 65, 297-333.

[4] White.

[5] Emmanuel Levinas, *Totality and Infinity* (The Hague: Nijhoff, 1969).

[6] John Watson, *Hedonistic Theories* (Glasgow: Macmillan, 1895).

[7] D.O. Hebb, *A Textbook of Psychology*, 2nd ed. (Philadelphia: Saunders, 1966).

[8] For example, D.E. Berlyne, "Novelty and Curiosity as Determinants of Exploratory Behavior," *British Journal of Psychology*, 41, 68-80; F.D. Sheffield and T.B. Roby, "Reward Value of a Non-nutritive Sweet Taste," *Journal of Comparative Physiological Psychology*, 43, 471-81; see also notes 11-22.

[9] For example, Skinner.

[10] Maslow; R.A. Butler, "Exploratory and Related Behavior," *Journal of Individual Psychology*, 14, 111-120; H.F. Harlow, "Learning Motivated by a Manipulation Drive," *Journal of Experimental Psychology*, 40, 228-34; see also notes 11-22.

[11] J.F. Dashiell, "A Quantitative Demonstration of Animal Drive," *Journal of Comparative Psychology*, 5, 205-8; H.W. Nisen, "A Study of Exploratory Behavior in the White Rat," *Journal of Genetic Psychology*, 37, 361-76.

[12] J.B. Wolfe and M.D. Kaplon, "Effect of Amount of Reward and Consummative Activity on Learning in Chickens," *Journal of Comparative Psychology*, 31, 353-61.

[13] See note 8.

[14] See note 8.

[15]Sheffield, *et. al.,* "Reward Value of Copulation Without Sex Drive Reduction," *Journal of Comparative Physiological Psychology*, 44, 3-8; J. Kagan, "Differential Reward Value of Incomplete and Complete Sexual Behavior," *Journal of Comparative Physiological Psychology*, 48, 526-30.

[16]See note 10.

[17]K.G. Montgomery, "The Role of the Exploratory Drive in Learning," *Journal of Comparative Physiological Psychology*, 47, 60-64.

[18]J. Kagan and M. Berkun, "The Reward Value of Running Activity," *Journal of Comparative Physiological Psychology*, 47, 108.

[19]See note 10.

[20]W.L. Welker, "Some Determinants of Play and Exploration in Chimpanzees," *Journal of Comparative Physiological Psychology*, 49, 84-89.

[21]C.T. Morgan, *Physiological Psychology*, New York: McGraw-Hill, 1943).

[22]H.E. Rosvold, "Physiological Psychology," *Annual Review of Psychology*, 10, 415-454; R.S. Woodworth, *Dynamics of Behavior* (New York: Holt, 1958).

[23]Gosling, 83-85.

[24]See note 3.

[25]White, 297.

[26]R.A. Spitz and K.M. Wolf, "Anaclitic Depression: An Inquiry into the Genesis of Psychiatric Conditions in Early Childhood," *P. A. Study of the Child, II* (New York: International University Press, 1946).

[27]M.J. Meldman, "A Nosology of the Attentional Diseases," *American Journal of Psychiatry*, 121, 377-8.

[28]John T. Saunders, "The Paradox of Self-Deception," *Philosophy and Phenomenological Research*, 35, 559-70.

[29]Husserl, *Logical Investigations*, I, 274.

[30]See Chapter I.

[31]Ellis, "Agent Causation, Chance and Determinism."

CHAPTER V

[1]Schopenhauer, *The Art of Controversy* (London: Aberdeen University Press, 1896), 7.

[2]*Logical Investigations*, I, 282-326.

[3]Ellis, "Existentialism and the Demonstrability of Ethical Theories."

[4]Karl Marx, *Economic and Philosophical Manuscripts of 1844*, T.B. Bottomore, ed. (London: McGraw-Hill, 1964), 44.

[5]Martin Heidegger, *What Is a Thing* (Chicago: Gateway, 1970).

[6]Heidegger, *Kant and the Problem of Metaphysics* (Bloomington: Indiana University Press, 1965).

[7]Husserl, *The Crisis of European Sciences*.

[8]David Hume, *An Abstract* (Cambridge: Keynes, 1938), 182.

[9]A.J. Ayer, *Language, Truth and Logic* (New York: Dover, 1946).

[10]H.H. Price, *Perception* (New York: McBride, 1933).

[11]J. Kockelmans, *Phenomenology* (Garden City: Doubleday, 1967).

[12]Merleau-Ponty, *The Phenomenology of Perception*.

[13]A.W. Watts, *Does It Matter?* (New York: Vintage, 1971).

[14]Sartre, *The Psychology of Imagination* (New York: Washington Square Press, 1966).

[15]See Chapter I, note 37.

[16]Calvin Schrag, "Phenomenology, Ontology, and History in the Philosophy of Heidegger" in J. Kockelmans, ed., *Phenomenology*.

MARTINUS NIJHOFF PHILOSOPHY LIBRARY

1. D. Lamb, Hegel – From Foundation to System. 1980. ISBN 90-247-2359-0
2. I.N. Bulhof, Wilhelm Dilthey: A Hermeneutic Approach to the Study of History and Culture. 1980. ISBN 90-247-2360-4
3. W.J. van der Dussen, History as a Science. The Philosophy of R.G. Collingwood. 1981. ISBN 90-247-2453-8
4. M. Chatterjee, The Language of Philosophy. 1981. ISBN 90-247-2372-8
5. E.-H.W. Kluge, The Metaphysics of Gottlob Frege. An Essay in Ontological Reconstruction. 1980. ISBN 90-247-2422-8
6. D. Dutton and M. Krausz (eds.), The Concept of Creativity in Science and Art. 1981. ISBN 90-247-2418-X
7. F.R. Ankersmit, Narrative Logic. A Semantic Analysis of the Historian's Language. 1983. ISBN 90-247-2731-6
8. T.P. Hohler, Imagination and Reflection: Intersubjectivity. Fichte's *Grundlage* of 1794. 1982. ISBN 90-247-2732-4
9. F.J. Adelmann (ed.), Contemporary Chinese Philosophy. 1982. ISBN 90-247-3057-0
10. E.N. Ostenfeld, Forms, Matter and Mind. Three Strands in Plato's Metaphysics. 1982. ISBN 90-247-3051-1
11. J.T.J. Srzednicki, The Place of Space and Other Themes. Variations on Kant's First Critique. 1983. ISBN 90-247-2844-4
12. D. Boucher, Texts in Context. Revisionist Methods for Studying the History of Ideas. 1985. ISBN 90-247-3121-6
13. Y. Yovel, Nietzsche as Affirmative Thinker. 1986. ISBN 90-247-3269-7
14. M.H. Mitias, Possibility of the Aesthetic Experience. 1986. ISBN 90-247-3278-6
15.
16.
17. W. Horosz, Search without Idols. 1986. ISBN 90-247-3327-8
18. R. Ellis, An Ontology of Consciousness. 1986. ISBN 90-247-3349-9

Series ISBN 90-247-2344-2